FROM TRENCH AND TURRET

FROM TRENCH AND TURRET

ROYAL MARINES'

Letters and Diaries 1914–18

In association with the Royal Marines Museum

S. M. Holloway

CONSTABLE • LONDON

Constable & Robinson Ltd
3 The Lanchesters
162 Fulham Palace Road
London W6 9ER
www.constablerobinson.com

First published in the UK by Constable,
an imprint of Constable & Robinson Ltd 2006

A copy of the British Library Cataloguing in
Publication data is available from the British Library

ISBN-13: 978-1-84529-321-5
ISBN-10: 1-84529-321-5

Printed and bound in the EU

This book is dedicated to the men whose words are reproduced within its pages. Though separated by time, it has been a privilege for me to work with them.

S.M.H. 2006

Acknowledgements

While every effort has been made to trace copyright holders for material featured in this work, the publishers will be glad to make proper acknowledgements in future editions in the event that any regrettable omissions have occurred.

The material within this book appears courtesy of the Royal Marines Museum, except where otherwise indicated.

Contents

Letter Writers and Diarists

The letters and diaries that appear in this book were written by the following men. The list shows their rank and unit at the date of writing.

'Albert', Pte RMLI, Deal Bn RMLI
Allen, John, Bandsman Royal Marine Band, attached Drake Bn RMLI
Barnes, John, Lt RMLI, Plymouth Bn RMLI
Black, W., Sgt RMLI, 2nd Bn RMLI
Blount, Harold, Capt. RMA, HMS *New Zealand*
Bourne, Alan, Capt. MVO, RMA, HMS *Tiger*
Bramley, G., CSM RMLI, Chatham Bn RMLI
Brookes, Frederick, Cpl RMLI, HMS *Triumph* (Dardanelles); Sgt, 2nd Bn RMLI (Somme)
Brown, William, Pte RMLI, Machine Gun Coy 190th Bde RND
Burge, Norman Ormsby, Maj. RMLI, Cyclist Coy RND; Lt Col. Howe Bn RND
Cauchey, Harold, Cpl RMLI, HMS *Iron Duke*
Chater, Arthur, Lt RMLI, Chatham Bn (Gallipoli); Capt., 4th Bn Royal Marines (Zeebrugge)
Conybeare, Charles, Lt RMLI, Plymouth Bn
Corbett-Williamson, William, Cpl RMLI, Cyclist Coy RND
Feeney, James, Pte RMLI, 4th Bn Royal Marines
Hallding, Percy, Chaplain Royal Navy, RND
Harvey, Francis, Maj. RMLI, HMS *Lion*
Hedges, Reginald, Clr Sgt RMLI, HMS *Implacable*
Hill, Chandos, Capt. RMLI, HMS *Colossus*
Hodgson, Philip, Pte RMLI, 4th Bn Royal Marines
Holloway, Ernest, Bugler RMLI, HMS *Lord Nelson*
Holloway, Harry, Clr Sgt RMLI (retired)
Hughes, Evan, Capt. RMLI, HMS *Revenge*
Inskip, S. Hope, Lt RMLI, Deal Bn RMLI
Jago, Norman, Sgt RMA, HMS *Agincourt*

Jerram, Charles, Maj. RMLI, RM Bde Staff (Gallipoli); 190th Bde RND (Somme)

Jollye, Godfrey, Capt. RMA, HMS *Malaya*

Kershaw, Edwin, Sgt RMLI, HMS *Albion*

Lamplough, Charles, Lt RMLI, Plymouth Bn RMLI (Gallipoli); 4th Bn Royal Marines (Zeebrugge)

Law, Francis, DSC, Lt RMLI, Plymouth Bn RMLI

Meatyard, William, MM, Sgt RMLI, Plymouth Bn RMLI (Gallipoli); 2nd Bn RMLI (Somme)

Montagu, Lionel, Maj. RMLI, Hood Bn RND

Morrison-Scott, R.C.S., Capt. RMA, No. 11 Gun Howitzer Bde

Moynahan, Cornelius, Pte RMLI, Plymouth Bn RMLI

Neasham, G., Pte RMLI, HMS *Yarmouth*

Oppenheim (later Orde), Godfrey, Capt. RMLI, HMS *Queen Elizabeth*

Pare, Herbert, Pte RMLI, HMS *Queen*

Pottinger, Robert, Pte RMLI, Chatham Bn RMLI

Richards, John, Lt RMLI, Plymouth Bn RMLI

Rooney, Gerald, Maj. RMLI, HMS *Queen Mary*

Saunders, Albert, Cpl RMA, HMS *Princess Royal*

Scorey, William, Pte RMLI, 4th Bn Royal Marines

Smith, Charles, Bugler RMLI, HMS *Inconstant*

Stapleton, Frederick, Clr Sgt RMLI, HMS *Ocean*

Swanborough, Thomas, Pte RMLI, HMS *Vanguard*

Thompson, James, Pte RMLI, Plymouth Bn RMLI

Tracey, Ernest, Pte RMLI, 4th Bn Royal Marines

Vickers, John, Pte RMLI, Plymouth Bn RMLI

Ward, Walter Wyon, Lt RMA, No. 12 Gun Howitzer Bde

Weekes, B. W., Capt. RMLI, 2nd Bn RMLI

Wells, W. E., Bugler RMLI, HMS *Bacchante*

Wilcox, Henry, Pte RMLI, HMS *Ocean*

Wright, Harry, Sgt RMLI, 4th Bn Royal Marines

Wyvill, Percy, Pte RMLI, HMS *Lord Nelson*

Photographs

All photographs, with the exception of those belonging to the author, are the copyright of the Royal Marines Museum collection and are credited *RMM*.

21 Lt Jack Barnes RMLI, killed aged 19 at Gallipoli, a few hours later. *RMM*
22 The grave of Capt. Andrews and Lt Barnes on the Gallipoli Peninsula. *RMM*

Maps

With the exception of numbers 2 and 6, which have been redrawn for clarity, these maps have been reproduced from contemporary sources.

1 Dardanelles: Attack on the Narrows, 18 March 1915.
  Source: *History of the Great War: Naval Operations*, Sir Julian Corbett (Longmans, Green and Co., 1921)
2 Battle of Jutland, 31 May 1916.
3 The landing beaches at Gallipoli, 25 April 1915.
  Source: *History of the Great War: Naval Operations*, Sir Julian Corbett (Longmans, Green and Co., 1921)
4 Gallipoli: Krithia and Y Beach some weeks after the landings.
  Source: Royal Marines Museum
5 Somme: Trench map showing attack on Beaucourt,
  13 November 1916.
  Source: Royal Marines Museum
6 Zeebrugge Harbour, 23 April 1918.

Foreword

by

Lieutenant General Sir Henry Beverley, KCB, OBE
Chairman of Trustees, the Royal Marines Museum

From Trench and Turret is an important contribution to the recorded history of the Royal Marines covering the major operations Per Mare Per Terram of the First World War. Utilizing letters and diaries, the realities of war are vividly portrayed in those campaigns and battles through the eyes of Officers, Non-Commissioned Officers, Privates and Gunners of the Royal Marine Light Infantry and Royal Marine Artillery, who were at the very forefront of the fighting.

At sea, the section covering the Battle of Jutland illustrates the realities of life afloat and the difficult and dangerous circumstances inherent in ship actions – with the results of the short-circuiting of safety procedures all too evident. Jutland was the last of the great actions between fleets, in which Admiral Sir John Jellicoe, indeed, could have 'lost the war in an afternoon', to quote Sir Winston Churchill. Although the terrible casualties of the great battles on land may well be uppermost in people's minds, the author notes that the loss of HM Ships *Queen Mary* and *Invincible* cost roughly the equivalent of two battalions in a matter of moments. The German 12-inch shell that exploded in 'Q' turret of HMS *Lion*, Vice Admiral Sir David Beatty's flagship, killed or wounded the whole turret's crew and the subsequent gallantry of Major Francis Harvey RMLI resulted in the posthumous award of the Victoria Cross. The depiction by Corporal Albert Saunders RMA of the appalling post-action scene aboard HMS *Princess Royal* brings the actuality of war at sea very much into focus.

In the Dardanelles campaign, Royal Marines units were confronted by the Turks defending their homeland with awesome tenacity and, on the Somme, they faced a tough, disciplined and well-trained foe. At Gallipoli much was learned about the sheer complexity of amphibious operations, which remains the *raison d'être* of the Corps. The sheer rawness of battle with man and rifle against artillery, machine guns, wire, disease and the elements leaves a deep impression but none more so than the cheerful, honest and largely unquestioning approach so symptomatic of that generation. It is impossible not to be deeply moved by the accounts of the various diarists and struck by the lucidity and command of the English language among men who, for the most part, left formal education by the age of fourteen; their words frequently illustrate the same degree of initiative expected of the Royal Marines of today. There is also a wide variety of age and experience, from the 'old sweats' such as Lieutenant John Richards, in his forties, through the middle range of military knowledge and understanding represented by Major Norman Burge, Sergeant Will Meatyard and Captain Lionel Montagu to the teenage officers mentioned below.

Zeebrugge was, in essence, a classic Royal Marines raiding operation demonstrating the projection of power from the sea into the land environment – later to be the speciality of the Commandos. Uniquely, two Victoria Crosses awarded to Royal Marines of the 4th Battalion RMLI were awarded by ballot (Captain Edward Bamford RMLI and Sergeant Norman Finch RMA) and the successful raid was a major boost to public morale after years of naval stalemate in the North Sea. Intriguingly, the 4th Battalion was permanently 'retired' from the RM order of battle as a special tribute. How much greater the honour, if a living influence could have been maintained and found expression in one of the Royal Marines Commandos! Here, the names of Charles Lamplough and Arthur Chater (both to become Major Generals) reappear, both men having cut their teeth in their teens at Gallipoli. The descriptions of the action by Sergeant Harry Wright and Private James Feeney are especially graphic. Throughout the book, it is so apparent that those who have experienced the realities of war avoid glorifying it.

The Royal Marines Museum possesses an outstanding collection of first-hand material and photographs. The future will see these slowly but surely digitalized to the huge benefit of the widest possible public but, for the moment, they cannot be on permanent display. In any event, the material has to be interpreted and set in context. That is what S. M. Holloway has done so admirably by using personal testimony to illustrate the Great War rather than the book being a history of that war illustrated by individual accounts. In so doing, she has created an enduring, and eminently readable contribution to the fascinating history of our great Corps.

Preface

The First World War cast a long shadow over the twentieth century; politically, socially and emotionally. The world has now moved on, and what was for so long relevant to the present is being consigned firmly to the past. The generation that lived through those years is gone, and that of the children who remember them diminishing. Yet for all that, the Great War, as it remained for those who survived it, will not lie quiet beneath the silt of time. It no longer influences the policies of politicians, or leaves an unnaturally high number of maiden ladies in pension queues, but retains a fascination for people who, for the most part, have never faced the realities of war. This is in part due to the scale of the war, not just in numbers of men or miles of trenches, but in its day-to-day horror. It is also due to the amount of written and oral material from the individuals involved: the human stories that do not date.

The oral history has an immediacy because it is possible to hear the emotion of an individual, but it is frequently clouded by the passage of time. Most combatants do not return home eager to tell all in gory detail. Indeed, the patient ladies, and it was usually ladies, who came to sit beside the recovering wounded to hunt down what happened to those listed as 'missing' were regarded with distaste by those whose memories they sought to probe. War experience was best kept in its own closed box, and only with the passage of decades, and on rare occasions, would it be opened. It is, I think, significant that in many cases it is grandchildren who have heard details, not children.

The written archive is often unable to put a face to a name, but much of what appears in the pages that follow was written within days, and often hours, of the actual event. The facts may not be totally accurate, but they are true as the writer saw them from a particular position, without thought of how they might be judged in the future, and without the distortion, often subconscious, of time and hindsight. Most of the diaries and letters used are in faded notebooks and pocketbooks, some scribbled over the tiny pages of daily diaries, and a few typed up from such diaries at a later date for the Royal Marines Museum, family or the Corps journal, *The Globe & Laurel.* Where this is the case, it is still clear that the reminiscences stem from records written at the time, and the gloss of hindsight is minimal. The Royal Marines Museum, at Eastney in Portsmouth, holds an outstanding collection of first-hand material and photographs, although the majority cannot be permanently on display and can only be viewed by appointment. This book is designed to bring some of the most interesting to a wider audience.

This is not a history of the Great War illustrated by personal testimony, but rather personal testimony illustrating the Great War. The words of the letter writers and diarists are paramount. My task has been to provide a context in which the events take place, and to weave the original material together in a logical and cohesive manner, providing corroboration where possible from others present. There is no attempt to cover all aspects or theatres of war, or even to focus on the most historically important events. What the book tries to convey is what men of widely differing ages and backgrounds saw and how they felt at specific times in their own small sector of action. When you are under fire, it does not matter how important an action may be or how it will be remembered in the history books. Such things are only known when the danger is past.

My thanks are due to Captain C. Page, Royal Navy, of the Naval Historical Branch, for his help in tracing several of the maps used here, and to Surgeon Captain P. J. Buxton OBE, Royal Navy, for assistance with the index. The photographs, excepting those few in my personal possession, are from the Royal Marines Museum Photographic & Picture Archive, and I am indebted to the Photograph & Picture Librarian, Mr John Ambler, for his ever prompt and helpful assistance hunting down particular images. I owe a particular debt of gratitude to Mr Matthew Little, the Royal Marines Museum Archivist, whose near encyclopaedic knowledge of what lies where, and unfailing good humour in the face of difficulties, prevented a labour of love becoming a labour of Hercules. I am also grateful to the editor of this new edition, Ms Liz Hornby, for her patience and sharp eye for ambiguities and errors. I also wish to add my thanks to Mr Stephen Dew, the cartographer who redrew the maps of Jutland and Zeebrugge. Some elements of this book were published by the Royal Marines Museum and with my authorship under the same title in a small publication designed for secondary schools in 1987 when a need for primary source material for educational purposes became apparent.

Other than my own grandfather, I have 'known' most of the men whose words appear in these pages for nigh on twenty years. When we 'met' I was a little older than the youngest subalterns, but could regard forty-years-old as pretty aged. In the intervening period, to paraphrase, 'time has not aged them, nor the years condemned', but I am now old enough to be the mother of those newly fledged second lieutenants and older than the oldest diarist who was killed.

S. M. Holloway

Prologue:
The Outbreak of War

The summer of 1914 was hot and sunny. In Britain, the biggest cloud on the political horizon was the threat of a civil war in Ireland. Attention was focused on this, rather than events in continental Europe. Thus, the assassination of the Archduke Franz Ferdinand in Sarajevo on 28 June was considered shocking but, to most people, of no immediate importance to their lives. The main news topic in the papers remained Sir Edward Carson's armed Protestants in Ireland, even as Europe advanced to the brink of war.

Franz Ferdinand's assassination did not make a general European war inevitable, nor even a war between Austria-Hungary and Serbia. The Archduke had not been popular in Vienna, and an inquiry after the assassination showed no proof that the Serbian government had been involved in the plot. The Austro-Hungarian government, however, decided to use the outrage as an excuse for war. One month after the assassination, following an ultimatum carefully worded so that the Serbs could not fully accept, the Austro-Hungarian army mobilized against them. The government in Vienna had first sought and received approval for their actions from Berlin, because they knew that Russia would not stand by and watch as the Serbs were overrun. The Tsar claimed to be the father of the Pan-Slav movement, and the Austrians hoped that warnings from Berlin of German support for the war against Serbia would be enough to keep the Russian bear, however irate, from war. It did mean that Russia initially declared only a partial mobilization on 28 July, but on the 31st this became a general mobilization. Germany gave Russia an ultimatum to cancel the mobilization, and, when this was ignored, Germany declared war on Russia. The date was 1 August. The Germans had planned for a war on two fronts, against Russia and its ally France. The armed forces were prepared not for 'if' there was a war, but 'when'. France duly mobilized on 1 August, but did not declare war. France was bound to its Russian ally, but Belgium, which mobilized at the same time, was simply preparing to defend its neutrality with its small army. The Germans' plan was to defeat the French swiftly in the West before turning against Russia, which could only achieve full mobilization slowly. They therefore wanted to get to grips with France as soon as possible. It was the Germans who declared war on France on 3 August, and the following day they entered Belgium. They had demanded free passage through Belgium, which the Belgians would not permit, so they simply marched over the border, to be held up only by whatever resistance the Belgian army could offer.

The invasion of Belgium finally brought Britain into the war. The British government had tried to assist in finding a peaceful solution to the crisis, and even towards the end of July was certainly not committed to joining a European struggle. In the House of Commons speeches were made in favour of the isolationist view, and there were hopes in Berlin that Britain would stand aloof from the conflict. However, Britain had been one of the countries which had stood as guarantor of Belgium's neutrality after that country had been formed in 1830. Whatever hopes the Germans might have held about keeping Britain uncommitted were soon dashed. On 4 August, after the Germans refused to respect Belgian neutrality, Britain declared war on Germany.

The Schlieffen Plan, even in the modified form the Germans used, demanded a sweep through Belgium to get to Paris – and quickly. The Germans made no attempt to hide the fact that harsh measures would be taken against those who tried to delay the advance. No doubt they hoped it would stifle further resistance. Tales of German atrocities in 'poor little Belgium' became banner headlines. Whilst claims that the Germans ate babies were wildly sensationalist, Belgian civilians certainly suffered at the hands of the invading army. In towns and villages where there had been any suggestion of armed resistance, reprisals took the form of summary executions of random selections of citizens, including women and infants, and arson. Reports of these events encouraged more men in Britain to flock to the recruiting offices. War fever was not universal, however. Amongst those who realized what war would really mean there was no hysteria. A Royal Marine pensioner wrote to his son, a 17-year-old bugler aboard the battleship HMS *Lord Nelson*, on 2 August. The letter does not rejoice, but is sadly determined.

Retd Clr Sgt H. A. Holloway RMLI to his son, Bugler E. E. Holloway RMLI, 2 August 1914

My Dear Boy,

This is an awkward day. We can get no news of the crisis, and last night's news were as bad they could [be]. However, while there's life there's hope, but everyone here is anxiously awaiting the latest news, although I expect that if the worst happens I shall get a telegram like you got on Thursday. The papers are absolutely silent as to the movements of the Fleet (and they ought to be; I'd like to shoot the Editor who gave the game away), but I shouldn't be surprised if you are off to the 'Straits'; however, wherever you may be if 'war' comes, do your best, remember you won't go before your time comes, and although we both very much want to see you home again, yet Mother and I would rather you died fighting (that is if you have to die) than of sickness at home, yet we pray and hope that if the fighting comes, that God will spare you and bring you home safe and sound.

May came home yesterday, quite well and happy, and in her feminine way considers the crisis very horrid and more so because you could not stay a few more days.

Mother, Winnie and I are all in the 'Pink of Condition' and only hope that you are still the same and that somehow or other this letter will reach you. Goodbye and God be with you; think of the man your ship is named after and his signal.

Your loving parents,
Mother and Dad

Sergeant Edwin Kershaw, aboard HMS *Albion*, was already experiencing the change from a peacetime to a war footing.

Sgt Edwin Kershaw RMLI, HMS *Albion*, 2 August 1914

Today bears no resemblance of the Sabbath, the dockyard humming with great activity such as suggests that great things are going to happen; in dry dock being refitted while the crew are busy getting rid of all woodwork which would be in the way, and a possible cause of fire during an action. Stores of every description are being taken in the ship and hustle is the order of the day.

Colour Sergeant Frederick Stapleton RMA, aboard HMS *Ocean,* was equally aware of the change from peacetime.

Clr Sgt Frederick Stapleton RMA, HMS *Ocean*, August 1914

. . . a number of men began to trickle down the hill from the Detention Quarters; carrying their bags and hammocks.

While we watched, the exodus continued, so it became evident that they were being released; especially as they were not accompanied by escorts, but were making their own way to the RN barracks.

On the afternoon of the first Saturday of August we moved to the coaling point, where we were to take in about a thousand tons of fuel, despite the fact that there were less than two hundred men to deal with such a quantity, instead of the usual seven or eight hundred.

To make matters worse it was landed on the upper deck by huge grabs, which deposited about a ton at a time; so, in a short time the pile was so high that it was impossible to remove it by barrows until a way had been cleared by shovels.

The full amount was soon deposited in immense heaps, which had to be dealt with from the top or sides, depending on the accessibility; there being all sorts of permanent obstructions such as guns and hawser reels.

During the day we were joined by a few men who had been recalled to active service. These were mostly coastguards, who were working under a different system to the present one.

As soon as these unfortunate men arrived, they had to shift into a coaling rig and join in the general task, which was the most heartbreaking in my experience.

We still struggled on after darkness added to our difficulties, but the pace was slackening and men, thoroughly exhausted, fell asleep on the black mounds, and although the officers were going round with words of encouragement, it was of no avail – nature would have its way – so, about midnight, the 'cease fire' was sounded.

Coaling ship was always an arduous and thankless task, but at least Frederick Stapleton was not working under the imminent threat of enemy torpedoes, which was the situation of Major Gerald Rooney RMLI, with HMS *Queen Mary* at Scapa.

Maj. Gerald Rooney RMLI, HMS *Queen Mary*, Wed. 5 August 1914

Returned to Scapa Flow 4 p.m., and started coaling at 4.30 p.m. overnight, finishing at 5 a.m. About midnight there was

an alarm, and it was stated that attack was imminent. White
Watch instantly manned the 4" guns while an effort was made
to carry on coaling in the dark. Ships further up the harbour
continued to burn their lights, which showed us up very
effectively; . . . coaling operations became excessively trying
and lingered on indefinitely, in the rain, which made the dirt
indescribable. Altogether a poor show.

Hard work prevailed over any sense of anticipation of what was to
come, and the officers and men simply got on with the job.

It has been popular to look with hindsight at the First World War
and claim that it was an 'unjustified' war, and that those who went
through it were brainwashed, blindly obedient to 'class' structure, and
led by officers who were idiots – if sometimes ridiculously brave idiots.
This is grossly unfair. The men who fought the war, and indeed the
families back in 'Blighty', faced life with very different attitudes to
those of today. The social structure was generally accepted, with its
limitations and boundaries, but the working man did not think of
himself as an 'inferior' human being. The war, by bringing men from
sectors of society to live and fight alongside each other, accelerated the
collapse of those old social boundaries, just as it advanced the cause of
female emancipation. Regardless of social position, the young man who
reached adulthood at the end of the Edwardian era had been brought
up to regard duty not just as something that applied to people in
uniform. Everyone understood duty. They accepted that there were
times when the individual would be lost for the sake of others. Captain
Oates' action in the Antarctic, walking out of the tent to his death, was
respected as brave, but others would have taken that course, or hoped
they would have. The men who made no attempt to find a place in the
lifeboats of the *Titanic*, so that the women and children could be got off,
conformed to that ethos.

They also understood and accepted the proximity of death. It was not
something that took place out of sight, sanitized, and only to the old.
Accident and disease were ever present and were faced by all classes to
varying degrees. Harry Holloway had lost a 15-year-old sister to
tuberculosis, and two cousins, drowned on the China Station with the
Royal Navy. Then in 1904 his wife had died within 24 hours of giving
birth to their fourth child. She was 34. Ernest Holloway was seven
when his mother died. The baby was handed over to Harry's unmarried
sister to bring up, and Harry, with three children under ten years of
age, remarried 16 months later. Grief was no less strong, the desire to
survive as great, but they accepted that one carried on. They were a
resilient generation whose resilience was about to be tested to the
extreme.

5

In the pages that follow there is no attempt to show the wider strategy of the First World War, or the influence of politics. Here are simply some of the events in which Royal Marines – both Royal Marine Light Infantry such as Bugler Ernest Holloway, and Royal Marine Artillery – took part, described as they themselves saw it.

I
PER MARE

1

The Dardanelles

In October of 1914 Turkey joined the Great War on the side of Germany and Austria-Hungary. In the past, Britain had been on good terms with Turkey, but in the years prior to the war Germany had replaced Britain as a trading partner, and German influence was in the ascendant. It was Germany that supplied the loans that Britain and France would not give, and Britain had soured relations with the Turks by cancelling delivery of two dreadnoughts to the Turkish navy. When war came, the Turks believed Germany and its allies would win. The Young Turks faction clamoured for Turkey to enter the conflict. If Turkey fought on the winning side, they foresaw valuable rewards at the end of hostilities. There were chances of gains in the oilfields of the Caucasus, and even of reclaiming control of Egypt if Britain was heavily defeated and its Empire crumbled. The Kaiser himself saw the possibility of damaging the Empire by encouraging *jihad* in the Middle East, and certainly Turkish soldiers defending Gallipoli wrote of becoming martyrs, but national rather than religious reasons remained predominant and the flame of Holy War never became the conflagration envisaged by Wilhelm II.

In August, at the very beginning of the war, two German ships, the *Goeben* and the *Breslau*, were in the Mediterranean, and they made a dash for the security of Constantinople. If they remained in a neutral port they would be interned, according to international law. To avoid this, Germany handed both the ships and their crews over to the Turks. The sailors wore Turkish fez hats and the ships flew Turkish ensigns, but they remained essentially a German threat at the eastern end of the Mediterranean. The Germans made further loans to Turkey and encouraged it to join the war. On 27 October the *Goeben* and the *Breslau*, with Turkish vessels, entered the Black Sea and caused damage to oil tanks and ships in the Russian port of Novorossiisk. Russia, ally of Britain and France, was thus facing war on two fronts. On 1 November Britain declared war on Turkey.

The idea of attacking the Dardanelles and the Gallipoli Peninsula

9

was put forward by the First Lord of the Admiralty, Winston Churchill, and Admiral of the Fleet Lord Fisher of Kilverstone, towards the end of November 1914. They recommended a joint naval and military attack as the best way to protect Egypt and Suez, by putting Turkey out of the war. This plan might also bring Italy and the neutral Balkan states into the war on the Allies' side. It would prevent Russian troops being diverted to the Caucasus from the Eastern Front against Germany. The claim was made that it could shorten the war.

This did not impress those who saw the war being won or lost on the Western Front. At that time the new Secretary of State for War, Lord Kitchener, declared that troops were not available. Men and materiel had been expended at a furious rate since the war began, and losses had been heavy among Britain's small regular army. All sides were building up supplies of armaments, ammunition and men for the spring offensive of 1915. As 1915 dawned, the politicians and generals who were committed to winning the war in France and Flanders wanted every available man there, not several thousand miles away in an Eastern Mediterranean sideshow. At the same time, those who saw stalemate in the trench warfare of the Western Front looked to the East for a breakthrough. There was therefore a division of opinion and effort that was to prove fatal.

In January 1915 the Russians asked Britain for some action against the Turks to take pressure off the Russian armies. Troops would not be ready for several months, so Kitchener decided that the 'action' against the Turks would be naval only.

Without troops being involved, Lord Fisher became extremely worried about a Dardanelles campaign. Churchill had telegraphed Admiral Carden, who commanded the British Squadron in the Aegean, to ask whether forcing the Dardanelles by ships alone was practicable. Carden's reply commented that the Dardanelles could not be rushed but 'might be forced by extended operations with large numbers of ships'. This 'might' came to be interpreted as 'can' and Carden was requested to draw up detailed plans.

Fisher could not see that an unsupported operation would work, and he was concerned that severe losses, even of old vessels, would damage the Grand Fleet's reserve. On 28 January 1915 he wrote to Asquith, the prime minister, 'Dardanelles bombardment can only be justified on naval grounds by military co-operation . . . As purely naval operations [bombardments] are unjustifiable.' At the War Council meeting that day he came close to resignation, but did not feel able to speak against the plans of Churchill, who was his chief. Instead he showed his disagreement by silence — which others took as assent to the plan. Later, Churchill persuaded him that as the decision to attack the Dardanelles had been taken, his duty was to support it. Churchill also convinced the elderly admiral that the plan was sound.

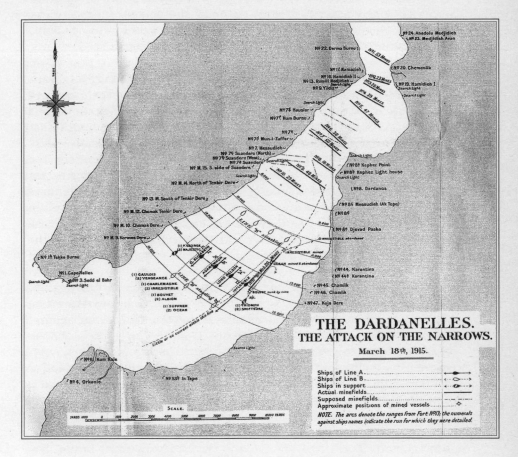

Bombarding the Narrows, 18 March 1915

Only afterwards did Fisher's doubts return, and then it was too late.

The Admiralty was told it should 'prepare for a naval expedition in February to bombard and take the Gallipoli Peninsula, with Constantinople as its object'. How the Royal Navy was going to 'take' the peninsula without troops was not mentioned. Two battalions of Royal Marines were sent out, but were 'to serve as the garrison for the Base, or for any small landing operation of a temporary nature'.

A force was assembled under Admiral Carden, consisting of old battleships, supplemented by the last two pre-dreadnoughts *Lord Nelson* and *Agamemnon*, and the new and powerful *Queen Elizabeth*. There was a battlecruiser, 4 light cruisers, an aircraft carrier, 16 destroyers, 21 minesweepers and 6 submarines. The French sent 4 old battleships, some submarines and small craft.

The plan involved several phases. First of all the outer defences of the Dardanelles were to be reduced by the battleships' gunfire and then by demolition parties if necessary. The minefields of the Narrows would then be swept and the Narrows forts reduced. The main minefield off Kephez Point would be swept, the forts above the Narrows silenced and the Fleet would enter the Sea of Marmara. It was estimated that this would take one month.

The Outer Forts were successfully reduced, though they did not fall as quickly as had been planned. One of the main problems was that the big guns of the new battleships, which were meant to have an immense effect, were not designed for use against fortresses. What were required were howitzers to lob high-explosive shells into the forts, not armour-piercing shells which came from guns with a shallow trajectory and entered through the side walls. The weather also hindered matters, as spotting aircraft were needed to direct the gunfire, and the winter conditions frequently kept them aboard their mother ship. However, by the end of February the Fleet could move up to pound the Intermediate Forts – once the mines had been cleared. That was easier said than done, and the Turks had the nasty habit of laying more mines. The 'minesweepers' were North Sea trawlers with fishermen crews and later a few Royal Navy and reservist officers and sailors. Enemy shellfire soon meant that mine-sweeping had to be undertaken at night, and even then under Turkish searchlights and gunfire. Colour Sergeant Frederick Stapleton of HMS *Ocean*, one of the elderly pre-dreadnoughts, described escorting one of the mine-sweeping operations.

Clr Sgt Stapleton RMA, HMS *Ocean*, March 1915

The *Ocean* was detailed to escort a number of trawlers which entered the Narrows to sweep for mines; so soon after dark, we steamed quietly to a point from which the Chanak light was clearly visible; where we were to remain until the moon arose at three the next morning. It was a weird experience, for we only spoke in whispers, for we could hear dogs barking and cocks crowing from shore; so any noise from us might make it uncomfortable for the sweepers, who went some miles further up.

There was little firing, however, probably because the Turks may have feared hitting their own positions across the water. The moon was high in the heavens before we departed, for one of the trawlers was late in arriving. She was followed by a small steam pinnace from one of the ships which was bobbing about on the waves in a manner that suggested that the whole affair was a joke.

Looking back, it is surprising to recall the number of hazardous and monotonous tasks that had to be continuously undertaken; jobs which were seldom performed by our allies.

By the second week in March, 'sweeping' was still in progress and the Turks had safely positioned mobile gun batteries on either side of the Dardanelles to harass the Allies further. On 18 March the Fleet made a supreme effort to force the Narrows, with the big guns of the battleships aiming to silence the Turkish forts before the minesweepers cleared the final path. The Line A ships (see map, page 11) – the dreadnought *Queen Elizabeth*, sister ships *Lord Nelson* and *Agamemnon*, and the battlecruiser *Inflexible* – sailed up the Dardanelles and began pounding away at the forts, supported by *Majestic*, *Prince George*, *Swiftsure* and *Triumph* tackling the intermediate mobile batteries. The Turks almost ran out of ammunition and the situation appeared serious for them. In the early afternoon, however, things began to go wrong for the Allied Fleet.

The French battleships *Gaulois, Charlemagne, Bouvet* and *Suffren* had passed through the British lines, and had made further progress in the destruction of the forts. The *Gaulois* took heavy damage in her bows and had to withdraw, almost sinking, to be beached on Rabbit Island. The other French battleships made their turn to come out of the front line. *Bouvet* had sustained some damage, but as she steamed swiftly back on the Asiatic side, a trail of reddish-black smoke emerged from her and she turned turtle and sank. Only a few survivors were rescued. Many of the men on the other vessels witnessed her demise, which was attributed by some to a shell hit in the magazine, but which was almost certainly the result of hitting a mine. The Turkish *Nusrat* had laid a line of mines at battleship depth, and in line with the current as opposed to across the Narrows, on the night of 8 March. It was the *Bouvet* that gave the first sign of their presence. Half a century later, senior bugler Ernest Holloway, whose action station had been on the bridge of *Lord Nelson*, recalled with horror how the *Bouvet* seemed to plough under the water, turning over as she went, in barely two minutes. The loss of over 600 men in so short a time made a big impact on the men of the Fleet.

HMS *Agamemnon* had sustained damage to her secondary armament but it was another two hours before the Royal Navy began to lose ships. Shortly after 4 p.m. HMS *Irresistible* struck one of the *Nusrat*'s mines and started to list badly. She sank during the night. HMS *Ocean* also fell victim to a mine and sank. Lesser damage was sustained by other ships, although the *Inflexible* limped back to Tenedos damaged by both shell and mine, and had to go to Malta for major repairs. Sweeps of the Narrows had been attempted but, under fire and in daylight, they were abandoned. The Allies did not know how close they had come to success, and were unwilling to try the same manoeuvre again, without the shores being free of Turks. They certainly did not realize that their best chance was gone.

Among the Royal Marines who took part in the abortive attempt of 18 March were Colour Sergeant Frederick Stapleton and Private Henry Wilcox aboard HMS *Ocean*, Corporal Fred Brookes of HMS *Triumph*, Sergeant Edwin Kershaw of HMS *Albion* and Private Percy Wyvill, who served, like Bugler Ernest Holloway, in HMS *Lord Nelson*.

Their accounts show the degree of confusion that existed at the time over what exactly had happened. Fred Brookes thought the *Irresistible* and *Ocean* had been hit by torpedoes fired from shore. Edwin Kershaw thought the *Bouvet* sank in 40 seconds, whilst Henry Wilcox thought she sank in 30 seconds, a time agreed upon by some other witnesses, and thought the number of survivors was 18 (in reality 35). Frederick Stapleton thought there were only six or seven, and heard that she had blown up. He, Kershaw, Brookes and Wilcox believed that *Ocean* was struck whilst going to the assistance of *Irresistible*.

Colour Sergeant Stapleton gives his description of preparations for the operation aboard *Ocean*.

Clr Sgt Stapleton RMA, HMS *Ocean*, 18 March 1915

We were summoned to the quarter deck, before we entered the Straits, where the captain addressed us, giving us an outline of the plan and of some of the difficulties that would probably be encountered. Finally, he advised us to wear clean clothing next to the skin, no matter how old. We could also change the white suits we already wore, for an older one, if clean; being careful to carry no unnecessary articles in the pockets, in case of wounds.

The guns' crews had been informed of the nature of the known Turkish defences and rumour had added others, such as the existence of torpedo tubes in caves at Chanak. We knew that mines existed in plenty, for we had seen them swept up, or exploded by gunfire. Apart from that, several small craft had limped out of the Straits showing the damage that they inflicted.

However, these considerations had no perceptible effect on the ship's company, except to form a grim determination to see it through, but they took the captain's advice and divested themselves of all unnecessary oddments, such as watches and tobacco tins.

I was only wearing a thin white suit at the time, torn at the shoulders, with canvas slippers on my feet and a hunting knife suspended by a lanyard from my neck. This latter was used for cutting the rope grommets which protected the driving bands on the projectiles.

Private Henry Wilcox makes no sartorial comments, but does mention the mine-sweeping that went on just before the 18th.

Pte Henry Wilcox RMLI, HMS *Ocean*, 18 March 1915

The Turks started to drop mines and these were being carried down towards us by the current. A bit further up was a place called Chanak, which was heavily fortified with 14-inch guns and from one side to the other was about 3,000 yards. Here also the Turks had laid a minefield. The following night six trawlers and ourself who was protecting them, went up and swept this minefield and picked up 108 mines. One trawler got blown up. We had to go astern as our ship was on the minefield all the time we were picking up mines. . . . The next day, March 17th [18th] 1915, we went up again to attack the big forts at Chanak. One half of the Fleet went up first and we were the flagship of the second line. Whilst steaming up in a single line we were in the centre of the line. Ahead of us were the *Inflexible* and two French battleships. The *Inflexible* got mined and had to drop out and one of the French was mined, and just ahead of us was the French battleship *Bouvet*. She struck another mine, turned over on her side and disappeared in thirty seconds. Eighteen out of six hundred were saved. We proceeded with the *Irresistible* and other ships up to Chanak and bombarded the forts. We were hit several times with 14-

inch shells and during the bombardment the *Irresistible* got mined. We went to try and tow her away. When we got near to her a 14-inch shell struck the foreturret 12-inch guns of *Irresistible*, and they rolled over into the water. A moment or two after, our ship, the *Ocean*, struck a mine and our engines were put out of action, so we were stuck there helpless, with shells coming over pretty thick. We got the order of abandon ship. Three or four Destroyers came alongside and took us off except one stoker who was below and could not get out.

Colour Sergeant Stapleton was in a gun casemate, with a restricted view of events, but gives a full account of how he and his gun's crew made it to a rescuing destroyer.

Clr Sgt Stapleton RMA, HMS *Ocean*, 18 March 1915

Some French ships had accompanied us, but it was impossible to see these from my position in a maindeck casemate, where the view was towards the Asiatic side, giving periodical glimpses of the cliffs referred to (Dardunas) and of Chanak.

We could only judge the time, but by about three o'clock the gunfire had become particularly heavy and light shells had burst on the protecting armour to such an extent that the ship's side was hot to the touch from the inside; but fortunately only a few splinters entered the space we occupied.

It was then that our voice tube failed, so we could not receive messages from our control position. While we waited, a man from the gun on the opposite side informed us that the French battleship had blown up and had disappeared under the water in a few seconds. A few minutes later, I saw the British battleship, *Irresistible*, lying helplessly out of action, with a big list, the water around her being filled with dark objects, which were men swimming for their lives.

We heard men scampering about on our upper deck, but had not been called up there ourselves, so remained at the gun while the *Ocean* attempted to tow the stricken ship out of danger; but whenever we got near, four heavy shells would drop from the cliffs, so we had to complete the circuit and come up again.

As we started on the third run, there was a dull, heavy explosion, somewhere aft below the waterline, which we at the gun thought was the burst of a large shell.

The *Ocean* at once took a heavy list to starboard, making it

impossible to elevate the gun in reply to the heavy gunfire
from the beaches round Dardunas, the cliffs previously
referred to. As we stood there, the port sill kept dipping
towards the sea and I realized that we would soon be flooded
out.

We were in a compartment which might be described as
being about ten or twelve feet square, with the corners
rounded off. A shaft ran down to the ammunition passage, two
decks below, and our exit was by a steel door, two inches thick
and probably weighing about half a ton.

As no sound could be heard from the deck above us, I sent a
man up to see what was happening. When he returned, he told
me that the voice tube was destroyed and that some seamen
had been getting the cable laid out, in readiness for towing the
Irresistible.

In the meantime, the crew remained quietly around the gun,
but one man asked why we did not fire. In reply, I drew his
attention to the helpless position the gun was in, for she
continued to dip towards the water. When we made a bigger
plunge a few minutes afterwards, another member of the crew
enquired what would happen when the water reached the port
sill. Being more logical than diplomatic, I replied, 'We shall
probably drown.' A few minutes later we received the order,
'Clear lower deck. Everyone aft.'

The armoured door of the ammunition hoist had already
been closed, so, thinking it might keep the ship afloat a few
minutes longer, I decided to close the casemate door also, but
found it impossible to remove the securing pin, as the ship's
list had thrown the weight of the door onto the fastener.

While looking round for some mechanical aid for removing
the pin, I was surprised to hear the ammunition door
commence to open, so I realized that it was being operated
from below. Then a voice called out, 'Topsides. Pass us down a
rope.'

When the men scrambled up the rope, they explained that
they had been in the flat above the torpedo room when the
explosion occurred, and finding themselves shut in, had
travelled along the ammunition passage, opening the
armoured doors by means of a large spanner that was kept
there for the purpose. The water there was above their knees
when they left. 'Did you close the doors after you?' I enquired.
'Yes,' replied the Leading Seaman in charge.

With their help, we closed the door of the casemate, which
slammed with a vicious snap that would have cut a man in
two, had one got in the way. By this time, the mess deck was

clear, but as I had to report that fact, I went along that way
until I reached the aft deck. When passing my mess I was
tempted to remove my watch and purse from the locker, but
decided to leave it until I had been on deck.

When I reached the quarter deck, an officer asked me which
way I had taken and if anyone was left there. When he
received my answer, he in turn informed the captain, who
stood behind him.

The deck sloped towards the side on which I stood, bringing
the other side up high. Just above it I could see the mast of
a destroyer, which at that moment sheered off. As she
dropped astern, I noticed that she was jammed with men
tighter than they can be got into a lift on a Tube railway. But
she had not left on that account, for at that moment four huge
shells struck the water near where she had been.

In the meantime, a few more men assembled on the quarter
deck, having made their way from all sorts of odd corners. One
of the last was a Marine bugler, probably the smallest I ever
met on a ship. He was struggling along with two large
baulks of timber. When I asked him what he intended doing
with the wood, he explained that he had hidden them near
the funnels some weeks before, in case anything like this
occurred, but on hearing that he would obtain passage in a
destroyer, he sat on the deck and removed the boots that were
hanging round his neck, suspended by the laces, and put them
on his feet, shouting joyously, 'Women and children first.'

By that time, two destroyers had reached our side, one being
the crowded one, the other having more room. So a few
passengers shifted over, while those waiting on our quarter
deck shinned down ropes to the nearest vessel.

While a few of us waited above, a Chief Engine Room
Artificer arrived and reported that he had dealt with certain
valves below, so the deafening roar due to escaping steam,
which had been moaning our departure, gradually ceased.
Being beckoned by the Major of Marines, I then slid down the
rope until my feet rested on some bridge rails, where I had to
balance myself for a few seconds until it was possible to
squeeze a foothold on the deck.

While we remained alongside I was able to push my way
through the crowd to some extent, to find out who was on
board. Apart from many men from the *Ocean,* there were six or
seven sailors from the *Bouvet*; the sole survivors.

Private Henry Wilcox was not quite as fortunate as Frederick Stapleton, for he found himself on a sinking ship for the second time that day.

Pte Wilcox RMLI, HMS *Ocean*, 18 March 1915

I got aboard the destroyer *Chelmer* when, before we left the side of the *Ocean*, the *Chelmer* got hit with a couple of shells and she started to sink, but she was able to get us alongside the *Lord Nelson* – who managed to keep her afloat and rescue us all. My word, we were glad when that Battle was over. As we were leaving the *Ocean* she was heeling over, and coming along the deck was a Sick Berth Attendant with two wounded men on each side of him – a brave act, but no notice taken of it.

Colour Sergeant Stapleton travelled to Tenedos aboard the destroyer and then transferred to *Lord Nelson*'s sister ship, *Agamemnon*, where he came upon a generous and tactful sergeant.

Clr Sgt Stapleton RMA, HMS *Ocean*, 18 March 1915

While on the way to Tenedos, the crew of the destroyer made some cocoa, which we welcomed, for apart from being hungry and thirsty, we were cold, most of us being lightly clothed.

When we reached the island, we went alongside the battleship *Agamemnon*. When we got inboard, we found that many other survivors had preceded us and that a number had been distributed elsewhere. Although burdened with over four hundred men at short notice, our hosts could not [do] too much for us. I was accommodated in the sergeants' mess, most of the members being already known to me.

After supper, one of the sergeants asked me to go round the ship with him, as he wished to point out the war scars. The chief of these was a hole on the upper deck, where a shell had entered and penetrated the deck below [and] had burst, the fragments disappearing.

This was a small thing to show one coming from the *Ocean*, for she had received a good battering during the six or seven weeks that she had spent in the area. This made me suspect that he had other motives for the inspection than those he had mentioned. This proved to be correct, for when we went on deck for a smoke, he slipped a florin in my hand, asking me to accept, as it was unlikely that I should receive any pay for a considerable time.

Although I tried hard to refuse, at last I had to accept, to avoid hurting his feelings. His conjecture was a correct one, for it was two months before I received any money; so I thank him for his kindly thought.

Corporal Fred Brookes had been in the thick of the action, but the damage to his ship was not too severe, and *Triumph* had been able to take survivors of *Irresistible* and *Ocean*, so that they were well spread through the Fleet.

Cpl Fred Brookes RMLI, HMS *Triumph*, 18 March 1915

Our ship was repeatedly hit and twenty-six times shells penetrated our armour. One howitzer shell went down five decks, but luckily it was too far aft to do any vital damage. Another shell pierced the Quarter Deck, setting fire to the woodwork in and about the Captain's cabin, but it also burst the water pipes in the bathroom which put out the fire. Another shell penetrated one of the Royal Marines casemates and killed a midshipman who was there at the time, and wounded the Marine Officer. None of the actual gun's crew were hit, as, being a lull in the firing, they were all behind the gun and having a round of cards out of sight of the Marine Officer.

The *Irresistible* was struck by a torpedo from a shore tube and the *Ocean* went to her assistance. Whilst taking off the crew of the doomed ship, she herself received a torpedo from the same tube. *Triumph* took the survivors from both these ships. (Not all.) We fitted them out in any clothes that we could spare from our kits, and they looked a motley crowd! Thus one Marine would be wearing a blue serge and white trousers, another the reverse. Some managed to get caps and others were without.

The action was called off at 5 p.m. and we steamed out of the Dardanelles. We had been in action from 9 a.m. and the weight of metal flung on shore must have been enormous. I was in charge of an ammunitioning party supplying the three Royal Marine 7.5-inch guns and we passed up seventy-four rounds – each of the shells fired weigh over 200 lb. Other of the fourteen 7.5-inch must have fired about the same and then to be added there was the shells fired by the four 10-inch guns.

When we were outside the Dardanelles and got out of range everyone crowded out on to the upper deck to get a breath of fresh air. By looking at a man's face you could tell if he had been stationed below as ammunition supply, or engine room or stokehole, or, in opposition, those who had been at the guns. The latter were full of fight, whereas those who had been below were white-faced and showed their nerve-wracking experience. They had not the excitement of fighting or the knowledge of what was going on. From 9 a.m. to 5 p.m. they had heard nothing but the crash of shells striking our ship and the sound of our own guns firing. Rumour passed from one to another often enlarged on the damage done by the enemy.

Aboard *Lord Nelson*, Private Percy Wyvill echoed the relief of having come through such a day, and was pleased to be in a 'lucky' ship.

Pte Percy Wyvill RMLI, HMS *Lord Nelson*, 18 March 1915

It is with very mixed feelings that I attempt to record today's doings, and it is only by the mercy of God that I am alive to do so. I will start from when we weighed anchor at 8.30 a.m. and steamed into the Dardanelles. *Inflexible* and *Queen Elizabeth*, *Agamemnon* and *Lord Nelson* – these ships went up first to engage the Forts in the Narrows. The remainder of British and French followed us in. The action started about 11 a.m. and we plugged them well with lyddite. The Forts replied very fiercely and all hell was let loose for a few hours. The *Inflexible* was the first to suffer, receiving some severe hits and losing her picket boat. Soon after this the French ship *Gaulois* had to withdraw in a sinking condition, another French ship was more unlucky still – the *Bouvet* was hit in several places and sank in three minutes. I do not know how many she lost. During this we were amidst it all, shells falling all around us and some striking or bursting over us, but we are still earning our name of the 'White Witch'. [This was *Lord Nelson*'s nickname in the Fleet, because of her ability to draw fire frequently without sustaining casualties.] Next to us was the *Irresistible,* and as soon as we saw she was sinking, we covered her with our fire while the Destroyers rescued her crew.

One Fort burst into flames and it is quite silenced, but from the other shore they kept up a heavy fire. HMS *Ocean* was now in trouble, believed to have struck a mine. She was sinking fast when the majority of her crew were taken off, and no sooner had some of them got into a Destroyer when the Destroyer was hit. She managed to get alongside of us, and we took aboard the *Ocean*'s men. The Commander of the Destroyer then said he would make for Tenedos. He said, 'I'll chance it and keep her going as long as the bulkheads hold together,' and away he went.

The failure of the Fleet to force the passage on 18 March effectively signalled that a combined naval and military operation would be required. Lieutenant General Birdwood, of the Australian and New Zealand Army Corps (ANZAC), had been sent by Lord Kitchener to report on the situation in the Dardanelles. On 19 March he wrote to Kitchener saying that he was reluctantly being 'driven' to the conclusion that ships alone would not force the Narrows and that military involvement would have to be a 'deliberate and progressive operation'. Too late, the men and materiel would be committed to the Dardanelles and Gallipoli Peninsula.

The ensuing campaign certainly did not mean that the Fleet was redundant. Throughout the landings and the efforts to extend the Allies' position on the Gallipoli Peninsula, the Fleet maintained vital bombardments in direct support of military actions and also indirect fire on Turkish guns on the far side of the peninsula. Several Royal Marines left diary accounts of this period, when attention had turned to the land war, which began on 25 April 1915. In the days after the failure at the Narrows, *Albion* and *Lord Nelson* were engaged in patrolling, as was HMS *Queen,* with Private Herbert Pare aboard, and HMS *Bacchante*, with Private W. E. Wells. Captain Godfrey Oppenheim, who changed his name to Orde at the end of 1915, was aboard the flagship, *Queen Elizabeth*. He joined her at the beginning of April, thus missing the 'excitement' of 18 March. He found 'marking time' frustrating, and was even more irritated when newspapers arrived from England with reports of what had been going on around the Dardanelles.

Capt. Godfrey Oppenheim RMLI, HMS *Queen Elizabeth*, 5 April 1915

Having finished our forty-eight hours at the work of protecting minesweepers, we retired for a rest. It is very funny to read the newspapers. For instance, the *Spectator* of 20th March says, 'From the Dardanelles there is not much news, due no doubt to the fact that the operations have reached a critical stage, and that the publication of the progress made might be injurious. All that we know is that we have cleared the Straits for about eleven miles, but that the problem of how to get through the Narrows without too great loss still confronts us.' The fact is – we have achieved nothing, up to date, beyond breaking up a few old forts and disabling permanently a small number of guns. The newspapers are full of rubbish about the *Queen Elizabeth* firing at 15 miles' range (i.e. 30,000 yards), when her guns are not sighted up to that distance. 'Eye witness' accounts of artillery operations viewed from Tenedos are also pure invention, owing to the fact that there is no suitable place to eye witness from. It is quite clear to everybody here that we are merely 'marking time', and have been for weeks. Nothing can be done until the army is landed, if they can find one to land.

Oppenheim was at this stage unaware that the 29th Division was on its way, and considered a Greek army, since he could not imagine one being spared from the Western Front. Nor did he view the enterprise with great hope. His account of that day continues:

It is possible that the Greeks let us down, and we depended on them to provide the army. If this is not so, the whole scheme has been conceived by men ignorant of war; we cannot spare an army of our own without weakening our forces in France more than we can afford to; on the other hand we cannot force the Dardanelles without strong land forces. Already we have lost several ships – expended millions of pounds of ammunition – for nothing. It's the old story of lack of co-operation – the co-operation of infantry and artillery. Furthermore the landing and supply of an army of the requisite size will be a matter of great difficulty, requiring much materiel, which can ill be spared just now.

A few days later his mood had become more hopeful.

Capt. Oppenheim RMLI, HMS *Queen Elizabeth*, 9 April 1915

From all accounts, troops are at Imbros and others are being landed at Lemnos, making with those at Alexandria about 120,000. On the 15th, 'the balloon goes up'. This may prove a very good show, if they can land sufficient troops on the Gulf of

Saros side of the Gallipoli Peninsula. This would cut off all the enemy to the south-west, and would enable the ships to get on with the bombardment of the Narrows. This prospect is much brighter. We must have an army – without it we can do nothing, with it we can carry the thing through.

Thursday 15 April passed without incident, and on the 16th HMS *Queen Elizabeth* received Australian troops for boat drills.

Capt. Oppenheim RMLI, HMS *Queen Elizabeth*, 16 April 1915

A Turkish torpedo boat tried to torpedo a Transport this morning. At a range of 100 yards she fired 3 torpedoes, all of which missed! The report says that 100 men were killed in the panic that ensued on the Transport. This is not good hearing.

The transport was the SS *Manitou,* whose captain had ordered the lowering of boats before the torpedo boat came in to finish her off. Some of the soldiers aboard panicked and 51 men drowned or died of hypothermia. The torpedo boat, having waited for boats to be lowered, got too close to the *Manitou* and fired three torpedoes which passed innocuously beneath her keel.

Capt. Oppenheim RMLI, HMS *Queen Elizabeth*, 16 April 1915

This evening we took 500 men of the 10th Brigade of Australian Infantry on board, and practised sending them away in boats in the dark. We shall do the same tomorrow. These men will come with us on 'the day'. The ships will evidently assemble under cover of darkness, and the men will be got into the boats in the dark: so as to attack at dawn.
    . . . The Australian Infantry did not come on board again tonight after all. It is to be hoped that these orders and counter orders are not indicative of confusion of ideas among the Staff.
    . . . The General and his staff have come on board this evening – the men come tomorrow morning. I suggest that a suitable signal would be 'England expects that every man will make the Turkey Trot' – although these operations are not looking quite such ragtime warfare as they were.
    The men came on board at 12.30 p.m. today, and we left Port

Mudros at 1.30 p.m. It was an inspiring sight to see the huge transports steaming out, their decks crowded with cheering men; our band of course playing 'appropriate airs'.

The *Queen* was also full of Australian troops, as Private Pare recorded, and was decidedly cramped.

Pte Herbert Pare RMLI, HMS *Queen*, 24 April 1915

There are about 500 of them and [they] are the 9th Battalion of the Australian Contingent. The same numbers have also gone on board the *Prince of Wales*, *London* and *Bacchante*. As soon as they got on board we got under way and left for Tenedos. The troops very soon made themselves comfortable. They are all Australians with the exception of a few New Zealanders who have got attached to them some way or other. The General went round among the soldiers to make sure that they were comfortable. At 9 p.m. they were served out with a hot meal and told to get as much rest as possible. We could not walk about the ship for soldiers and equipment which was lying all around. No hammocks were allowed to be slung tonight.

Colour Sergeant Reginald Hedges, serving in HMS *Implacable*, found it just as crowded.

Clr Sgt Reginald Hedges RMLI, HMS *Implacable*, 25 April 1915

At 5 p.m. on the 24th April we embarked about 700 men of the Fusiliers. We did our best to make them comfortable.

No man was allowed to have his hammock so soldier, Marine and sailor slept side by side on the decks. It was a very curious sight to witness on a battleship.

We steamed very slowly from Tenedos to the 'Dards'. We were now entering the enemy's country so all guns crews were manned and kept watch all night.

I had occasion to leave my gun about midnight, and I saw the soldiers. Some were asleep, some were talking yarns and some were writing home, the last time for a good many poor fellows.

The landings commenced in the early hours of 25 April. The warships provided 'artillery' support and also boats' crews to tow in the boats crammed with soldiers. The command of these towing boats was given to midshipmen, some of whom were as young as 15 years old. The men aboard the ships did not come under much fire which actually caused damage, but had clear views of what went on as the troops reached shore, and their memories stayed fresh. *Lord Nelson* was positioned off Morto Bay, in support of the landing at S beach, which was made by men of the South Wales Borderers, and which was achieved with comparatively low casualties. But Bugler Holloway was able to see what was going on where gaining a toehold on the peninsula proved grim and costly. He recalled, as men from other ships did also, the sea turned red with blood, and bodies and parts of bodies floating in the tide. Private Percy Wyvill, whilst not dwelling on the horrors, was aware of the day's importance.

Pte Wyvill RMLI, HMS *Lord Nelson*, 25 April 1915

I take up my pen now to record one of the most glorious days in the world's history. It is impossible to describe it all, it would take weeks to do so. We got underway at 2.20 a.m. with all the Allied Fleets and transports and steamed towards the Dardanelles. At 5 a.m. we started to sweep the country on each side with heavy gun fire, each ship taking a certain area. The Turks replied fiercely with howitzers and field guns, this ship being hit once or twice besides several shrapnel bursting over us. After about two hours' bombardment the landing of troops began and the way it was carried out was splendid – the French on the Asiatic side and British and Colonials on the European side. The place we were covering was Sedd ul Bahr and the country beyond. The troops that landed at Sedd ul Bahr found the town swarming with the Turkish soldiers, so they withdrew, and the town was bombarded again for several hours. Meanwhile, the Australians had landed in another place in the Gulf of Saros, and made splendid progress, capturing some Krupp guns.

Captain Godfrey Oppenheim, aboard *Queen Elizabeth*, knew about the Krupp guns, though his pleasure was diminished by the knowledge that the Anzac landing had not taken place in the correct location.

Capt. Oppenheim RMLI, HMS *Queen Elizabeth*, 25 April 1915

Got to our rendezvous about 12.30 a.m. The position was
marked by the *Triumph*. The men were got into boats, placed
in tow of steam launches and the whole proceeded at 5 knots to
a spot one mile from land. It was discovered afterwards that
we were nearly two miles north of our proper landing place: a
very serious and inexcusable error – must have been due to
the *Triumph*. She ought to have been able to fix her position
accurately by cross bearings – all we had to do was to steam
four miles due east.

In reality, the positioning error was not that of HMS *Triumph* but a
combination of factors, most importantly the towing launches keeping
closer together than intended, because they were otherwise invisible to
each other, and an act of initiative by the midshipman in command of
the most northerly tow. He made an alteration of two points to port to
take his line of boats ashore in a less exposed position, and this in turn
brought all the other tows to the north. Captain Oppenheim's account
continues:

The first party got ashore all right and it was apparently some
time before the enemy discovered them. Musketry fire then
became fairly brisk, also some howitzer fire at the troops'
transports. The *London* replied – somewhat inadequately –
with 6–inch. About 6 a.m. the musketry fire had died down,
and we received a signal from the shore that the landing was
progressing favourably. We seem to have taken possession of a
high ridge.
  9 a.m. Landing very successful in spite of making a mess of
the actual spot. The Australians charged magnificently up the
hill – 900 feet – after a fine burst of fire, and now hold the
ridge, having capture three Krupp guns. The landing will now
be extended to the south so as to embrace the proper landing
place.

Private Pare, who watched the Australian troops head ashore from the
Queen, gives a detailed account of the night's events.

Clr Sgt Hedges RMLI, HMS *Implacable*, 25 April 1915

It was a terrible time, we sweated hard feeding the guns. The
thundering of guns and being choked with smoke was horrible.
We were very pleased at sending a Turkish field gun into the
air, but when we saw the soldiers had reached the top of the
cliffs I cannot describe our feelings. We were elated with proud
British victory . . . Then there came a lull in the firing and one
of my guns crew fainted. He was choked by fumes, [but] he
soon came round and was as right as rain afterwards.

We were then ordered to get out the steam pinnace. I and
others caught hold of the boat's falls and walked onto the
Quarter Deck. Here the bullets were whistling around us and
falling into the water.

As it was so dangerous to life I said to myself, 'Reginald –
hop it,' because I would sooner be a live nobody than a dead
hero. We finished that job, closed up round our guns and
bombarded up till noon . . .

About 1 p.m. one of the realities of war was brought home to
us. Our Fleet Surgeon [Adrien Forrester] was shot through the
stomach on the Quarter Deck. We buried him at sea next day.
The ship's company were very sorry as he was very popular
and a thorough gentleman. During the rest of the day we
continually bombarded the Turks, meanwhile our troops had
entrenched themselves and were advancing slowly but
steadily.

Captain Oppenheim was receiving more information on the progress of
the landing and saw his first Turkish prisoner of the day.

Capt. Oppenheim RMLI, HMS *Queen Elizabeth*, 25 April 1915

It now transpires that on first landing the Australians
dumped down their packs and rushed the first three trenches
without firing a shot, climbing the hill like cats. What
casualties we have had so far is not known. One Turkish
prisoner was just brought on board; poor devil, he looked
fearfully frightened and was trembling like a leaf. I don't know
what he thought was going to be done to him! However, he'll
be well treated – in a cell – and ought to think himself lucky
he's out of it all.

12.30 p.m. We have seized De Tott's battery on [the] hill
above Morto Bay (1st Squadron). The Australians state they

require more ammunition at once. There has been a continuous roar of musketry all the forenoon.

4.30 p.m. The landing is not going very well here now. Apparently our men advanced a bit too far on the other side of the hill and about 3 p.m. came in for a regular storm of shrapnel from all sides. After the Neuve Chapelle incident the soldiers seem very afraid of our firing. [British shells dropping short had caused significant casualties at Neuve Chapelle in March.] As a result, having no guns themselves at the time, the enemy's howitzers were able to fire undisturbed, doing tremendous execution. We have at least 500 casualties – the Hospital Ship is now full – and the total is now about 1500. After the shrapnel storm mentioned above our men had to retire, and could be seen running back over the crest of the hill, carrying their wounded with them. To add to our difficulties all our aeroplanes disappeared – for some reason not yet known.

The *Majestic* opened up about 1 p.m., but was stopped for some inexplicable reason by the *Queen*, because the soldiers had reported '2000 short'. At 4 p.m. she opened fire again with aeroplane spotting and quickly knocked out a battery of three guns. This might have been done three hours earlier. All we can hope for now is to entrench ourselves on the crest of the hill for the night and wait for the other attacks to develop. The soldiers keep on urgently asking for their howitzer batteries to be landed: poor devils, they must be suffering fearful losses from the enemy's unchallenged batteries. All our tremendous strength in ships' guns is being wasted – we are lying idle. The battle continues with unceasing roar and rattle.

5.30 p.m. There are known to be 600 wounded in the Hospital Ship, 350 in a transport and many more on the beach waiting to be taken off. A Sergeant reported to the PMO [Principal Medical Officer] that of the men on board here, in two companies, only two men remained unwounded. We advanced three miles inland over the ridge and were then beaten back, but afterwards regained our ground. The operations at Sedd ul Bahr continue satisfactorily but slowly. All firing has ceased for the moment, except for some enemy howitzers. Mules have been landed, and it is to be hoped that the guns will soon follow, so as to be able to get into position during the night. Much will depend on tomorrow.

7.20 p.m. ... Yesterday I repaired the eye piece of Col. Weir's glasses, presented to him on leaving Australia by his 'fellow workers in the Govt. Service'. Poor chap, he's rendered his last service – he's dead.

Captain Oppenheim was in a position to know more of what was really going on than the average man afloat, which meant that he ended 25 April in less than buoyant mood. One thing at least proved less depressing, for his diary entry has an amendment regarding Colonel Weir, made on 30 April: 'Only wounded.'

Colour Sergeant Hedges was suffering from the effects of cordite fumes aboard *Implacable*, but was well aware how much better off he was than the wounded from the beaches.

Clr Sgt Hedges RMLI, HMS *Implacable*, 25 April 1915

By this time I had swallowed enough cordite fumes that I suffered greatly from a rampaging headache. It drove me nearly cranky. I have forgotten to mention that at 4 p.m. we managed to get some of the wounded aboard from shore. We dressed them and made them a bit easier and then sent them to the hospital ship.

It was a pitiful sight, but the poor fellows were very plucky and cheerful. Their wounds were ugly, bleeding and terribly swollen. Some had been hit in the head, some arms and others in the legs.

Feeling a bit queer I turned in about 9 p.m. and had just got to sleep when about 11 p.m. I was shook to close up around my gun.

The Turks were making a very fierce night attack to drive our fellows into the sea . . . We ceased firing at 4 a.m. next morning and laid down to rest. Reveille sounded at 6.15 a.m., had breakfast at 8, afterwards we again commenced firing.

Private Wells, of HMS *Bacchante*, wrote a comparatively short entry in his diary, which shows that not all the Marines who were off the beaches were unaware of the seriousness of the situation ashore.

Pte W. E. Wells RMLI, HMS *Bacchante*, 25 April 1915

The Allied Fleets were divided into two Fleets and the *Bacchante* had to cover the landing of the British troops. The landing commenced about 3.00 [a.m.], and the boats full of troops approached the shore, when a terrific fire of Maxim and rifle was showered upon our troops. Many boats were blown up in the attempt. The [men in] boats that did land charged up the hill, clearing the Turks from their positions. Many a foul deed was committed by the Turks, but no prisoners were taken until sometime afterwards. The shrapnel fire was deadly, and many a Red Cross man was killed in the attempt of saving the wounded exposed to the enemy fire. Very heavy casualties on both sides. Fierce fighting all day, the salt water turned red for some hours, but our troops captured the hill at 2.15. The Australians charged too far, and were cut off from our lines.

Sergeant Edwin Kershaw, in HMS *Albion*, made equally grim notes of how the landings had gone at Helles, where his ship was in support of V Beach, but concluded with a positive thought.

Sgt Kershaw RMLI, HMS *Albion*, 25 April 1915

The day progresses. SS *River Clyde* with 2,000 troops, DF [Royal Dublin Fusiliers, one quarter of the battalion; the rest came ashore in tows], Munsters and Liverpool Regt [in reality half of the 2nd Battalion Hampshire Regiment], ran ashore and dropped her sides for troops to get out. This was very bad for the troops that were in the boats [the majority of the Royal Dublin Fusiliers] coming under Maxim fire between the ship and shore, roughly 250 being either killed or wounded.

The Royal Dublin Fusiliers lost over 400 of the 700 men attempting to land, and many of the 300 who made it ashore were wounded. It had been intended that the *River Clyde*'s steam hopper should be moved into position to link ship to shore, but this had gone awry at the outset. A brave attempt to use lighters as a bridging device proved only a temporary solution, and one where the men were being mown down as they crossed the lighters to shore. A second attempt, using boats and then a bridge of boats, was met with equally devastating fire and resultant carnage. Sergeant Kershaw continues:

Warspite opened fire with 6" Lyddite, sweeping the whole of the Valley, while our guns were shelling trenches with 6" and 12 pdr [pounder], which was excellent firing. How troops could live in that fire, [they] could live anywhere. It was Hell upon earth for nearly four hours. During the evening boat loads of wounded were removed from the beach to different ships. The sights that came aboard us were ghastly, in fact they won't bear describing, it was awful. We finished up firing about

8 p.m. Then under darkness we got rid of the wounded and dead. About 10.30 p.m. there were Maxims firing from both sides, some bullets came inboard, but did no damage. On the whole the day was very successful. What was carried out could never have been accomplished had it not been for the ships of the navy, on whom the whole Empire are relying for the taking of the Dardanelles.

Private Percy Wyvill, whose diary entry opened this account of 'Anzac Day', concludes his entry with a paragraph about the landings at S Beach and the French diversionary attack at Kum Kale.

Pte Wyvill, HMS *Lord Nelson*, 25 April 1915

Another lot of troops, South Wales Borderers, landed a few miles past Sedd ul Bahr, directly under cover of our own fire. They were met with raking fire from the enemy entrenched, and I could see the brave lads falling very fast, but they soon gained a sheltered position and held on there. We carried on shelling the enemy's trenches and the Queen Lizzie was then pouring salvoes into Sedd ul Bahr. In the other side, Kum Kale was receiving plenty of attention from the French ships and fire broke out in several places. The French troops made very good progress and effected the landing of their Field Artillery, and it was a fine sight to see them limber up and then gallop into position. The wounded were now being brought down to the boats on the European side and the *Cornwallis* took them aboard while still under shrapnel fire. The fighting on each side was now getting very fierce, and we were kept very busy at our guns assisting the troops ashore by covering their advances and blowing the Turks to pieces whenever their positions were located. This was carried on until nightfall, and then the sound of rifle and Maxim fire was audible throughout the whole night.

Once the initial landings had been effected, a routine emerged for the ships working in support, providing barrages and targeted fire. In the few days after 25 April the consolidation of the beachheads and landing of more troops meant that there was a lot of work for the Royal Marines gun crews, and little rest or opportunity for meals. Whilst undoubtedly in a far safer position than those ashore, the men aboard the warships faced the risk of Turkish gunfire and the ever present threat of torpedo attack from enemy destroyers and then submarines. A selection of diary entries from the ensuing week illustrates the hard work undertaken. The first is from Private Percy Wyvill in *Lord Nelson*.

Pte Wyvill RMLI, HMS *Lord Nelson*, Tuesday 27 April 1915

As soon as daylight appeared we started again, very little rest and nothing to eat except corn beef. Troops are making steady progress and many prisoners have been taken. Today there seems to be something doing on the Asiatic side and several shells fell round us, fired from somewhere near the Dardanelles. TBD [Torpedo-boat destroyer] *Raccoon* was hit by a shell which penetrated the foremost boiler. The 'Aggie' [*Agamemnon*] covered her while *Raccoon* got her collision mat over the side, then she made for Tenedos and beached herself. Another TBD, *Scorpion*, had a boiler burst injuring several hands. The troops did very well today and hold good positions where they are entrenched for the night. 6 p.m. we are relieved by sister Aggie and proceed to Rabbit Island to take in ammunition, that took all night. We have no doubt used more ammunition in two days than the North Sea Fleet will use in ten years. Mail received good. No sleep tonight and battle again tomorrow. Changed, had fresh meat.

Sgt Kershaw RMLI, HMS *Albion*, Wednesday 28 April 1915

4 a.m. turned hands out and went into action 4.45 a.m. . . . A big shell hit us in the bows causing a hole 12' by 10', another one hit on the quarter port side, but only broke away the rubbing strake, the water from the splash drenching us in the Port Battery. At noon we were relieved by three ships, these going to do what the Old *Albion* had been doing herself. Great progress has been made throughout the day. Went to Rabbit Island to ammunition ship but found her nearly empty, and couldn't fill up. Left Rabbit Island during mid watch, for Lemnos, Friday morning [30 April]. Arrived at Lemnos we prepared to coal but took ammunition first, then took in stores, then coaled, then provisioning, having had four ships alongside during the day. Turned in after 21 hours' hard work.

Pte Wyvill RMLI, HMS *Lord Nelson*, Thursday 29 April 1915

Action again this morning and we are catching it pretty warm. Shells from guns on Asiatic shore, hit several times, but no one very much hurt. Lord Graham [Lieutenant Commander] slightly scratched by splinter when shell struck fore turret. *Agamemnon* not so lucky, one shell burst on her flying deck injuring about nine men. Queen Lizzie, firing overland from Gulf of Saros, sank a Turkish transport in the Narrows.

HMS *Albion* had divers over the side on 30 April, working on the damaged bows, and Sergeant Edwin Kershaw notes that two compartments were pumped out, then the carpenter's party worked inside on the hole. Work was still in progress on 1 May.

Sgt Kershaw RMLI, HMS *Albion*, Wednesday 1 May 1915

Still working on the bows, getting ready for sea. Working party down getting ammunition ready, taking off grommets and baseplates. Stowed Lyddite in shell room and common [shell] all round passages. Finished the bows about 8 p.m. and then put to sea for Dardanelles.

The rest of Edwin Kershaw's diary, following this matter-of-fact entry, is blank. The next day, 2 May, he was killed when *Albion* sustained further damage in action.

Captain Godfrey Oppenheim was again despairing of the strategic situation, as he reflected on 3 May.

Capt. Oppenheim RMLI, HMS *Queen Elizabeth*, 3 May 1915

I hear that General French [Field Marshal Sir John French] is very annoyed that these operations have been commenced, as it takes away so much men and materiel – but if they deal with the matter promptly and send us sufficient reinforcements – another 20,000 men – we shall be able to bring the matter to a successful conclusion; a result which will have a very marked effect on the operations both in the East and West, and will justify the course taken. But if they send insufficient men, the operation will drag slowly on, no decision will be obtained, and the men and materiel employed here will have been really wasted . . .

4th May . . . If they are going to starve us for men, we had much better pack up and acknowledge ourselves beaten. If we send troops out in detail, we shall be beaten in detail. If they again try to force the Narrows before the land campaign has achieved its object we shall suffer considerable loss and even then shall have attained no lasting result. So it appears to me, at any rate. Doubtless I shall change my mind!

The threat from torpedoes was a cause for concern, with so many warships engaged in such a small area, and frequently in static positions. German submarines did not make their appearance off the Dardanelles until mid May, but their anticipated arrival meant a change of routine for the Fleet, with only a couple of battleships directly off the coast at one time, with the rest in more protected waters at Imbros unless called up for a particular task. In fact it was a torpedo attack from a destroyer which first caused a major loss. At 1.15 a.m. on 13 May the Turkish destroyer *Muavenet-i Millet*, commanded by Kapitän-Leutnant Rudolph Firle of the Imperial German Navy, torpedoed the battleship *Goliath*, scoring three hits. *Goliath* turned turtle and the majority of her 750 complement were lost. Only 183 survivors were picked up. Private Percy Wyvill was asleep in his hammock aboard HMS *Lord Nelson* when he was called out with the boats' crews to rescue survivors. In such a situation, the men nearest the boats formed the crew, so a boat could have oars manned by Royal Marines, seamen, stokers and telegraphists.

Pte Wyvill RMLI, HMS *Lord Nelson*, 13 May 1915

About 1.30 a.m. this morning HMS *Goliath* was sunk by torpedoes fired from a Turkish torpedo boat. This is a terrible thing to write about and the scenes were indescribable. The first I heard of it, was waking up to hear the pipe 'Away lifeboats crews'. I immediately jumped from my hammock and took a place in the cutter. Now the *Goliath* was lying a good way ahead of us in the Dardanelles, and as there was an eight-knot current the survivors and wreckage were soon abreast of us. We left the ship and started our work of rescue; the cries of the men in the water and the darkness of the night broken here and there by the beams of the *Lord Nelson*'s searchlights, made a scene I shall never forget. We had not gone far from the ship when we picked two up, a marine and a midshipman

[Midshipman Wolstan Forester] were the first. Then we heard cries in all directions and we were kept hard at it pulling here and there, then dragging the drowning men into the boat. Some were in a pitiful state, quite delirious. After pulling round through all the wreckage for some time, we started to pull back to the ship, but we could see nothing of her and her searchlights had been switched off long before, so we came to the conclusion that she had gone out to sea for safety. Our position was then, all the boats' crew were naked or nearly so, because we had given our dry things to the men we saved. Well, we could see nothing and we could not tell where we were pulling to, but at last we sighted a trawler and hailed her. She took the rescued men aboard, and we made the boat fast and went aboard ourselves. At daylight there was no sign of our ship, but she came steaming up about 6 a.m. and we lost no time in getting aboard again. The ship was full of survivors all walking about with blankets round them – three lay dead.

The medical officer, Fleet Surgeon Menary, recorded in his journal that he had had preparations made – including hot blankets and Bovril – and that 116 men were attended to, suffering from the effects of submersion. All these men recovered, though there were three men dead on arrival. These were the men seen by Private Wyvill.

On 25 May, the German submarine U21, commanded by Kapitän-Leutnant Otto Hershing, arrived off Gallipoli and commenced her task. An attempt to sink HMS *Vengeance* was foiled when the ship took avoiding action, but just after midday a second target was found, HMS *Triumph*. Although the torpedo was again seen, this time it could not be avoided. Corporal Fred Brookes was at his action station on the starboard side.

Cpl Brookes RMLI, HMS *Triumph*, 25 May 1915

Up to now the Fleet here assembled had not been troubled with submarines and had things much their own way. They were strung out along the coast line, in some cases anchored, as they bombarded enemy positions in support of our troops on shore. We were near Gaba Tepe off Anzac [Cove] supporting the Australians and New Zealanders.

The appearance of the submarine that morning put a different complexion on matters. Each ship still continued to shell its target but steamed in circles at speed to elude the attentions of the sub. We did not conform to this pattern but kept just a little steerage way on the ship and trusted to our outspanned torpedo-nets for protection. Other precautions were taken [such] as closing watertight doors, [and] manning the lesser armament, which were loaded and with a presumed range on the sights. Everyone not actually required for duty below decks had to remain on the upper deck and hatches leading below were dropped.

I was at my station as NCO in charge of the two 14-pounders, in the waist on the starboard side. I controlled these guns from the foot of the starboard crane.

At about one bell (12.30 p.m.) the submarine's periscope was sighted abreast of the ship on the starboard side. I gave the order to fire to my two guns but the shells dropped over. I reduced the range but before I could fire the second salvo a torpedo was speeding towards us. My foremost gun tried to depress and hit the torpedo in a forlorn effort.

The torpedo struck the ship just below my foremost gun. The explosion shook the ship and she heeled to starboard and then she righted herself, before heeling again to starboard and turning turtle in twelve minutes. The explosion blew off all the bunker lids and covered everyone on the starboard side in coal dust. The water cast up by the explosion came down in torrents and I hung on to a stanchion to prevent myself being washed over the side. When it subsided I missed the Private whose duty was beside me and I surmised that he had been washed overboard.

I had often rehearsed in my mind what route I would take under such circumstances and I found that I subconsciously followed that route. I seemed to be two personalities, one talking to the other. The subconscious voice was saying, 'Over to the fore-and-after bridge, along the bridge, and on to the after shelter deck, drop on the quarterdeck, down the ladder to the torpedo net-shelf, out on the after torpedo boom, and drop in the "ditch".' As the voice directed so I took that route and dropped into the sea and swam clear of the ship.

As I climbed down the iron ladder to the net-shelf the Chinese Messman was clinging to that ladder and would not let go despite the ship sinking. When I was clear of the ship I watched the ship heeling over and the torpedo boom on the port side rising up with the nets hanging down from them, and caught in the meshes of the net by their fingers and toes, were men who had attempted to climb down them. I saw the Chinese Messman had left the ladder and had climbed out to the end of the after torpedo boom. At this moment the cranes and upper deck casemates, at the extreme angle, took charge and the ship gave a sudden lurch. This shot the Chinaman up into the air to come down, plop, into the sea. I thought, 'That is the last of John Chinaman,' as I knew that he could not swim.

Destroyers and trawlers raced toward the stricken ship and one destroyer managed to take many off by nosing in and backing off repeatedly, each time taking off as many as she could. The operation was perilous, as the *Triumph* was heeling over rapidly, but the Captain of that destroyer took the risk to save life.

The destroyer in question was the *Chelmer*, yet again proving invaluable to a sinking ship. Much credit must be given to her captain, Lieutenant Commander Hugh England, for his seamanship and determination. Corporal Brookes continues:

The sea was covered with men swimming and the rescue ships moved to where there were groups and in doing so many isolated men were run down or left. I swam well clear and waited until the first scurry was over and then swam over to a destroyer that was nearest. A midshipman threw me a rope and I secured this under my armpits and hung on. It was a good job that I did so, for the destroyer forged ahead towards another group of men in the water. I was towed under till she stopped. I was then hauled on board and joined many of my shipmates who had been picked up from the water.

Most of us had discarded clothing when we left the ship [so] as to have a better chance in the sea. I had stripped all but my flannel [underwear] and a pair of socks. Thus arrayed we were fell in and mustered by the Sergeant Major similarly undressed; how he managed to salvage his 'Watch Bill' puzzled us but he checked our names off by this list as if nothing unusual had occurred.

Our old friend, 'The Count', conductor of the Band and the ship's clown, still lived up to his innate humour. He could not swim, but as the ship turned over he had climbed right around the ship and stood posed upon the keel in imitation of the Kaiser. He struck an attitude and twirled his moustache until he slipped on the wet seaweed and slid in the 'ditch'. The Commander dived in off the deck of a destroyer and saved him as he did to many others.

The *Triumph* had no boats to lower as these had been taken out of the ship as a fire risk at the commencement of the Dardanelles campaign. A 'copper-punt' (used by the side-party for painting ship) was the only thing resembling a boat and a group of seamen had dropped it into the water and manned it, and as they paddled away from the ship kept time as they sung the popular song 'It's a long way to Tipperary'. This was typical of the morale of the ship's company, and many jokes were passed one to the other as men swam waiting to be picked up.

The Engineer Commander sacrificed his life in an effort to prevent the ship blowing up. [This was Engineer Commander Ernest F. Baker, Royal Navy.] The ship had been stopped and the boilers were in danger of bursting if the steam was not eased off. He knew the risk, and, as the ship went over, went below and started the engines, knowing he had little hope of escape. Before he went below he said 'good-bye' to his Royal Marine attendant, saying that he had no-one to grieve for him and described what he was going to do.

Another Officer, who had a dread of drowning, had made himself a life-saving jacket with numerous corks from bottles. This jacket should have kept him afloat for ever, but unfortunately he jumped over the stern of the ship at the moment that the Engineer Commander had started the engines, and was killed by the revolving screw.

Another Officer was run over by a destroyer as she dashed from group to group. These were the three officers that we lost additional to fifty-three men. Everyone else was saved, mostly from the water and much can be said for the efficiency of the inflated rubber life-belt that had been issued to all: without those belts we would have lost many more.

The destroyer that had picked me up steamed post haste for Mudros Harbour, and, as we steamed away, passed our chummy ship of Tsingtao days, who was racing to the rescue. When the *Chelmer* heard the news by wireless, she was coaling from a collier at Rabbit Island; she broke away from the collier and raced to Anzac. She cheered as we passed and we cheered back.

On arrival at Mudros we were placed on board a French merchant ship called the *Fouvette*, which ship collected all the survivors from the *Triumph*. As the rescuing ships came in, survivors were transferred to the *Fouvette* . . .

As we collected up on the *Fouvette* we had a few surprises as many shipmates turned up who we thought had died. We were all asked if we knew of anyone who we could definitely say was lost. I had mentioned two persons under this heading, one, who was the Private who was my assistant at the foot of the starboard crane. I said he must have been washed overboard and drowned. I was wrong: he turned up the following day, having been picked up by a trawler. The other person I named was the Chinese Messman and I described what I saw. Three days afterwards John Chinaman turned up from a destroyer. I asked him how he had been saved and he said, 'Fall in water, no can swim, come up, no can swim, come up and see wood, catch wood, can do. Commander, he good man, he save me.'

What is particularly interesting about the accounts of being sunk is the calm, almost detached way in which Private Wilcox and Corporal Brookes describe events. They had lost their 'home' and all their belongings, and could easily have lost their lives. Despite this there is a matter-of-fact quality to what they recorded. The same can be said of accounts of the Battle of Jutland. They are in marked contrast to the more personal and emotional writings of men serving ashore. The man afloat is physically an element of his ship; the man ashore is part of a close-knit unit but, when the shrapnel and the bullets fly, very much aware that he is on his own.

2

Jutland

On the afternoon of 31 May 1916, the Grand Fleet and the German High Seas Fleet met after nearly two years of move and countermove, in what proved to be the last great battleship battle. Both sides sought a breakthrough: Britain wanted to show that the German fleet could not challenge its command of the seas, and the Germans wanted to weaken the British, who had superiority of numbers, and thus strengthen their challenge. The British were looking for an equivalent of Trafalgar, a decisive victory. In reality the 'fog' of war and of the North Sea meant that the result of the clash of the two fleets could be seen as victory or defeat by either side.

In May of 1916 Admiral Reinhard Scheer, Commander-in-Chief of the High Seas Fleet, put a plan into action which was designed to trap and destroy the British battlecruisers commanded by Vice Admiral Sir David Beatty. The German battlecruisers under Admiral Hipper would act as bait to tempt the British into the North Sea, whilst the main German fleet stood by, out of sight. The trap would then be sprung and the British battlecruisers, hopefully already damaged by submarine attacks, would be devastated. Unfortunately for Scheer, British Naval Intelligence knew his plan and, several hours before the Germans had even put to sea, sent out both the Grand Fleet under Admiral Sir John Jellicoe aboard HMS *Iron Duke* and the Battlecruiser Force under Beatty in HMS *Lion*. Since 1914 the German signalling codes had been known by 'Room 40' Naval Intelligence, at least sufficiently to know when the Germans were putting to sea and their likely area of operations. In fact, had Room 40's intercepts been correctly passed on and given credence during the pursuit, Jellicoe might have achieved the victory he sought. Nevertheless, the Germans were intercepted before they could set their trap. The two forces met off the Danish coast in a battle which the Germans called Skagerrak and the British called Jutland.

The men aboard the warships could only see the part of the battle as it took shape around them in their own small area. Without going into

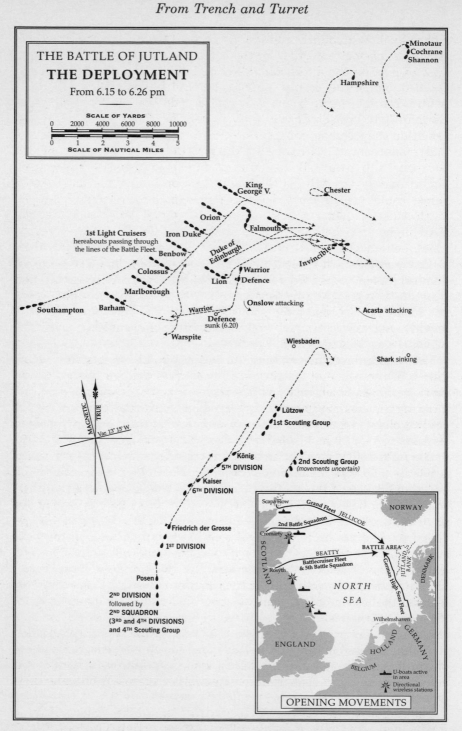

THE BATTLE OF JUTLAND
THE DEPLOYMENT
From 6.15 to 6.26 pm

SCALE OF YARDS
0   2000   4000   6000   8000   10000
0   1   2   3   4   5
SCALE OF NAUTICAL MILES

Minotaur
Cochrane
Shannon

Hampshire

King
George V.

Chester

Orion

Falmouth

1st Light Cruisers
hereabouts passing through
the lines of the Battle Fleet.

Iron Duke

Benbow

Duke of
Edinburgh

Invincible

Colossus

Warrior
Defence

Lion

Marlborough

Warrior

Onslow attacking

Acasta attacking

Southampton

Barham

Defence
sunk (6.20)

Warspite

Wiesbaden

Shark sinking

MAGNETIC
TRUE

Var. 13° 15' W

Lützow

1st Scouting Group

König
5TH DIVISION

2nd Scouting Group
(movements uncertain)

Kaiser
6TH DIVISION

Friedrich der Grosse

1ST DIVISION

Posen

2ND DIVISION
followed by
2ND SQUADRON
(3RD and 4TH DIVISIONS)
and 4TH Scouting Group

Scapa Flow

Grand Fleet JELLICOE

NORWAY

2nd Battle Squadron

Cromarty

BATTLE AREA

SCOTLAND

BEATTY

Battlecruiser Fleet
& 5th Battle Squadron

JUTLAND
BANK

Rosyth

NORTH
SEA

German High Seas Fleet

DENMARK

Wilhelmshaven

GERMANY

ENGLAND

HOLLAND

BELGIUM

U-boats active
in area

Directional
wireless stations

OPENING MOVEMENTS

Jutland, 31 May 1916

a blow-by-blow account of the course of the battle, it is necessary to give an outline of events in order for the personal accounts to fall into place. At 2.15 p.m. on the afternoon of Wednesday 31 May, the light cruiser *Galatea*, one of the 'scouts' for Vice Admiral Beatty's force, sighted a neutral steamer being boarded by the torpedo boats ordered in by the German light cruiser *Elbing*. *Galatea* and *Elbing* exchanged fire and called up their companions. *Galatea* also signalled to Beatty that she had made contact with enemy vessels. Determined not to let the Germans slip away, Beatty turned his force towards the action. Unfortunately the 5th Battle Squadron, containing his four battle-ships, could not properly see the flag signal being passed by the battlecruisers. Some minutes later the signal was confirmed by searchlight and they altered course, but by this time they were ten miles behind. The battlecruiser forces headed towards each other. Beatty wanted to hit hard at Hipper's squadrons, but the German admiral aimed to lead Beatty onto the main part of the German High Seas Fleet. When the two battlecruiser forces came into contact, Hipper turned as if running for home. Beatty turned south as well, on a slightly converging course, and a fierce engagement took place, in which Beatty's battlecruisers suffered badly.

This was in large measure due to failures in following safety proce-dures, in the name of speed and convenience, and the design of the British ships, which were vulnerable to shells hitting turrets and allowing the ensuing flash to pass down and cause the explosion of the cordite charges below. It was a problem that had occurred in the German navy, and had been highlighted by the damage to the *Seydlitz* at the Battle of Dogger Bank in 1915. A 13.5-inch shell, which weighed 1,400 lb (635 kg), had been fired from HMS *Lion* and struck the barbette armour of the aft turret, at the level of the working chamber, immediately below deck level. The bagged charges had ignited and a flash fire had wrecked the gunhouse and magazine. When the maga-zine crew had attempted to escape via the handling room of the next turret, the flash fire had destroyed that turret as well. Only the swift action of the Executive Officer in ordering the flooding of the maga-zines had saved the ship, though lives had been lost. The Germans had learned the lesson of this near disaster, and had not only made mod-ifications to their ships but also ensured strict adherence to the rule that flash doors be closed in action. The Royal Navy, determined upon the highest possible rate of fire, continued to bring up excess numbers of charge bags, removed from their leather 'Clarkson' cases, ready for action, and did not pay attention to the leaving open of watertight doors.

The senior Royal Marine officer aboard *Lion*, Major Francis Harvey RMLI, had written to a fellow officer, Major Arthur Grattan RMLI, serving in HMS *Orion*, after the battle. Major Harvey was unaware how close his ship had been to destroying the *Seydlitz* in spectacular fashion.

Maj. Francis Harvey RMLI, HMS *Lion*, 13 February 1915

> As to the fighting in a turret, one doesn't suffer any discomfort and my chief feeling has been of 'curiosity' mixed with the idea that whoever else is coming to grief, oneself will be all right. I am under no delusion though, that if a proj[ectile] does hit one's turret it will in all probability come right in and send one to glory.

At Jutland, after missing the first vital signal and delaying their turn, the battleships of the 5th Battle Squadron arrived on the scene only after two battlecruisers had been sunk and damage caused to others. It was then about 4.15 p.m. and the main fleets had not yet come into contact. The light cruisers were engaging each other and searching for further units. At 4.38 p.m. the light cruiser *Southampton* reported sighting the German High Seas Fleet under Scheer. Beatty then reversed his force, heading northwest, to lead the enemy onto the Grand Fleet under Admiral Jellicoe – exactly the same move that Hipper had attempted.

As the two battle fleets closed, the light cruisers clashed again. This time, however, the Germans found themselves suddenly under heavy fire from three battlecruisers, Rear Admiral Hood's 3rd Battlecruiser Squadron. They had been sent ahead by Jellicoe to help Beatty. At about 6.20 p.m. Hood and Beatty joined, and they were swiftly engaged in an intense battle with Hipper's battlecruisers, outnumbering the Germans by seven ships to five. Within a few minutes, however, Hood's flagship, HMS *Invincible*, blew up. Once again cordite flash was to blame. Hood and over 1,000 officers and men were lost. Six were saved. Hipper's ships withstood the punishment much better, but were severely damaged and slipped off, awash, into the increasing mist. *Derfflinger* was holed in the bow, *Von der Tann*'s guns were out of action and the *Moltke* remained the only one of his squadron in anything approaching fighting condition.

Scheer now saw the trap Jellicoe and Beatty had sprung. Jellicoe began to 'cross the T', the move that would bring the British across the Germans' bows. Scheer ordered a battle turn which turned all his ships individually 180 degrees and headed them away from the oncoming British fleet. The Germans disappeared into the mist before the Grand Fleet had time to fire more than a few salvoes.

Just after 7 p.m. *Southampton* found the German fleet and reported their position to Jellicoe. The British fleet began pounding Scheer's force. The damaged *Lützow* was so badly crippled that her ship's company had to be taken off and she was sunk by a German torpedo. Other ships sustained heavy damage but German construction meant that almost all the damaged vessels were able to reach port. Scheer again turned away into the mist and fading daylight, leaving torpedo craft to dissuade Jellicoe from following. During the night a series of actions took place between the homeward-bound Germans and British destroyers and cruisers, which cost ships on both sides, but the battle was effectively over. Scheer reached Wilhelmshaven and Jellicoe and Beatty likewise returned to port. Thereafter the battle would be one of words as each side considered the outcome of the clash. More British ships had been sunk, but the British had had a greater number at the outset. The Germans had not inflicted enough damage to erode the British 'command of the sea' and had more ships that would require lengthy repairs before being ready for sea again. Victory was claimed by both sides in public, whilst in London and Berlin complaints were also made of failure to achieve the desired breakthrough.

A battle on this scale, and in such weather conditions, could only be seen by the combatants from the narrow view they had from their vessel. Indeed, the majority of men would never see the battle at all, as they had action stations within the ship and could only hear the sounds of battle and the orders being piped, with occasional snippets of information being broadcast. Many Royal Marines were in gun turrets or serving secondary armament. It was usual for major warships to have one main armament turret run by 'Royals', and in general this was 'X' turret. The turrets were lettered bow to stern. The foremost turret was 'A', manned by the fo'castle division, then 'B' manned by the top division. The two aft turrets had the Royal Marines in 'X' and the quarterdeck division in 'Y'. Where there were turrets amidships, between the funnels, they would be 'Q', or if two, 'P' and 'Q'. There was always competition to be the first turret ready. Several officers wrote accounts of what happened in 'their' turret, and they are worth comparing, especially in view of what happened to 'Q' turret in HMS *Lion*, which happened to be the Royal Marines' turret.

Lion was Beatty's flagship, and it was very nearly lost early in the battle. Just before 4 p.m., 'Q' turret, which had fired 12 rounds, was hit by a 12-inch shell (415 kg) from the *Lützow*. The round hit at the junction of the roof plates, blowing out the front roof plate and front plate and detonating in the gunhouse. The occupants were all killed or badly wounded and a fire started amidst the wreckage. The explosion had blown the breech lever of the left gun into the open position. The shell and the bagged cordite charge slid back and fell into the well and ignited in the fire. The resulting flash fire ignited all the cordite charges in the hoists and handing room, as far down as the magazine.

There the fire was halted, because the Officer of the Turret, Major Francis Harvey, had, in spite of mortal wounds, ordered that the magazine doors be locked shut and the magazine flooded.

Only a sick-berth attendant and a wounded sergeant of the Royal Marines, whom Harvey had sent to the bridge to report the damage, survived from 'Q' turret. Captain Francis Jones RMLI, also of *Lion*, identified the charred and blasted bodies at the close of action and recognized the remains of Francis Harvey, horrifically burnt but not, as reported elsewhere, with his legs blown off. As Jones noted, he could not have reached the voice pipe if he had suffered such an injury. [*The Globe & Laurel*, October 1956, p. 202.] Major Harvey's actions saved his ship, though he was indeed 'sent to glory' in an unenviable fashion. Major Gerald Rooney outlived him by only half an hour, for he was killed when *Queen Mary* blew up. Harvey's widow was presented with his posthumous Victoria Cross.

Aboard HMS *Malaya* Major Godfrey Jollye had narrowly avoided a similar fate.

Maj. Godfrey Jollye RMA, HMS *Malaya*

About 5.27 p.m. GMT, rather more than an hour after the Squadron had first come into action, the Ship was struck several times, the enemy had our range exactly. We had just completed a 16-point turn, and were drawing the High Seas Fleet to the Northwestward and towards the Grand Fleet.

At this time the roof of 'X' Turret (15") was struck by a 12" Shell, the Shell struck almost exactly in the centre of the roof. This turret was manned by Marines. Owing to an exceptionally good piece of Plating, only 4½" thick, the Projectile did not penetrate. It probably did not burst in contact with the roof, but as the Rangefinder hood was plastered with splinters, it must have burst almost instantaneously. The effect on the roof was to bulge it downwards at the point of impact, which caused all the holding down bolts, 1½" diameter, on the right side of the roof, to be sheared, and the whole of the centre plate of the roof to lift on that side.

A splinter entered the right port of the Rangefinder hood, and put the Rangefinder out of action, and another entered the port of the Officer of Turret's Periscope, rendering that instrument useless. The effect on the Gunhouse Crew was nil, and it is interesting to be able to report that none of the Electrical Instruments were affected, nor did they get out of step, and strange to say none of the Electric Lights were extinguished.

Up to this time the loading of the Guns had been quite normal, but it was now reported from the Shellroom, that the Carrier taking the Projectile could not be run into the Central Hoist, unless the Turret was trained Fore and Aft, and from now onwards secondary loading from the Shellroom to the Working Chamber had to be resorted to. This brought a heavy strain on the Crews of these two compartments, and they responded splendidly, a steady supply reaching the Guns throughout the rest of the Action, which intermittently lasted another hour and a half. Each Projectile weighing nearly a ton, and a great deal of manhandling having to be done in the process, [this] required stamina. Their task was made all the more difficult, by the ship having a very considerable list to Starboard, due to a Projectile penetrating below the Waterline, forward, abreast the Bridge, and flooding several compartments.

Godfrey Jollye may have put the survival of his turret down to a strong piece of armour plating, but Captain Alan Bourne, MVO, of the Royal Marine Artillery, who was on HMS *Tiger*, recognized that the survival of his turret, and indeed the ship, had more to do with the idea of a young Royal Marine private.

Capt. Alan Bourne, MVO, RMA, HMS *Tiger*

At 3.56 p.m. 'X' Turret hit by 11" shell on the barbette, directly between the guns. The body of the shell and a large piece of the barbette lodged on top of the lever for jacking up the guns, and two more large pieces covered the manhole between the centre sight setter's position and the working chamber. The central training shaft was knocked into the dynamo compartment and bent across the dynamo. There was a shower of sparks, like a rocket, in the gunhouse and working chamber, and thick fumes. The central trainer (Sgt Magson) was hit by a small piece of burning waste, which he put out with his water bottle. Some of the lights were extinguished and the remainder for a few minutes only glowed. Respirators were found to be very effective. The control cabinet door and manhole in the roof of the turret were left open for two or three minutes to clear the fumes. The centre sight setter was reported probably killed.

This was confirmed when 'check fire' was ordered at 5.10 p.m., but his body could not be removed until just before dusk. Numerous problems were encountered within the turret, from water leaking onto the charge bags to broken electrical wiring, and a large rivet jamming open a flash door, but the gun was back in action once the fumes had cleared. Bourne realized the potential for disaster, but a seemingly unimportant change before action had averted calamity.

Just before the action the projectiles in the Receiving Tray several times slipped into the Gun-loading Cage, which was already loaded, and had to be hauled back again. To avoid this, Private Lambert, a young soldier of 19 years of age, who had been brought up as spare No. 5 at the left gun in place of the No. 5 on leave, suggested to the Second Captain of the Turret that the Main Cage should not be brought up until the Gun-loading Cage was raised. This was done at both guns for the rest of the firing and did not delay the loading at all. This Private performed his work as No. 5 very ably and without a single hitch, although he had never actually done the work before during a firing, only during drill . . .

The following I wrote at the time but did not include in the Report. When Pte Lambert, RMLI, suggested to Sgt Gliddon, RMA (the 2nd Captain of the Turret and in charge of the Working Chamber) that the Main Cage should not be brought up until the Gun-loading Cage was raised to the gun, the latter was not certain of the effect and so voice-piped up to me. I saw at once that it was an excellent idea, hence the following –

'I ordered the rounds in the Receiving Trays to be put back into the Hoist Cages (after emptying) and lowered to the bottom of the hoist. This was completed a few minutes before 'Open Fire' and before the German 11" shell entered the turret. Burning material fell all over the two empty Receiving Trays, and the fact of them being empty of exposed charges probably saved the ship from blowing up.'

Clr Sgt Magson got a 'mention in despatches' for Jutland, but Pte Lambert got nothing – to my regret, as I think he deserved it.

In fact, Private Percival Lambert was given a foreign decoration, the Russian Medal of St George, Fourth Class. He was killed, not by enemy action, but 'accidentally' on Christmas Eve the following year, and was buried in Dunfermline Cemetery.

Away from the gun turrets, other Royal Marines found themselves above decks and with a view of more than just the inside of a metal box, and left their impressions of what they saw. They did not all see the same events, and those they did were all from different viewpoints, but they give us an impression of the battle in all its confusion. There was certainly a feeling of anticipation in the Fleet. Sergeant Norman Jago, serving in HMS *Agincourt*, made note of the preparations.

Sgt Norman Jago RMA, HMS *Agincourt*

At 2.45 p.m. the rumour we had heard appeared to be coming true at last (which pleased us very much), because the order came, 'Clear ship for battle.'

At this order (of course every man in the ship has got his own bit to do), all woodwork, such as tables, chairs and stools, and all bedding was put down below under armour, out of reach of enemy's shells, which would set it on fire if it were hit.

The salt water mains were started and allowed to run over the deck, against fire. While this was being done the guns were being cleared away, shells placed in rear of the guns, and everything appertaining to the working of the guns cleared for action.

All ships were now flying the battle flag and extra white ensigns. All the work of clearing ship for battle was done in a very short space of time.

The excitement was just beginning now, as we were pretty sure of having a scrap, after nearly two years of waiting.

Bugler Charles Smith RMLI was serving in HMS *Inconstant*, one of the light cruisers which first sighted the enemy, and it is he who opens the narrative.

Bugler Charles Smith RMLI, HMS *Inconstant*

On Thursday [Wednesday] 31st May we were on scouting duty off the Dutch [Danish] coast and were in company with HM Ships *Galatea* (flag), *Phaeton* and *Cordelia*. We sighted the enemy's scouting forces at 3.15 p.m. and immediately went to action stations. The *Galatea* and *Phaeton* being in range, opened fire on a large three-funnelled enemy vessel at 3.30 p.m. It replied with heavy guns and seemed to concentrate its fire on *Phaeton*, which was not touched however. Our battlecruisers were now coming up with the 3rd Light Cruiser Squadron. They engaged the enemy as soon as they were within effective range. Soon five enemy battlecruisers were made out and were immediately taken on by our battlecruisers.

One of the battlecruisers engaging the enemy was HMS *Princess Royal*, of Beatty's First Battlecruiser Squadron, in which Corporal Albert Saunders RMA was serving. Corporal Saunders quotes from the gunnery lieutenant's report to give details of the action, and then comments upon it from his point of view.

Cpl Albert Saunders RMA, HMS *Princess Royal*

3.47 p.m. Opened fire. Speed about 25 knots. Enemy opened fire first, *Lion* and *Princess Royal* concentrated on leading ship, either *Derrflinger* or *Lützow*. [It was the *Lützow*.] The weather was hazy and hung around our glasses. 3.50 p.m. Straddled enemy. 3.51 p.m. *Lion* hit in 'Q' turret and shortly after *Princess Royal* hit port side forward. 4.20 p.m. *Indefatigable* hit by salvo and blew up. 4.36 p.m. *Queen Mary* ditto. Magazine hit in both cases . . .

The first shots we fired it was like the letting off of steam. All the bottled up anxiety of the past months was let loose then. Everyone was ready and eager for whatever was to come and I think I can safely say that had those who died been able to foresee the future, they would still have 'gone in'. As the time passed so news of the fight came trickling through. We heard of the loss of the *Queen* Mary, our chummy ship, and many a heart beat a little faster when they thought of chums gone for good. It made everyone more than ever determined to fight on. Of the ultimate result we had no doubt. We knew we should have to lose some ships – that is part of the game.

Captain Alan Bourne, aboard HMS *Tiger*, did not feel that his men would have quite so sanguine an approach.

Capt. Alan Bourne, MVO, RMA, HMS *Tiger*

I saw three of our ships, and one German ship, blow up, but did not tell the Turret's Crew. However, during a 'Cease fire' when I could not see any enemy ships, I got the Gun House Crew onto the top of the turret to give them a change, and we passed the remains of the *Invincible* sticking up out of the sea – she had broken in half and the broken parts were on the seabed with the ends sticking up. The three or four survivors were standing on a raft and cheering as the ship went past. Whilst we were discussing this, there was a crack and an enemy salvo landed just over us. I bundled the Crew back into the turret.

The battlecruiser HMS *New Zealand* was the companion ship to *Indefatigable* in the Second Battlecruiser Squadron. When *New Zealand* had gone to action stations her captain, Captain J. F. Green RN, had put on the piu-piu and tiki given to the ship by a Maori chieftain to be worn on such occasions. Here, in a foggy battle in the North Sea, stood a senior naval captain wearing the additional 'uniform' of a Maori ceremonial flax skirt and with a green stone weapon on a flax cord around his neck. This was regarded as good luck by 'jolly Jack' and when *New Zealand* sighted some German light cruisers in November 1917, several bridge officers noticed a sailor pop his head up through the hatchway onto the bridge, then duck back and shout 'It's alright, he's got it on.'

Captain Harold Blount RMA was Officer of the Turret in *New Zealand's* 'X' turret.

Capt. Harold Blount RMA, HMS *New Zealand*

At 3.57 p.m. *New Zealand* opened fire at the enemy's fourth ship (*Moltke* or *Derrflinger*) range 18,100. There was however a very large closing rate, and the sights had to come down to nearly 13,000 before a straddle was obtained at 4 p.m. At 4.06 p.m. course was altered to S.S.E., and during the run down, courses varied between S.E. and S., more or less on a parallel course to the enemy. At 4.08 p.m. the *Indefatigable* blew up, evidently having been caught with a salvo when on the turn. Our fire was consequently shifted to the 5th ship (?*Seydlitz*), whom we straddled with the first salvo at 14,000 yards . . . At about 4.22 p.m. the 5th ship was obscured by mist, the range having now increased to 18,000 yards, and fire was shifted to the 4th ship, which was straddled almost at once, and hits were again observed. About this time 'X' Turret was hit by an 11" shell which exploded against the glacis, port side forward, filling the Turret with thick yellow fumes. Respirators were used, but the fumes were found to have no ill effects. Considerable blast was also felt in the centre sighting position and working chamber, but luckily no one was hurt. Two more rounds were fired from the Turret which then jammed, and there was a delay of some 25 minutes while splinters of the shell and armour were removed from the roller path [part of the turret turntable mechanism]. A piece of 9″ armour, 2′ 6″ in diameter, was blown into the danger space, and rested on the rollers, but this did not impede the training of the Turret. At 4.32 p.m. the *Queen Mary* blew up; when sighted from this ship her stern was still visible and her propellers were still going round, but when abreast of us, there was another explosion, after which there was nothing left of her.

Sergeant Jago was still waiting to come into action in the heavily armed *Agincourt*, with her fourteen 12-inch guns.

Sgt Jago, RMA, HMS *Agincourt*

At four o'clock the word was passed round the ship that our battlecruisers were in action with the German High Sea Fleet, about 50 miles ahead. There was loud cheering and shouting at this news, and such remarks were heard, as 'Hammer 'em David, give Big Willie some iron pills,' and 'Save a few of 'em for us to have a go at.'

Corporal Harold Cauchey RMLI was in the shell room of the Royal Marines turret aboard Jellicoe's flagship HMS *Iron Duke*, and had been at action stations since 4 p.m.

Cpl Harold Cauchey RMLI, HMS *Iron Duke*

About 5.30 they sent down to the Shell Room that there was heavy firing on the starboard bow, and that the flashes of the guns could be plainly seen.

Shortly after that we had the order to load all cages with common shell and full charges.

At 6.25 p.m. we opened fire. Could hardly realize it. Everybody cheered in our Shell Room and Magazine. Even then we thought it was only a sighting shot, but we were firing rapidly so we knew that we were at it at last . . . We opened fire on a German battleship of the *König* class and I heard afterwards that our first salvo straddled her and the next struck her between her A and B turret and she burst into flames. Whether she went under or not I don't know, but she was done a little bit of no good at any rate.

At 6.37 we checked fire.

This check fire was ordered because Admiral Scheer had just ordered a *Gefechtskehrtwendung* to starboard. The *Gefechtskehrtwendung*, literally 'Action about-turn manoeuvre', was an unusual battle manoeuvre in which the rearmost ship in the line turned first, followed by the others putting over their helm in succession as the next astern of them commenced turning.

Captain Evan Hughes RMLI was a turret officer aboard the battleship HMS *Revenge*, one of Jellicoe's First Battle Squadron. Evan Hughes had been at action stations since 2.45 p.m. and after three hours of preparation and testing of equipment he could hear gunfire.

Capt. Evan Hughes RMLI, HMS *Revenge*

Somewhere about 5.30 p.m. the sound of the guns could be heard [and] shortly afterwards small 'flickers' of light could be seen away on our starboard bow. Orders now arrived to load and stand by, so we closed up quickly and reported. When the 'director' started moving it took the turret round on to the port bow so we evidently were expecting to deploy to starboard. The 'banging' was now coming nearer and nearer, when suddenly the battlecruisers streamed past our bows, firing hard. The *Lion* was followed by the *Tiger*. The latter looked a fine sight, with flame and smoke pouring from large rents in her funnels and large columns of water springing up on each side of her. Some of the 'overs' fired at her came well down to us.

The squadrons of the Battle Fleet now altered course to port, so round the turret went, following the director on the starboard foremost bearing. No sooner were we 'on' by director than 'bang' went the first salvo, followed by a cheer from the depths of the turret. 'X' turret's blast screens sailed away like seagulls, the starboard water-tight screen door turned a circle, the starboard ladder disappeared and the salvo fell well short. The left guns then joined in, but were also short. Our 'target' was one of the *König* class.

Piteous wails from the TS (transmitting station) for ranges, but you can't see in a thick mist. Having loosed several salvoes at the ?*König*, the mist blotted her right out, so we shifted on to the third ship to the right (there seemed to be lots more of them further to the right still).

This target was put down as one of the *Kaiser* class. More wails from the TS for ranges. One of our destroyers now drifted past quite close to us, out of action and apparently sinking. The crew were standing about waving caps and odds and ends, and cheering.

I then saw two of our cruisers coming down between the lines going 'all out'. The first was a flagship and was noted down as the *Minotaur*: the second was of the *Warrior* or *Black Prince* class. They were being simply smothered by shell, but were both firing hard in return.

When the leading ship was bearing about green 120° from us and at a distance of about 3,000 yds, a salvo hit her aft, and the after turret blew up; almost immediately another salvo hit her forward, the fore turret seemed to explode and the remaining turrets went off in a ripple from forward aft. When the smoke cleared there was no sign of her left. (This proved to be the *Defence* later.) The other cruiser was still being hit hard, but appeared to be escaping some of the punishment by zigzagging. Immediately beyond her (the *Warrior*) was the 5th Battle Squadron led by the *Barham*. One of the squadron seemed a long way out of station on the starboard beam, and a large flare as if from an explosion appeared for a moment in one of the others. The *Warrior* disappeared in the mist astern.

We had 'checked' fire for a few minutes, whilst these cruisers passed, owing to the mist, but now opened again at what appeared to be the fourth ship of a squadron. However, the mist intervened again so we shifted on to the leading ship of the squadron. The range varied from 11,500 to 9,800 yds.

There then appeared an enemy ship drifting down between the lines; she apparently had two masts and three funnels to start with, but soon lost them.

Each battleship in turn seemed to give her a few salvoes as she passed; but she declined to sink, though hopelessly out of action and with no signs of life. It was impossible to tell what class of vessel she belonged to. We then passed another wreck, the bow and stern of which were sticking high out of the water, with the centre apparently resting on the bottom. We all thought at the time it was one of the enemy, but it turned out to be the poor old *Invincible*.

Private G. Neasham had actually watched the *Invincible* blow up, during a respite from gun loading aboard HMS *Yarmouth*, of the 3rd Light Cruiser Squadron.

Pte G. Neasham RMLI, HMS *Yarmouth*

Shells were falling all round, and very close to us; too close for comfort . . . Two of our destroyers were being made a target of by the enemy heavy ships. One went up in smoke and the other came up on our port beam and sunk just as the *Invincible* blew up on our port quarter. The destroyer just got ahead of the ill-fated Battlecruiser and they both went down together. Two of us had been loading as hard as possible and just had a spell for a few minutes and went over to our port side to see what was doing. We could see the after part of our Battlecruiser Fleet line and were watching the *Invincible* die . . . the last belches of smoke came out of her muzzles. A salvo from an enemy ship hit her fair amidships and must have penetrated her midship turret magazine for she went up in a cloud of smoke and flame . . . When everything had cleared away all that was to be seen was two riblike parts, sticking out of the water like pieces of rock. We nearly turned sick on seeing this lot!

Private Thomas Swanborough, at actions stations with the secondary armament four-inch guns of HMS *Vanguard* in the Fourth Battle Squadron, had a similar view of *Invincible*'s demise.

Pte Thomas Swanborough RMLI, HMS *Vanguard*

Then we were well at it with an enemy battleship. We had been standing idle and men were beginning to use rather strong language, round the light battery, at having to wait so long. Suddenly, there was a terrific explosion which was that of a torpedo, followed by broadside from an enemy ship, catching as near as one could make out, in the vitals of the unfortunate *Invincible*. Things are beginning to get red hot now, fire and smoke and the choking fumes of the shells fill the air like a cloud, causing it to be terribly uncomfortable; everywhere you look there seem to be wrecks of destroyers and torpedo boats – these floating around in their helpless position, battered to pieces, with practically nothing standing above the water line; men dying or dead about the remaining intact part.

The secondary armament of the *Malaya* had themselves taken heavy punishment. The starboard six-inch battery was hit and a flash fire wreaked havoc.

Maj. Jollye RMA, HMS *Malaya*

The flash from the Shell ignited our own Ammunition, which was being supplied to the Guns which were in action, and in a very short time the whole Battery was on fire. The Marines in this Battery formed the Ammunition Supply Party, and not a single one escaped very severe burns, seventeen out of a total of twenty-seven losing their lives.

At 6 p.m. HMS *Colossus*, part of the First Battle Squadron, was drawing close to the fray. Captain Chandos Hill RMLI was in charge of the four-inch guns, and his action station was on the fore bridge. Interestingly, he wrote of the action in a private letter a few days afterwards, and in a more measured account in a report to his ship's captain, Captain A. D. P. R. Pound (who, as Admiral of the Fleet Sir Dudley Pound, was First Sea Lord for much of the Second World War). The opening description in his letter shows his exposed position.

Capt. Chandos Hill RMLI, HMS *Colossus*

Personally I had a pretty hot time of it as my action station was the fore-bridge, with no cover at all. The only thing to be said in its favour is that you get a fine view of what is going on. The direct hits did not worry me much, what I objected to were the misses short which burst and spattered the whole forepart of the ship with splinters which penetrated the unarmoured position.

At just before 6 p.m. we heard heavy firing, and ten minutes later we saw our battlecruisers firing hard. Soon after 6 p.m. we had our first taste of the Huns as a large projectile hit the water on our starboard bow, ricocheted into the air and passed over. We could see plainly it turning over and over. It was painted yellow with a black band.

The next point of interest we saw was the armoured cruisers in action. They made a very gallant fight but were outclassed by the German Battle Fleet. As you know the *Defence, Warrior* and *Black Prince* were sunk. We saw one blow up in a mass of heavy smoke that towered into the sky.

By this time we had deployed into line, and the Fleet presented a beautiful sight. Miles of ships all with their guns pointed to where we knew the invisible enemy were. Every ship was flying three or four huge new White Ensigns, and strings of flags were continually going up. When the action became imminent the Admiral, Captain and Navigator left the bridge and retired to the Conning Tower just underneath, leaving myself, a midshipman (Hervey) and the Admiral's Secretary [Paymaster Lieutenant Commander Foot], whose job it was to take notes and from whose diary I am able now to reconstruct what did take place. Events happened so fast and one so lost all sense of time, that without actual notes made at the time it is very hard to piece the story together again.

I also had two splendid boys stationed at voice pipes to pass orders. Both these little fellows were splendid. They never lost their heads and did their job perfectly. They and I were hardly off the bridge from 3 p.m. that day till 11 a.m. the next. In addition I had with me two range finder operators.

In his report to Captain Pound, Captain Hill wrote: 'I would also bring to your notice Boy Jones whose duty it was to repeat Mr Hervey's orders to the after group. He remained calm both while our 4" guns were in action and under the enemy's fire. Boy Lawrence was excellent at his post at the voice pipe and when he was left by me to keep taut the tourniquet I had placed round Ld. Sea. Beddow's arm.' His letter continued:

Just before 6.30 p.m. we saw in the mist a four-funnelled enemy cruiser. She was apparently disabled but still firing. We let her have four salvoes of 12 in., but whether we actually finished her off, I don't know. We also got a glimpse of the enemy Battle Fleet and let them have three salvoes, but the fog closed down and we could not see the result of our fire. Often when we could not see the ships we could see the angry red glow of their guns through the fog.

A little later we passed quite close to one of our own destroyers, damaged. We recognized on her poop a Warrant Officer who had been in *Colossus*. They appeared very happy though their ship was in a bad way, and they cheered us heartily. I hear she got home all right.

Our next target was a three-funnelled cruiser who appeared out of the mist. She was only under fire from us for a short time, and then we passed her on to our next astern while we stood by for the next. It all reminded me of shooting pigeons in the caves and cliffs. You never know when they are going to bolt.

About 7 p.m. we passed the remains of the *Invincible*, her bow and stern both sticking out of the water. A destroyer was standing by picking up survivors. We thought at first she was a Hun and only found out later that it was one of our own ships. We could not spend much time looking at her as a destroyer attacked us on our starboard bow. That was where Hervey and I came in. We fired eight salvoes of 4 in. at her. The big guns, having nothing better to do, plastered her too. It was rather like using a sledge hammer to kill a wasp. We left her stopped and sinking.

Up to this time I don't think any big ship had fired directly at us though shots were continually passing over or falling short. Then suddenly out of the mist, only 10,000 yds away, emerged a battlecruiser of the *Lützow* class. Here was worthy game at last. We let her have five salvoes, there was no time for more as she was passing us. The last two hit her well and we saw flames bursting from her decks. She also disappeared into the mist, turning directly away from us. But before she got away she put two 12 in. shells into our superstructure. Both missed the mast by a few inches, indeed both passed between the main and side struts of the mast. One burst, wrecking the lower part of the superstructure and setting fire to the Cordite for the 4 in. guns. This produced a tremendous blaze, but it was soon over and the smouldering remains were quickly put out before even the fire parties arrived on the scene.

One or two shots from the same salvo burst short and spattered the whole forepart of the ship with splinters. Nearly all the cabins in line with the burst had holes in them. The Captain's office was wrecked, and the damage was increased by a water pipe being shot away and flooding everything. Two pieces went right through the funnel and one piece wrecked a searchlight immediately under where I was standing. We all on the bridge had very narrow escapes as bits of steel were flying like hail. It was here that our only bad casualty took place. The rangefinder operator [Leading Seaman Beddow] who was on his platform immediately behind me had his right arm nearly shot off. It was a ghastly sight. I put on a tourniquet improvised out of a handkerchief and a bit of stick, and had the satisfaction of seeing the flow of blood stop. I then sent for a first aid party who took him away to the Dressing Station. As soon as he was taken below the doctors amputated his arm. He is now I believe in a hospital ship and doing well.

The foretop was spattered with splinters from the same burst. One man had his collar bone broken. A midshipman up there had a splinter right through his cap, which just grazed his head. Three marines were slightly wounded but after having their wounds dressed returned to their stations. The top of the semaphore on the fore-bridge was carried away and also the vane of a bearing instrument.

Several ships ahead and astern of us told us after that they saw *Colossus* pass through a sheet of fire, spray and smoke. After that we saw no more of them [the *Lützow*].

The *Lützow* had in fact taken such a pounding that a few hours later her remaining ship's company were rescued, and her torpedo boat destroyer escort sank her.

Other German torpedo boat destroyers had taken on enemy targets. Sergeant Norman Jago noted those that came in range of *Agincourt*.

Sgt Jago RMA, HMS *Agincourt*

Enemy destroyers now appeared off our starboard quarter, but our 6 in. guns engaged them. The first destroyer was hit by a few direct hits and blew up, the second was so badly hit that she stopped and the others retired, some on fire.

Corporal Harold Cauchey, aboard *Iron Duke*, found the attack by the torpedo boat destroyer too close for comfort.

Cpl Cauchey RMLI, HMS *Iron Duke*

At 7.15 we were attacked by 3 German destroyers which came tearing straight towards us. The starboard 6 in. battery opened fire on them and firing was very heavy till 7.25. They all went under. One torpedo just missed our stern.

Captain Chandos Hill also experienced torpedo attack, but was unsure of its origin.

Capt. Hill RMLI, HMS *Colossus*

About 7.30 p.m. a torpedo was fired at us, but I do not know if
it came from a submarine or destroyer. We did not ourselves
come into action again but some small local battles raged at
short intervals up to nearly midnight. A destroyer action was
particularly spectacular especially when one burst into flames.

About midnight I got down and had some ham, bread and
butter and tea and dozed in my chair for about 20 minutes and
woke up quite refreshed.

We fully expected to meet the German Battle Fleet at dawn,
but they had escaped home. At 3.15 a.m. we heard heavy
firing, and about half an hour after a Zep [Zeppelin] hove in
sight and had a look at us. Several ships fired but it was miles
out of range, and anyhow the Zep cleared off!

As things began to quieten down for various ships there was a chance
to assess the damage, both to men and the ship itself. Captain Hill
made note of a quirk of fate:

One of our doctors had two budgerigars in a cage in his cabin.
Before going into action he placed them on the deck. The side
of his cabin was pierced twice, pictures and looking glass
broken and other damage done, but the birds were none the
worse for what they had gone through.

The *Princess Royal* had at one stage been reported to Admiral Beatty
as having been blown up, as she had disappeared in a pall of smoke
just after the loss of her 'chummy ship' *Queen Mary*. In fact the damage
did not prove nearly as desperate as this report. Corporal Albert
Saunders describes the scene.

Cpl Saunders RMA, HMS *Princess Royal*

At 11 p.m. we fell out from our day action stations to close up
at our night defence stations. Some managed to get something
to eat and drink. Below decks the sight was awful – just
gaping holes, decks flooded with water, dead and wounded
everywhere and an awful smell where the shells had burst. It
was a never to be forgotten sight and one that one never
wishes to see again. As you walked round you heard of familiar

names who had paid the supreme penalty. You looked down at a burnt, battered mess of what was a few hours previous a splendid specimen of British manhood, and now you could only tell who it was by a label tied on the coat. The remains of some were awful.

Admiral Brock CB came down from the bridge for a short while to speak to the wounded and give them a word of encouragement. A rush was made, after everything was over, for pieces of shell as a memento. In their eagerness to obtain a bit they forgot the fact that they were hungry. The gruesomeness of the thing did not strike them. They did not give it a thought that probably that particular piece had laid low someone in the prime of life. It was not from lack of reverence, but rather a feeling of perfect sang-froid.

The ship was hit twice forward, port side (one to the Admiral's pantry and one below the Admiral's cabin). One came through the foremost struts and funnel, one through the Canteen, starboard side, one into the Issue Room, port side aft. One in 'X' turret, cutting the gunlayer's foot off and killing a couple more. The upper deck was completely cut up and the centre funnel and the after screen on the quarterdeck were one mass of holes. One shell struck 'Q' turret left gun on the muzzle and glanced off. Our total casualties were exactly 100 viz. killed 19, wounded 81, of these three died during the next two or three days, 73 being sent to hospital and five cases being kept on board.

The cost in human terms only really became apparent after the battle. Men thought in terms of ships as a whole, rather than the individuals within them. When a ship went down it was a collective loss. When Corporal Saunders heard that the *Queen Mary* had 'gone', he thought of his lost friends but mostly of the 'Chummy Ship'. The destroyer that Captain Chandos Hill saw pass by 'in a bad way' had a ship's company that could cheer because 'she', the ship, was still going. The loss of the *Queen Mary* and *Invincible* cost roughly the equivalent of two battalions in a matter of moments. To think of the loss of the ships as single 'beings' rather than all those men was the best way to cope, but the survivors had to face the realities of burials at sea with hammock-shrouded corpses slipping from beneath the Union flag. The sound of the splash was not one forgotten by those who heard it. The *Lion* put the remains of 95 men into the North Sea.

On the evening of 1 June, Corporal Harold Cauchey made a note when *Iron Duke* was called to attention for the burials from other ships.

Cpl Cauchey RMLI, HMS *Iron Duke*

At 7 p.m. the attention was sounded and everyone on deck had to face aft while they buried the killed of the Battleships *Malaya* and *Barham*.

Captain Godfrey Jollye was promoted Major in 1917, awarded the OBE in 1919, and retired from the Royal Marines in 1920, becoming Secretary of Liphook Golf Course; he died in 1934, aged 51. Captain Alan Bourne eventually rose to be General Sir Alan Bourne, KCB, DSO, MVO, and died in 1967, aged 85. Captain Harold Blount attained the rank of Major General and also died in 1967, at the same age. Bugler Charles Albert Smith was lost, aged 19, when the *Louvain*, in which he was taking passage, was sunk by a U-boat in the Eastern Mediterranean on 20 January 1918. Corporal Albert Percy Saunders survived the war and reached the rank of Colour Sergeant; he died in Portsmouth in 1971. Captain Evan Jukes Hughes went on to reach the rank of Major and was awarded the OBE. Captain Chandos Egerton Walter Hill also survived the war and reached the rank of Lieutenant Colonel; he died in 1948.

II
PER TERRAM

3

Gallipoli

Naval efforts in the Dardanelles reached a peak on 18 March 1915. The plan was for a major landing to take place at various points on the Gallipoli Peninsula, using the Royal Naval Division (RND), the 29th Division, the Australian and New Zealand Army Corps (ANZAC) and the rest of the Royal Marine Brigade. If large numbers of troops had been able to land at Gallipoli at that time, the campaign might possibly have succeeded. As it was, major landings did not take place until late April. The Turks had been able to place mobile gun batteries on the Gallipoli Peninsula and the Asiatic side without hindrance. This made Allied advances to the Narrows very slow. When the landings were eventually made, the Turks had also been able to create well-prepared positions where an attacker would have grave difficulties. Getting onto the peninsula and holding ground, let alone advancing to Constantinople, would be a long and extremely costly business.

The Plymouth Battalion of the Royal Marines left England on 6 February 1915, accompanied by the Chatham Battalion. At that time it was only planned that they would act as support troops for the Royal Navy, making raids and destroying forts. The decision to deploy any large number of troops in Gallipoli was taken in February, but in the form of 'when we have troops available'. Only when the 29th Division arrived in the Aegean in April was any action assured.

When the Plymouth Battalion left England, their final destination was not known by those on board, although the Dardanelles was the most commonly rumoured. Among the Battalion aboard the SS *Braemar Castle* were Private John Vickers and Lieutenant John Barnes of No. 1 Company, Private James Thompson of No. 2 Company, Private Cornelius Moynahan and Sergeant Will Meatyard, Lieutenant Francis Law and Lieutenant Charles Conybeare of No. 3 Company, and Lieutenant John Richards and Lieutenant Charles Lamplough of No. 4 Company. John Vickers came from Stoke-on-Trent and had enlisted in November 1914, aged 19. John Clixby Barnes had only recently been

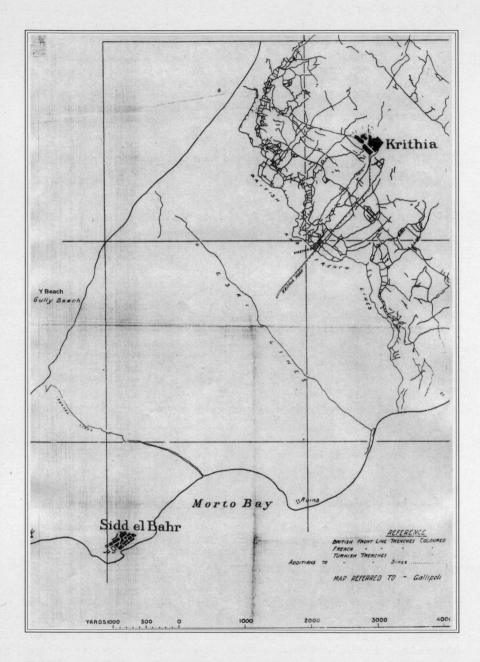

Krithia and Y Beach, with the trenches as they were some weeks after
the landing of 25 April 1915

commissioned and was also 19. Sergeant Will Meatyard was the Battalion Signal Sergeant.

Charles Lamplough was 18, and during the journey eastwards his diary shows the youthful attitude which combined excitement with a determination not to fail anyone – rather like being picked as opening bat for the First XI at school. As Gallipoli approached, Lamplough began to grow up swiftly, as the alteration in tone of his diary illustrates.

After a rough passage, which saw everyone seasick, the SS *Braemar Castle* reached Malta on Sunday 14 February. The Companies went ashore for route marching. Private Vickers noted on the 17th that they were 'inspected by several apparently important officers', and then returned to the ship. As an officer, Lamplough was able to get shore leave on the evening of his route march. His diary comments for the Tuesday are worth noting to compare with his later entries.

Lt Charles Lamplough RMLI, No. 4 Coy Plymouth Bn, 16 Feb. 1915

. . . We went through the town and one's first impression was that the Maltese people were mad, as it was their carnival day yesterday and today and they nearly all rush about in fancy dress and masks – absolutely mad. However, we went to dinner at the Royal Hotel and met some of the Chatham fellows after dinner. We thought we might go mad as well so we went to the Mask Ball and had a fine rag. We came across quite a lot of Naval Officers and some of our own. It was good fun, much the best since I left England.

Fun was not something Charles Lamplough or the rest of his battalion would see much of in the months to come, and they were to be the first battalion to see action at Gallipoli. In the course of the campaign, 5 of the 25 officers in the battalion were killed, 14 were wounded and 4 invalided through illness. Only the medical officer, Surgeon Mellor RN, and the adjutant, Captain Lough, emerged unscathed. This was a typical casualty rate for the Royal Marines Battalions.

The SS *Braemar Castle* and her sister ship SS *Cawdor Castle*, carrying the Chatham Battalion, reached Lemnos on 24 February. On the 27th the battalions were told to be ready to land at Kum Kale and Sedd ul Bahr, at either side of the entrance to the Dardanelles, the next day, but bad weather delayed the action until 4 March. The troops landed were to act as demolition parties and to reconnoitre. Waiting was not easy, especially for young Lamplough, who knew his Company was to land.

Lt Lamplough RMLI, No. 4 Coy Ply. Bn, Monday 1 March 1915

Well I wonder what today will bring forth. It makes one wonder when writing this at 7.30 a.m. in the morning and you know that you are going in for your first scrap at 11 a.m. or thereabouts. However, I don't feel a bit worried now and treat the whole thing as a usual Tavistock Field Day, although somehow I don't think there will be so much work to do. I am quite happy now that I have received a Mail and sent one. That is what worried me and I practically told them where we were as old Andrews [Christopher Andrews, his Company Commander, who was actually 34] never looks at mine . . . I shall pack up all my things and close this diary in case I don't come back and then they can see what I have been doing.

Of course the landing being cancelled meant emotional let-down and repeating the mental preparations all over again. However, three days later No. 4 Company landed at Sedd ul Bahr and Charles Lamplough got his first taste of war. He was fortunate in having with him not only experienced NCOs but also a far older subaltern. Lieutenant John Richards was almost 50, and had enlisted in the RMLI in 1879. He had risen through the ranks, becoming a Sergeant Major in 1904, and eventually gained a commission. He was undoubtedly old for active service, especially at the Platoon Commander level, but was an ideal man to have among totally inexperienced young subalterns. The presence of someone who was of the same rank, and thus approachable, but with years of experience, would be a very steadying influence on a green 18-year-old such as Charles Lamplough.

Charles Lamplough wrote out the Company Operations Orders in detail in his pocket book. In his account of what went on, published in the Corps journal *The Globe & Laurel*, Lieutenant John Richards summed them up as follows.

Lt John Richards RMLI, No. 4 Coy Ply. Bn, *Globe & Laurel*, Jan. 1920

Five patrols under Sergeant Major Goldring were to search ground, including fort, for enemy. When 'all clear' was reported an escort of Lt Edwards and twelve men, with the demolition party, would move up and make good the fort.

The patrols were to move out about half a mile in advance of the points to be covered by the platoons, and remain in observation.

Three platoons, each of about forty-six strong, were to cover the ground in front of the village; the right wing resting on the cliff passing in front of old fort, Hill 141, to Cape Helles Batteries and Hill 138, its left overlooking what was later known as 'Lancashire Landing' or 'W' Beach. Machine guns to accompany platoon on the right. One platoon in reserve.

On the signal 'retire,' patrols to fall back on platoons, who would retire to boats, commencing from the left.

It all sounded very much like a 'Tavistock Field Day' on paper, and in fact it began quite easily. The Company was transferred from the *Braemar Castle* to two destroyers and thence, for the last half mile, to towed ships' boats, five to a tow, as used on the main landings on 25 April. The tows were dropped for the last hundred yards to shore, when the men rowed to a small boat camber and disembarked. Thus far they were unopposed, except for a little long-range artillery fire. Lieutenant Charles Lamplough recounted his view of the day's events in his diary, where his youthful optimism returned.

Lt Lamplough RMLI, No. 4 Coy Ply. Bn, Thursday 4 March 1915

Well, this has been the day of my life. We were called at 5 a.m. I had breakfast as 6.15 a.m. and got onto one of the destroyers at 7 a.m. and sailed off at 18 knots. When we got just off Sedd ul Bahr the fleet started bombarding like blazes. It looked very nice and as if we should have no opposition. Well, we got into our cutters and finally got ashore and everything looked in our favour. The patrols got out and went up the cliff. One went to the top through the fort and the others straight up. When they got to the top they got it thick – poor old Baldwin [Clr Sgt Alfred Baldwin] was very soon caught. He got one through the head and died a little time after. Then we had a good deal of firing.

According to John Richards, Colour Sergeant Baldwin was killed whilst trying to dislodge some enemy snipers.

Lt Richards RMLI, No. 4 Coy Ply. Bn, *Globe & Laurel*, February 1920

There was no opposition to our landing . . . until the leading men of the patrol started to debouch from the path at the head of the camber into the road which ran between the fort and village. They were immediately met by rifle fire, and had to take cover behind a drinking fountain in the middle of the road. The remainder closed up under cover of a low stone wall behind it. It was here that Clr Sgt Baldwin was killed in trying to pick off some snipers who were in the houses.

The party detailed for the fort got in there without any trouble. The advance by the road being held up, the right platoon was ordered to move up the face of the cliff into the village, the houses being flush with it. As soon as they got among the first houses they also came under rifle fire, but not a single enemy could be seen.

The machine-guns, under Lt Williams, were grouped at the foot of the camber, and opened fire occasionally on an old hut on high ground on our right, from which effective enfilade fire could have been used on us.

Finding themselves pinned down, the landing party called up supporting fire from the ships offshore. Charles Lamplough sent the message.

Lt Lamplough RMLI, No. 4 Coy Ply. Bn, Thursday 4 March 1915

I finally found we could not get up there [the fort] as they were in the ruined houses sniping us, so we found where they were. I came down to the beach and signalled which houses we wanted shelling and they [the Fleet] let them have it. Then I took my patrol up and we did not have much opposition. Dickinson got hit in the leg and had to be taken off but he is alright – but Jones of 14 Platoon was killed and also Dyter of 13 Platoon. We had quite a nice little scrap and then they sent a lot of shrapnel over, but they did not get us. A sniper killed one man in the picket boat. We found several Turks, some dead and one wounded, and sent for a stretcher party. The old fool flung himself off the stretcher down the cliff – he died on the way to the *Braemar*.

Lieutenant Richards did not see the injured Turk but did see some scavenging by the men.

Lt Richards RMLI, No. 4 Coy Ply. Bn, *Globe & Laurel,* **February 1920**

The right platoon passed through the village, searching the houses as they went. As the time allotted for our task was drawing near, orders were given that the advance was not to go beyond the village, but on reaching the further end to turn about and retire back on the boats.

This was done without any molestation from the enemy . . . Whilst advancing through the village, on going into one house a number of fowls were discovered. The eggs were promptly confiscated, some of the men promising themselves poultry for dinner on their way back, but much to their disgust missed the locality and had to depart without them.

No. 3 Company, undertaking a similar task at Kum Kale, on the Asiatic side, would have liked the luxury of egg hunting. Unfortunately for them, the enemy turned out to be far more formidable, and they found themselves under sustained fire. The Colonel of the Battalion, Lieutenant Colonel Matthews, went ashore with No. 3 Company under Major Bewes. Major Charles Jerram was with the Brigade Staff who watched the landings, and was aware of the original plans. When things began to go awry, he was sent ashore to inform Colonel Matthews of the decision to withdraw, and to assist as required. During the first part of the action his impressions were those based on a view through binoculars and from hearsay, but once ashore his is a very vivid account. Although far more experienced than the fledgling subalterns like Charles Lamplough, it was still his first taste of being under fire.

Maj. Charles Jerram RMLI, 3rd RM Bde Staff Captain, Notes on landings of 4 March 1915

The landing was for the purpose of covering a demolition party of Seamen, who were to complete the destruction of certain forts which had been shelled by the Fleet. A good deal of uncertainty existed as to the strength and whereabouts of the enemy . . .

At Kum Kale the landing was opposed, but was pressed and the Coy eventually landed under the walls of the Fort. The first attempt was made at a short pier, but this was swept by shrapnel and MG fire and several casualties ensued, whilst the Machine Guns, which had been landed, had to be left. They were soon recovered by the MG Crews under Lts Conybeare and Law with some loss.

Private Cornelius Moynahan and Sergeant Will Meatyard were two of those who landed at that pier.

Pte Cornelius Moynahan RMLI, No. 3 Coy Ply. Bn, 4 March 1915

At 6.30 a.m., Nos 3 & 4 Companies transferred from the Transport onto Torpedo Boat Destroyers and were taken to the Dardanelles; when at the entrance we were transferred to small boats which were towed by armed picket boats . . . We (that is No. 3 Company) landed against a fairly strong opposition, sustaining about half a dozen casualties in the boats.

Enemy shells began to fall around the boats, and there were also casualties from well directed rifle fire. Had the enemy had machine guns I don't think many would have landed. Sgt Minns was killed by a rifle bullet before we got ashore, the bullet having first passed through and wounding Pte Liversedge, who was sitting on his lap.

We got alongside a wooden landing stage that was about 40 yards long, and clambered up onto it. Being flat, without rails and clear of obstacles it afforded no cover. We were subjected now to a good deal of rifle fire. On reaching the top we laid down flat until the first boat load had assembled.

Lieutenant Francis Law, with classic understatement, described the pier as 'a most uncomfortable landing position'.

Lt Francis Law RMLI, No. 3 Coy Ply. Bn, *Globe & Laurel*, May 1920

Only about 80 men landed here, the remainder of the Company reached the edge of the fort practically unopposed . . . The enemy commenced sniping from two windmills situated close to the fort. The men were ordered to get off the pier and take cover behind the fort. The machine guns and ammunition had meanwhile been left behind.

Sgt Cook DSM and Pte Trelfall volunteered to rescue a gun and ammunition, and it was here that Cook was dangerously wounded, after a very gallant attempt to save his guns. Another attempt was made, the party this time successfully bringing off a gun and a box of ammunition.

Will Meatyard and Private Moynahan were glad to get off the pier.

Sgt Will Meatyard RMLI, No. 3 Coy Ply. Bn

We were given the order to stand by, and all rising together
doubled to the shore. There were two who could not obey the
order.

Pte Moynahan RMLI, No. 3 Coy Ply. Bn, 4 March 1915

. . . we rushed for the road to the village and the majority of us
managed to get off the pier which was exposed to heavy rifle
fire from the village.

There were two windmills on the left of the pier and inside
were several snipers and as they were causing a lot of
annoyance, we sent a signal to the *Cornwallis* and in less than
a quarter of an hour there were no windmills to be seen.

Francis Law watched the next move.

Lt Law RMLI, No. 3 Coy Ply. Bn, *Globe & Laurel*, May 1920

Meanwhile, the patrol, under Lt May, had met with strong
opposition, but this officer succeeded in entering the fort and
reported 'All Clear.' The fort was then thoroughly searched.
The first stage of the operations having been completed, the
advance towards Yeni Shir was at once commenced.

Will Meatyard was one of the patrol detailed to follow the road into the
village itself, but he did not get far.

Sgt Meatyard RMLI, No. 3 Coy Ply. Bn

We were now at the foot of the Fort, and at the commencement
of the road that led direct into the village. This road I had been
detailed to follow with the advanced patrol, which consisted of
ten men under Capt. [Lieut.] Brown[e]. The advance of this
patrol was not successful, we had only gone a few yards when
we were compelled to lay prone and look for targets to return
fire. Out of the ten, three only remained who were not either
killed or wounded. The enemy were well concealed and
apparently firing from houses. It was when on aim, having

spotted one of the enemy coming up to fire from behind a garden wall, that I was hit by two bullets from the flank, one in the chest and the other in the left foot. I wriggled back around the corner of the Fort and got my wounds dressed. Fortunately the wounds were not serious and after a breather [I] did not feel much the worse, although lamed . . .

A section was told off to man the crest of the bank overlooking the Fort, and now I joined up with this party, being anxious to get my own back on the enemy, but they still kept well concealed. Meanwhile the party on the right of the Fort had made good progress, in fact being too eager I think they went too far . . .

It was at this point that Major Charles Jerram began to take a more active part in proceedings.

Maj. Jerram RMLI, Notes on landings of 4 March 1915

Major Bewes with the advanced guard of two Platoons moved south and was followed by another Platoon, and the Naval demolition party for the 'small Fort'. They had a few casualties from the Houses and then appear to have advanced without loss, but under considerable fire until the Ad. Gd. [Advanced Guard] reached the Nullah and the remainder a position between the low hill and that spot. Here the party was held up by an hot fire from trenches on Yeni Shir and from the windmills.

This was about noon and the Brigadier wishing to be nearer the Naval Commander, transferred his Headquarters to the Flagship. Whilst a conference was being held on the bridge, I saw and reported a number of the enemy, some 200 or 300 strong, move down from Yeni Shir round the hill behind the Small Fort. It looked as if they would cut off our men and it was decided to withdraw both parties. The Brigade Major was sent to Sedd ul Bahr to order their withdrawal . . . I was sent to Kum Kale for a similar purpose and to remain to help Colonel Matthews. I went ashore in a whaler and felt very uncomfortable as occasional shell burst over and around us, but we arrived without incident. At the landing place were the boats and their crews, the Doctor, one Platoon and the MG Section doing little but taking cover. The Doctor took my cap, which was a staff one and conspicuous, and told me that I was certain to be killed if I left the shelter of the Fort, but that it was suicide to leave in that cap. Colonel Matthews was somewhere out at the Front. I ran the gauntlet of snipers in the Houses and, being fresh, escaped being hit. There was no cover and the houses were only 150 yds to 200 yds from the sea, by wading in which one's height was reduced to about 4 feet.

There were several dead about, and being by oneself was very uncomfortable. I found that my puttees after getting wet were unbearably tight and, after passing this point I had to stop and take them off and gave them to a midshipman, who was going back. He duly returned them next day. I found Col. Matthews by the Low Hill and delivered my message, when he told me that he had already come to the conclusion that to advance was impossible. He sent me to tell the Naval party to withdraw – then to get B's Platoon into a position on the Low Hill facing East to watch the flank, and then go on to Bewes and get him back.

I found the Naval Party scattered along the spit, under an hot fire, one man in true Naval style taking cover behind a box of detonators, and ordered them back. B's Platoon I found in about the same place. They had had several casualties and were under an hot fire. B, who was a 'Temporary', I found quite hopeless – he was pale with funk and refused to move. I then found the Platoon Sergt who was wounded in the head, and although a gallant soldier, could do little. The Platoon, under such leadership, was hard to move and it was not until I said that I proposed standing there until they did and that it was unusual for Marines to watch their officers being killed that a fellow got up and said, 'I'll come with you Sir.' I said, 'I'll put you into the position I want and then the remainder rush forward and line out on you.' Unluckily he was shot in the chest as I got him up, but we had succeeded in moving the Platoon, which only required an example and very naturally saw no reason for moving if their officer didn't. Just then Col. Matthews came up and as this had taken some time asked if I had got in touch with Bewes. I said no, but that I was told that these were the most advanced troops. He told me that he thought Bewes was in the Nullah and I went forward again. Whilst with the men I don't think I felt any fear; but now it was horrid – the bullets were cracking round on every side and I certainly did not feel as if I wanted to go on. At last I came to the last bit of cover and there were 300–400 yds of bare open sand, with, as I believed, nothing but enemy in front.

Col. Matthews hailed and stopped me and I brought him up to this point. He agreed that nothing could live between us and the Nullah and sent me back to signal to the Fleet for every gun to open on Yeni Shir in order that Bewes' party could get back. I was never so glad of an order in my life, but I soon found going back almost as bad as going forward. I ran zig-zag – like a snipe – and I think that saved me, as I was the only thing visible to shoot at and there must have been about 500 of the enemy firing. About half way I had to get my wind and dropped into a slight depression in the sand. However, they had seen me drop, and the bullets rained around, knocking up the sand into my face and doing all but actually hit me. It was not easy to make up one's mind what to do, as I made sure that immediately I began to get up I should be hit. However I wasn't, and soon got out of range. This side of the narrow strip I met Capt Lough, the Adjutant, who asked me what was happening; I told him the party was coming back so he decided to return, but said if we were together we'd both be killed from the Houses – so I gave him the messages and if I failed to get across he would try.

Why they didn't hit me I can't tell. Bullets must have been less than inches off my head and between my legs. The people in the Fort shouted to me to run or crawl but by then I was too exhausted to do more than walk. When half way across, in sheer desperation and anger I drew my revolver and emptied it at the Houses. Whether one took effect or not I don't know, but the enemy never fired another shot, nor did they fire at Lough who followed. He was however hit in the back by a spent bullet and knocked into the crater, but was only bruised. The Doctor gave me a strong dose of brandy and I then got off the message and was delighted to see the guns open fire.

In the meantime something had to be done about the Houses and I told Conybeare to get his two MGs [machine guns] on to the parapet of the Fort and open on the windows. This we did with some difficulty as the enemy had got back into the near face of the Fort and was keeping up a sniping fire. We then swept the trenches on Yeni Shir and soon saw the Adv. Party coming back. They arrived in a very exhausted state, bringing their wounded, and were embarked. Just as the last of them were going we saw two men out in the spit, believed dead, get up and stagger back. Lts Conybeare and Law took a stretcher and went out for them and I called for a volunteer to follow – a midshipman at once did and we started off but were recalled by Col. Matthews who said he would send a boat into the spit. Conybeare and Law were left in an enemy country and in any other war would have earned a VC. As it was they received nothing, though each member of the boat's crew which went in after dark in no danger at all received the CG Medal [Conspicuous Gallantry Medal].

Needless to say, Francis Law's short account of the action makes no mention of Conybeare or himself taking the stretcher, and covers the evacuation in two sentences.

Lt Law RMLI, No. 3 Coy Ply. Bn, *Globe & Laurel*, **May 1920**

It was realized that the enemy were in great strength, and to continue the advance would be inadvisable. Machine guns from the top of Kum Kale fort assisted in covering the retirement, which was successfully carried out, but not without considerable loss. In response to a signal, the fleet bombarded the enemy trenches and strong points, thus rendering valuable assistance to the retirement.

As soon the Company had returned to Kum Kale, it was decided to evacuate our position, and this was done without any further opposition. All the wounded were successfully taken off.

Charles Lamplough, back aboard *Braemar Castle*, did not know what had happened to No. 3 Company, as the men were picked up by *Lord Nelson* and *Irresistible,* and could work only from rumour and report.

Lt Lamplough RMLI, No. 4 Coy Ply. Bn, 4 March 1915, 11.45 p.m.

We have just heard that the *Lord Nelson* has got off 96 men and three wounded of No. 3 Company on board and that is all we heard so far but hope for better news tomorrow.

Private Percy Wyvill, of HMS *Lord Nelson*, wrote almost regretfully of not quite getting his full share of the day's action.

Pte Wyvill RMLI, HMS *Lord Nelson*, 4 March 1915

Got under way at 7.30 a.m., arrived at the entrance of Dardanelles at 9 a.m. Started bombarding. Landed demolition party first, open fire on No. 7 fort. At action stations for about three hours when the Marines have orders to land to reinforce the Marine Brigade which landed from *Braemar Castle*. Off we go, 200 rounds of ammunition per man – this is life at any rate. We get almost within jumping distance from shore when we are fired on from snipers. We can see all the troops ashore taking cover under the cliff. They have obviously been driven back. Boats recall – we have got to return to the ship, what rotten luck. Still firing at us from shore, no one hit in the boats. We receive the wounded of the Brigade and about 70 men who have thrilling tales to tell of work on shore. One man of the Brigade died before we got him inboard. It appears our troops are hopelessly outnumbered by the Turks. What of our demolition party, consisting of the First Lieutenant and Lieut. Mack, about 20 torpedo ratings and 4 marines. They have suffered 1 PO [petty officer] killed and 2 ABs [able seamen] wounded, 2 marines wounded. It appears Corporal Snelling was carrying another wounded comrade out of the hail of bullets when he got hit himself!

The same feeling was not shared by Charles Lamplough, who had been there.

Lt Lamplough RMLI, No. 4 Coy Ply. Bn, 5 March 1915

Friday, 5th March 1915 – Total casualties now are 20 killed, 24 wounded and 3 missing. It is a sad sight seeing their equipment etc all bloodstained, being brought back on board. They have only brought three bodies back with them and they died on the ships. We went to sea in the afternoon and buried them – six of ours and one Turk. It was by far the most moving thing I have ever witnessed. Poor old Baldwin had to go.

In the cold light of day, and after the adrenalin had passed, the day's action did not seem quite such a 'nice little scrap'. It was not only Lamplough who was impressed by the Burial at Sea, however. It was mentioned both by young Private Moynahan and Lieutenant John Richards.

Pte Moynahan RMLI, No. 3 Coy Ply. Bn, Friday 5 March 1915

We remained all night on the battleship and in the morning we returned to the transport while the wounded were taken on board the Hospital Ship *Soudan*.

The dead were brought aboard the transport also, to be taken to sea for burial, including the body of one Turkish prisoner who had been captured by No. 4 Company, and had since died. At 2 p.m. we proceeded to sea and at 2.30 everyone was paraded for the funeral service. The Chaplain of the Battalion read the service over the bodies which were laid out on stretchers on the poop, each being covered by a large Union Jack. Our people were buried first and afterwards the Turk was consigned to the deep. The whole service was very impressive and touching. It was my first burial at sea and I was very deeply touched by it.

John Richards must have seen a number of such burials over his many years of service, but closed his account with the same scene.

Lt Richards RMLI, No. 4 Coy Ply. Bn, *Globe & Laurel*, **February 1920**

We then went to sea, where an impressive Funeral Service was conducted by our chaplain, the Rev. Moore, and our dead, whom we had been able to bring back, were committed to the deep.

The wounded Turk we had brought on board having died, was also buried, our chaplain holding a separate service for him.

This had been the first experience of action and the sensation that someone was actually trying to kill them, as opposed to an action involving risk, for the youngsters, officer and man alike, and even for more senior Royal Marines such as Charles Jerram. Some coped very well, but not all. 'Lieutenant B', castigated by Charles Jerram, obviously found the experience overwhelming and froze. The only lieutenant of No. 3 Company whose surname began with 'B' was Lieutenant M. C. Browne, whom Sergeant Will Meatyard had followed up the road. If it was this officer then this was clearly 'first night nerves', as his obituary illustrates after his death at Beaucourt in 1916.

The Globe & Laurel, **January 1917**

Captain M. Campbell Browne, DSC RM, killed on November 13th, aged 28 years, was the youngest son of Dr Sam Browne, MD, late RN, of Esher. Educated at Cheltenham College and

Heidelburg, he joined the Royal Marines in November, 1914. He served in February, 1915, at the defence of the Suez Canal, and in April, 1915, landed at 'V' Beach, Gallipoli, with the Marine Brigade. In May he was wounded in the arm, and after recovering returned to the trenches. On July 12th and 13th he held for nearly two days, without food or water, half a trench. He and four men, all wounded, were the only ones left of the platoon. He was promoted captain and awarded the DSC. At the evacuation of Gallipoli he was the last in his trench, and swam off to the ship under a heavy fire. Last June he was ordered to the front, and took part in several engagements.

There is one other candidate for 'Lieutenant B'. Nineteen-year-old John Clixby Barnes, known as Jack, was in No. 1 Company, and therefore should not have been in action on 4 March, but he wrote to an old friend on 8 March, describing his first taste of action. The description is clearly that of the landing at Kum Kale.

Lt Jack Barnes RMLI, No. 1 Coy Ply. Bn, 8 March 1915

It is now a month since I left England and [I] have been in action once, and I can tell you it was damned rotten. We lost about twenty men and about twenty-three wounded, I managed to scrape through quite safely, tho' rumours went about that I had been killed, a lot of men seemed quite surprised to see me again. We had snipers shooting at us the whole time. I didn't see the enemy once. We were only in action about twelve hours, the worst part of the whole thing is seeing other men wounded, it absolutely takes the vim out of one, the No. 1 of my maxim gun was the third man to be wounded, I rather think that it is a pretty rotten hit. Another had his canteen on his back and a bullet went clean through it and smashed his razor. We were fortunate not to lose any officers. I don't expect that we shall return to England for a considerable time, but I think that we are better off here than in the trenches.

Why young Barnes was at Kum Kale is not noted, but he did not get much time to grow accustomed to warfare, and never returned to England. Two months after writing this letter, on 11 May, he was killed. Charles Lamplough noted in his diary that 'poor old Barnes got killed, shrapnel bullet through the head'. There is no way of knowing whether John Barnes became accustomed to being under fire, or had to steel himself every time, and was thoroughly miserable. Some men are naturally more suited to facing danger than others, and a brave man is not one who is without fear, but one who does what needs to be done in spite of it.

The Royal Marine battalions spent the next few weeks in a military limbo. They remained off the Dardanelles until after the attempt to force the Narrows on 18 March, then were sent to Port Said and spent about a week ashore, whilst the Royal Naval Division was drawn together and inspected. They then re-embarked and returned to Lemnos, which they reached on 12 April. On 18 April Colonel Matthews and the officers of the Plymouth Battalion were taken by HMS *Dublin* to take a look at the Gallipoli coastline. On Saturday 24 April the men were prepared for a landing. James Thompson, a signaller in No. 2 Company, noted the practical preparations in his diary.

Pte James Thompson RMLI, No. 2 Coy Ply. Bn, 24 April 1915

Signalmen paraded before Adjutant, Captain Lough. We were told by him to be very careful of water as our water bottles had to last three days. We were served out with two 1 lb tins of beef and two bags of biscuits, which has to last us five days.

In a similar vein are the details recorded by Private John Vickers of No. 1 Company.

Pte John Vickers RMLI, No. 1 Coy Ply. Bn, 23 & 24 April 1915

Preparing to land. Fell in with 'Field Dressing' and Identity Discs. Prepared our marching order (which is rather weighty). It contains greatcoat, three pairs of socks, canteen and cover, towel and soap, flannel, hard brush, holdall containing knife, fork, spoon, comb, razor and brush, three days iron rations consisting of 2 lb 'bully' beef and 2 lb biscuits, a waterproof sheet weighing about 5 lbs. We were to carry 250 rounds of ammunition weighing about 10 lbs, a full waterbottle, rifle and bayonet. This completed our equipment and we could take what private property we wished.

Charles Lamplough's preparations were more spiritual than temporal.

Lt Lamplough RMLI, No. 4 Coy Ply. Bn, 24 April 1915

Well we are getting into the outer anchorage this morning and hope to sail for Imbros this afternoon or evening and land about 5.30 tomorrow morning. I wonder how we shall get on – I should like to be able to see this time next week – may be finished, may be alive – some poor fellows will be finished but I think I shall be alright. I feel quite safe somehow or other, and with God's help I shall be.

The landings took place on the morning of Sunday 25 April. The Plymouth Battalion was sent with the 1st Battalion King's Own Scottish Borderers (KOSB), under Lieutenant Colonel Koe, and a company of the South Wales Borderers (SWB) to Y Beach, the northernmost of the British beaches. The objective was to gain a foothold on the peninsula and prevent Turkish reinforcements from reaching the main British landings on the end of the peninsula. The actual orders given to the officer in command, Lieutenant Colonel Matthews, were vague and only oral. The landing was made successfully, but as the day drew to a close the small force of Plymouth Marines, KOSB and SWB came under severe attack from the Turks. When the Turks realized that a landing had taken place they quickly sent troops to push the British from their new position. During the night, repeated attacks were made and by dawn the British were short of ammunition and had suffered many casualties. Lieutenant Colonel Matthews sent a signal to his commander, Lieutenant General Hunter-Weston, saying that he could not hold on without reinforcements. He did not receive a reply. Hunter-Weston was more concerned with the landings further south, and merely passed on Matthews' message with the comment that he had no troops to spare. The previous night Hunter-Weston had been offered the Worcestershire Regiment as a support for the Y Beach force and had declined it.

Matthews found himself unsupported and without the likelihood of assistance in the foreseeable future. A few troops and wounded had been removed from the beach itself by the Royal Navy, and seeing that take place led to others thinking that an order to retire had been given. In view of the number of casualties and the difficulties with ammunition, this was not an unrealistic assumption. The evacuation began, and by the time Matthews became aware of it, there was little alternative. Rearguards were formed and Y beach was finally evacuated in good order. The troops had held out against increasing Turkish forces, but had received neither assistance nor further orders from the Staff. Their failure was not due to lack of effort, but an apparent lack of interest from Hunter-Weston. Signals were not acknowledged, requests for ammunition ignored, except by HMS *Queen Elizabeth*, which authorized a supply of ammunition from HMS *Goliath*, and no officer was sent by Hunter-Weston to accurately report the situation and liaise with the troops on the ground, as happened elsewhere.

Hunter-Weston bears heavy responsibility for these failings. He did originally suffer from the misconception that the landing on Y Beach, unopposed and successful, had been followed by a linking of the line with X Beach to the south. There were also the obvious distractions of the carnage and desperate problems being faced by the troops at V and W Beaches. Yet as the day progressed, others were clearly aware of the increasing problem at Y Beach. Hunter-Weston saw no reason to exploit the initial advantage, stuck rigidly to his original plan regardless of the run of events, and then proceeded to ignore his left flank 'sideshow'.

Lieutenant Charles Lamplough and Private John Vickers left long entries in their diaries about Y Beach, and there are also detailed accounts from Lieutenant Charles Conybeare, Private James Thompson and Sergeant Will Meatyard, now recovered from his wounds and back with the Battalion. Meatyard's notes on the signals sent are most telling. All of these men were in a small area, often within a few yards of each other, and, whilst there are discrepancies, many of the details tally. Charles Conybeare begins his account with the objective and some interesting details on headgear.

Lt Conybeare RMLI, No. 3 Coy Ply. Bn, *Globe & Laurel*, April, May 1919

. . . the object of it [the landing] was to attack the Turk in the rear, engage his reserves, which were stationed somewhere close (which we found to our cost later in the day), and to cut them off, when they were driven out of their positions round the main landings at Cape Helles.

We were told we might expect to be isolated thus for about six hours, after which the troops from the end would be up with us, when we would join in with them in the attack on Krithia and Achi Baba . . .

We landed with full packs, three days' iron ration, and 250 rounds per man. We were warned that the wells would probably be poisoned, so that the water-bottles would have to last two or three days, till the Engineers bored some new ones. The Plymouth Bn. landed in 'cap comforters', as we had left our caps in Egypt and only had our helmets with us; later it was discovered that every time one lay down to fire the pack caught the back of the helmet and pushed the peak of it over one's eyes. We were rather afraid of the cap comforter being mistaken for a 'fez' and being fired on by our own troops, so all the 29th Division were informed.

Private John Vickers' account begins the night before the landing.

Pte Vickers RMLI, No. 1 Coy Ply. Bn, 24 April 1915

We turned in early on the 24th, at 8 p.m., and left the bay after dark with several battleships and destroyers. Every light on the ships was extinguished so as not to be detected by the Turks who would probably be on the alert when we drew near the Peninsula. We slept till 1 a.m. When we turned out we had something to eat and drink and prepared ourselves generally for the landing. As we got ready we went on deck. The moon was shining and every one of us was very excited, and wondered what dawn would bring.

The ship slowed down and stopped some three miles from the Peninsula, where the trawlers, which had been detailed to land us, came alongside. We got into the trawlers which soon moved off in the direction of the Peninsula. It was rather dark now and we could see several small lights on the Peninsula, but they were very distant. As we drew near the land it grew light quite suddenly and we were able to see the point at which we were to land.

Charles Lamplough describes it as 'a lovely moonlight morning', but Sergeant Will Meatyard did not enjoy his early morning 'dip'.

Sgt Meatyard RMLI, HQ Coy Ply. Bn, 25 April 1915

Getting out of the boats dropped into water waist deep. It was rather a cold shock at first. We waded towards shore keeping rifles in the air clear of the water, and eventually reached the narrow bit of beach.

John Vickers found the wade ashore difficult, though he was relieved to have found the landing beach easier than initially thought.

Pte Vickers RMLI, No. 1 Coy Ply. Bn, 25 April 1915

It appeared from the distance to be an impossible landing, but as we drew nearer it was not so sheer as at first supposed – although the cliffs were some 200 feet high.

The next few minutes were the most exciting I had experienced. The Turks opened fire from all sides and our battlecruisers and destroyers replied. The intensity of the fire increased and it was plain that the Troops who were landing on the other beaches were having a hot time. We got out of the trawlers into small boats holding about 30 men, and went inland. The boats grounded some 50 yards from shore and we jumped in to water and waded ashore – a very difficult task, as the water was over our waists and we had a decent weight to carry. A few snipers made their presence felt from the top of the cliff but were shelled off before causing any casualties.

As soon as we reached land we took cover under the cliffs and scouts were sent out. The KOSB's scouts (two of them) were killed by a shell from our own ship, who took them for Turks. This mistake happened several times, for a shell from a ship pitched into a section killing and wounding six. We were in an awkward fix, for we were being wiped out by our own men – very disheartening. The scouts returned and reported all clear. There were no enemy in sight and we climbed the cliffs, extended, and commenced digging in.

Having endured the 'shock' of the cold water, Sergeant Meatyard faced what he noted as 'a stiff climb' up the cliff; words repeated in Lieutenant Conybeare's account of the approach to the beach.

Sgt Meatyard RMLI, HQ Coy Ply. Bn, 25 April 1915

We had a stiff climb before us, the part we scrambled up being called the 'Gully' and the beach 'Y Beach'. The scouts went ahead and actually reached the outskirts of Krithia, a small village which we saw but never reached again during the whole campaign. Our scouts came in contact with one or two Turkish scouts during the advance. Two were shot and one brought in as a prisoner. He looked very depressed about it, being under the opinion, as told by his German leaders, that all prisoners would be shot by the British.

Lt Conybeare RMLI, No. 3 Coy Ply. Bn, *Globe & Laurel*, April, May 1919

It was just getting light (about 4.30 a.m.) when we got close in shore. We could see our covering ships, the *Goliath, Dublin, Amethyst,* and *Sapphire,* and the cliffs in front of us, and far away to our left the shell bursts which had just started and let us know that the Australians were off. Those of us who had done the landings at Kum Kale or Sedd ul Bahr on the 4th March began to wonder if we were going to be treated better or worse this time.

When we got close in, we realized what a stiff climb we had before us, and we could see the KOS Borderers crawling up the cliff; still no shot had been fired at us . . .

By now the sun was up and it was a very pleasant day. The bombardments at the other beaches had started and were going full belt.

Despite the physical difficulty of getting to the top of the cliff with all their equipment, the Royal Marines soon found themselves at the top, and Charles Conybeare could see explosions from the other landing beaches.

Lt Conybeare RMLI, No. 3 Coy Ply. Bn, *Globe & Laurel*, April, May 1919

Across the peninsula we could see the Dardanelles with Morto Bay full of ships, which were firing hard, making the cliffs round the main landings look like 'young volcanoes'.

The KOSBs and the 1st and 4th Companies of the Plymouth Bn. now started to dig in close to the edge of the cliff, and the 2nd and 3rd Companies of the Plymouth and the S. W. Borderer Coy started to advance inland to cover the Krithia road, which was the main road of retreat for the Turks from Cape Helles. We now had another climb as we had to cross the 'Gulley Ravine', a gulley about 120 feet deep, with very steep sides. We fell most of the way down one side and crawled up the other. It was just after crossing this gully we got our first prisoner, a Turkish officer, who seemed very surprised to see us.

James Thompson of No. 2 Company was at the top of the cliff, with his signallers just behind a forward trench of the King's Own Scottish Borderers.

Pte Thompson RMLI, No. 2 Coy Ply. Bn, 25 April 1915

Are now awaiting the result of scouts' reconnaissance. This is
a beautiful morning, we have reached the top of the slope I
mentioned and are in extended order with the KOSB
entrenching themselves in front.

The Battleships are still tearing the country to pieces and
aeroplanes and seaplanes are flying overhead.

A lot of rifle firing is going on off to our right rear. I am on
the left flank of the firing line with my group of signallers
looking out for orders from HQs . . .

We have been under rifle fire for about an hour. Just now a
party left here to try and deliver a flank attack. Do not know
how they are getting on.

As I write this a continual 'swish' 'swish' is going on.

Charles Lamplough was one of No. 4 Company still in the gully.

Lt Lamplough RMLI, No. 4 Coy Ply. Bn, 25 April 1915

. . . we stayed in the Gully as reserves. We got up the
ammunition, which was a rotten job. Well, we did not have
half a bad time in the morning, but with a little sniping.
However, at midday it got much worse and we entrenched
ourselves. It got worse all the time till about 4.30 p.m. and
during the afternoon we had several casualties, including
Major Palmer. I also had a jolly close shave with some
shrapnel and also the ships hit the cliff above us twice,
blowing one man's eye and leg off.

Meanwhile Sergeant Will Meatyard was with his commanding officer,
on hand for communications up and down the chain of command.

Sgt Meatyard RMLI, HQ Coy Ply. Bn, 25 April 1915

After the first line of skirmishers had gone on some distance,
the enemy's artillery came to bear, and dealt out shrapnel on
them with some accuracy. Having established a signal station
on the side of the cliff to communicate with HM Ships I
proceeded with the CO, having sent two signallers with the
advanced line of skirmishers. I was ordered to make the signal

'Retire to your original positions', a blue flag being necessary and advisable.

Lieutenant Charles Conybeare was one of the 'advanced line of skirmishers' and was most relieved to be called back from a difficult position.

Lt Conybeare RMLI, No. 3 Coy Ply. Bn, *Globe & Laurel*, **April, May 1919**

Presently one of our range-takers discovered a Turkish battery about 2,500 yards away coming into action [from Serafim Farm]. We all got our glasses out and watched it, thinking it very pretty, till we discovered we were target! They gave us a very unpleasant ten minutes with shrapnel, before we got orders to get back to the top of the cliff and dig in. We staggered back across the gulley, where a certain amount of sniping was going on, as the Turk appeared to have at last sat up and taken notice of us . . . We'd just got back to the top of the cliff (about 11 a.m.) when the lid came off with a bump; shells and bullets appeared to come over in a sheet, in the midst of which we were trying to dig in again. The KOS Borderers and our two advance companies, who had stopped behind when we advanced inland, had been digging for some time, so had fairly decent trenches. The force was now in a rough semicircle, the two flanks resting on the edge of the cliff above the beach, two Companies of Marines being on both flanks, with the KOS Borderers in the centre and the SW Borderer Coy next to them.

Turks began to show in small groups, chiefly on the left flank and centre, and our machine guns had a bit of practice. Our covering ships were firing hard now, and it was a very fine sight to see the 4-inch guns of the *Amethyst* and *Sapphire* going as hard as they could, to all appearance with very good results.

Col. Matthews, who walked about in the open all that day encouraging everybody by his coolness, appeared to bear a charmed life; anybody else who tried it promptly got hit. During the afternoon we got in touch with 'X' Beach by heliograph, when we found out things weren't going too well with the main landings, and that we would have to stick it considerably longer than the six hours. About the same time an aeroplane reported two battalions coming from the Krithia direction to attack us.

Sergeant Will Meatyard was a Royal Marine with years of experience and, like many of the senior NCOs, considered himself a true professional. He was the Signal Sergeant and his job was to send and receive signals, regardless of whatever else might be happening around him, and if necessary by improvisation. Communication with the ships proved awkward but fulfilling, as they responded as desired.

Sgt Meatyard RMLI, HQ Coy Ply. Bn, 25 April 1915

This all happened within a very short time and the trenches were very far from being deep or completed in any way, and it now became necessary to bring fire to bear on the advancing enemy . . .

By laying on the back, on the slope of the cliff, it was possible to use a large flag and keep communication with the Ships. It was necessary to lay on the back as bullets passed over from each flank and dropped somewhere inside the semi-circle. Men on each flank complained that their own men were firing at them, but it was the indirect fire of the enemy that passed over the heads of our men on one flank and so caught the men on the other flank, the flanks being so close together and our position being of a semi-circular formation.

Private John Vickers had been digging in earlier and had seen 'others hauling ammunition, barbed wire, machine guns etc. up the cliffs'. He describes his position.

Pte Vickers RMLI, No. 1 Coy Ply. Bn, 25 April 1915

The village of Krithia was about half a mile to our right front, and about 600 yds in front was a trench already dug by the Turks. This was found to be unoccupied by our scouts. We did not take possession [of] it for we guessed it would be mined. The day wore on and we had dug well in. The fire from our ships and the Turks' batteries was terrific. All went well until about 4 p.m. in the afternoon when the enemy scouts and snipers got busy and it became necessary not to expose ourselves unnecessarily, as they had already picked several off. The first casualty was Pte McGuirk, shot through the head. He died shortly after being hit.

Charles Lamplough also found the afternoon becoming increasingly dangerous at his location.

Lt Lamplough RMLI, No. 4 Coy Ply. Bn, 25 April 1915

At 5 o'clock the order came to reinforce and the bullets were simply coming like rain and our front trenches had to retire a little lower. We ran up the gully and I honestly never thought we should get out of it as the fire was terrible, but we got up to the 2nd line ready. The order came to get off packs, and so we had to leave our packs containing our food etc. Then the whole of us advanced under frightfully heavy fire and got to the trench. We had a large number of casualties during this advance. We could not get up, but crawled along on our stomachs. The bullets were buzzing past our heads and ears. It was awful, and I honestly thought I had met my end, but by God's grace I was spared. Well, after a few more adventures we reached the trench and there was terrible fire on both sides, but our difficulty was getting up ammunition. This went on every bit of the night and we were also being enfiladed by the Turks attacking our other trench, so that we had bullets coming behind us as well.

Lieutenant Charles Conybeare was in a similar position as the light failed and the Turkish attacks became more fierce.

Lt Conybeare RMLI, No. 3. Coy Ply. Bn, *Globe & Laurel*, April, May 1919

About 5 or 6 p.m. the firing got hotter than ever, and the Turk started to try and attack the left and centre again with infantry, but he never came to grips during the day.

Our casualties had been fairly heavy, but the KOS Borderers had lost a good many of their officers. The wounded were put under the top of the cliff, but even there bullets dropped from somewhere. The 'overs' were very troublesome, many of the bullets aimed, say, at the right flank, would go over and hit the left flank in the rear, whereupon those on the left flank would want to know who the ——— were firing at their backs.

It wasn't till darkness came on that the show really started, and things really got mixed. A few Turks got round our flanks on the cliff, and there was hide-and-seek going on among the bushes on the cliff in the dark, our wounded, who were there, having a very unpleasant time.

James Thompson was one of those playing 'hide and seek', and did not enjoy it.

Pte Thompson RMLI, No. 2 Coy Ply. Bn, 25 April 1915

We remained in our small trench until about 7 p.m. with continual fire going on from our trenches in front. At the above time Captain Tetley came running back to gather any troops that were about, to repel an attack on the cliffs to our left. I fixed my bayonet, left my pack and signal gear in the trench and ran forward and down the cliffs, being joined by about thirty men under a Lieutenant who was wounded just as I lay down alongside of him.

The Turks made an attack on us at once with hand grenades, so we were ordered to retire in consequence. We all got mixed up and were shouting 'Who are you?' to anyone that came running along. If they failed to answer in English, we fired! We continued to retire until I eventually found myself on the sea shore with three wounded men and one chap who was alright. I shall never forget our experience that night. All three of the wounded were able to walk so we tried to hail a boat but were immediately fired on from above so ran along the beach with the devils above chasing us along the top. Luckily nobody was hit, and at last we reached a sort of split in the rock, so took shelter and waited all night with our rifles ready. To make matters worse it came on to rain and we didn't have a waterproof sheet or coat between us.

Meanwhile, the engagement at the top of the cliff was as furious as ever.

Lt Conybeare RMLI, No. 3 Coy Ply. Bn, *Globe & Laurel*, April, May 1919

They [the Turks] broke in amongst the KOS Borderers' left, and so No. 3 Coy (Major Bewes) was taken away from the right and sent over to strengthen them. No. 2 Coy (Capt. Knight) had to withdraw slightly and dig in again in the dark so as not to lose touch with the next company, which was the

SW Borderers. Beyond rifle fire, which was terrific, and a Nordenfeldt, the right flank was not worried during the night, like the centre and left flank, where there was hand to hand fighting going on the whole time. Sometimes with the flanks in the air, at other times with the Turks behind them, it became all the more bitter when it was discovered our wounded were being killed by the Turks, if they got hold of them.

Private John Vickers was one of those in the thick of the fighting.

Pte Vickers RMLI, No. 1 Coy Ply. Bn, 25/26 April 1915

Shortly after the snipers made their appearance the order was passed along the line: 'A large body of Troops advancing over the skyline'. This message was followed by another: 'A *larger* body of Troops advancing over the skyline'. As our platoon had taken up a position about 10 yds from the top of the cliff it was not possible to see them advancing for some time after. They were 800 to 900 yds away, advancing in massed formation, shouting and waving their rifles above their heads. As soon as they came within a reasonable distance we opened fire upon them. They still rushed on, until the two cruisers who were supporting us, HMS *Goliath* and HMS *Dublin*, each fired a broadside which completely scattered them. It was growing dark now and the Turks had taken possession of the trench 600 yds away . . . We had prepared ourselves for the worst. Every man had as much ammunition as he could find room for, and had plenty of reserve. Shortly after dark they made their first charge as expected. They came up within 10 yds of our trench, but by keeping up a rapid fire we held them back. They retired for a short time but there was a regular hail of bullets hitting the parapet of the trench and almost blinding us with dirt. The dirt was also getting into the mechanism of our rifles, which added to the difficulty of keeping up a rapid fire.

Shortly after they retired, their bombers got to work and came within a few yards of our trenches. They were shot down however, but it was very difficult to see more than 15 yds away from our position. Apart from being very dark and the ground shrubby it was a dark background. They then made another attack in their usual close formation but it was no trouble to hit them, we simply mowed them down, although we could not actually see the effect of our fire. The fact that they never got into our trenches told that they were having a lot of casualties.

The noise was awful – wounded groaning and calling for stretchers (which never came) – the incessant rattle of the machine guns and rifles – the wounded and dying Turks in front calling for 'Allah' (their God). To make matters more cheerful it began to rain. We beat off the second attack but they were not to be denied and soon came on again with greater force. Things were looking sick for us now. We were only 2,000 strong to begin with and we were quickly getting weaker with casualties, which were not being replaced. The Turks were easily five to one and were being reinforced. We had great difficulty in beating off their third attack and our ammunition was running short. The night wore on, but so slowly. How we would welcome dawn.

Sergeant Will Meatyard was well aware of the seriousness of the situation, both from the volume of fire and because it was he who was sending out the Colonel's increasingly desperate signals, and not receiving replies. Will Meatyard focussed on his task and put other concerns aside.

Sgt Meatyard RMLI, HQ Coy Ply. Bn, 25/26 April 1915

Another unfortunate instance was that I had received orders to take no signal lamps whatever when we landed, but when night came on we found that a Signal Lamp was badly needed, there being no other means of communication. By a stroke of luck I thought of the CO's torchlight pocket lamp, and with this I was able to send quite a number of important signals, my fingers got rather sore working the small slide up and down, but a handkerchief helped matters. Words were not wasted and signals (as they should be) were short and to the point. Some I remember were, 'Send in boats for wounded, the spot will be indicated by a light', 'Send 30,000 rounds of small arms ammunition, running short' and to the GOC [General Officer Commanding], 'Can't hold on without reinforcements of at least one Battalion'. 'We are in a serious position . . . '

Throughout all my experience I have not heard a greater volume of rifle and machine gun fire, considering the hours that it lasted. It never ceased during the night.

John Vickers and Charles Lamplough were in the midst of that enemy fire through the night of 25 to 26 April.

Pte Vickers RMLI, No. 1 Coy Ply. Bn, 25/26 April 1915

Our Captain (Tetley) gave the order 'Stand by to charge'. It was then that another terrible mistake happened. The Turks, who were still trying to break through, made a rush and our second line, thinking they had got past us, commenced firing into us. They were quickly informed of their mistake but not before they had caused some casualties. We managed, however, to hold them [the Turks] back, and they retired again for a little while. During the lull we were able to get more ammunition and the gaps in our front line were filled up with our only supports. We could hear them [the Turks] jabbering not many yards away. It may have been their Officers giving orders, but not knowing the language we were not much the wiser.

Lt Lamplough RMLI, No. 4 Coy Ply. Bn, 25/26 April 1915

Well, this was the same all through the night but at 3.45 a.m. Monday we took a few (two platoons) about 50 yds back and dug ourselves in as we expected to be shelled, but instead of this they made a very desperate attack on our right flank and this enfiladed us badly especially my party in dugouts. Soon after this the ships burst a 12" in the trench and this caused the Borderers to retire and in fact it was a stampede [most of their officers had become casualties] and they came rushing down into the gully, but I was there with Captain Andrews and my platoon and we rallied them again and went up the cliff again to make a counter attack, however some more shrapnel came over and we had to scatter. Finally I got hold of five KOSBs and two of my men and we went on our own; getting across the open we came across a few of them [Turks] and three of my party got killed so that only five of us arrived and we were very lucky. Of course the other platoon had come up on our right and the Colonel was there.

It was at about this time, during a counter-attack, that Lieutenant May was killed and Lieutenant Francis Law wounded. Law was later awarded the DSC for his actions. Down on the beach, James Thompson and his bedraggled party were cold and wet, but on the alert.

Pte Thompson RMLI, No. 2 Coy Ply. Bn, 25/26 April 1915

In the early hours of the morning I suddenly saw something creeping along the beach, so thinking it was a Turk I challenged him and found him to be a wounded soldier who had tried to swim to the ships but had returned exhausted. This poor devil turned out to be the man whom we had heard calling for help the night before, but [we] could not help as we could not see him and he seemed to be a long way out. The Turks were also firing down at him from the top of the cliffs. His cries were pitiful and we thought when he had ceased calling for help that it was all up with him. He hadn't a stitch to his back, but was as happy as could be to see I was English. He made our party up to six, but only two of us had rifles.

John Vickers was still up on the cliff top, facing heavy attacks.

Pte Vickers RMLI, No. 1 Coy Ply. Bn, 26 April 1915

We held our ground, but for how much longer we did not know. They made another stronger attack still, and seeing they could not break through their officers (German) began shouting out to us in good English to retire. We were, however, up to these tricks. Our ammunition was almost spent and we knew we must soon trust to the bayonet. We could not retire for we had nowhere to go, only into the sea.

This problem was fully understood by Lieutenant Charles Conybeare, with No. 3 Company.

Lt Conybeare RMLI, No. 3 Coy Ply. Bn, *Globe & Laurel*, April, May 1919

Dawn broke with the fight going as hard as ever, but we began to see where we were and counter-attacks were organized to adjust the line; also the Turks on the cliff behind us decided it was time to go, but we bagged a few who started too late.

There was still no sign of our troops approaching from the other beaches; casualties were very heavy, the KOS Borderers had lost practically all their officers, the cliff and beach were covered with our wounded, ammunition and water were low, so we were in rather a tight corner. In an ordinary scrap if you go back a few yards it probably doesn't matter, but here if we went back we should go over the cliff. Apparently it was the same at the other beaches, they couldn't go back a yard, as if they had, they would have been in the sea . . .

At about 6.30 a.m. the KOS Borderers made a splendid counter-attack, the remnants of the battalion getting up and going forward with a rush, cheering like mad; it was a very fine sight to watch. An hour or so after this the Turk appeared to have had enough and beyond an occasional shot nothing happened. The boats which came in for the wounded were not fired on, though we saw several Turks further down watching the wounded on the beach. Two Turkish prisoners taken on the left were on the beach when the boats arrived; they had evidently had enough scrapping, and dived into one of the boats before you could say knife. Soon after this orders were given to evacuate 'Y' Beach.

Sergeant Will Meatyard described the orderly withdrawal.

Sgt Meatyard RMLI, HQ Coy Ply. Bn, 26 April 1915

Platoons were told off to form rearguard while the re-embarking commenced. They retired down the cliff, right and left sections retiring alternately. Many of the enemy dead were left in front of our trenches, many lying there only within a few yards. At dawn they had apparently had enough for the time, as they had retired some distance from the front of our position but were still pressing on our flanks. With the exception of considerable sniping we were allowed to re-embark unmolested. It may have been the enemy had had enough, or the presence of our warships (with memories of the morn's bombardment), that checked them. The boats for re-embarking were organized remarkably well, and this assisted us to get away smartly.

Private John Vickers was heartily glad of the lull, and the chance to leave without making it a fighting re-embarkation.

Bugler E.E. Holloway RMLI and his father, Clr Sgt H.A. Holloway RMLI, who was recalled for duty in Britain. This photograph was taken shortly before HMS *Lord Nelson* left for the Dardanelles.

Capt. Harold Blount RMA and Capt. Alan Bourne, MVO, RMA when they were majors.

Bugler Charles Smith RMLI, lost at sea in HMS *Louvain*, January 1918.

Capt. Chandos Hill RMLI, HMS *Colossus*.

Gallipoli

Officers of the Plymouth Bn RMLI aboard SS *Braemar Castle*. The photograph was taken with Lt Lamplough's camera. Left to right: Lt A.N. Williams, Lt Charles Tuckey (killed 23 April 1918), Lt Charles Lamplough.

Gallipoli, Y Beach. Although this picture was taken later in the campaign, the 'stiff climb' that faced the Plymouth Bn is still daunting.

Gallipoli landings, 25 April 1915. Men clambering over the dead to get ashore. The carnage in the boats was horrific.

Zeebrugge

Officers of the 4th Bn Royal Marines. *Left to right, rear rank:* 2nd Lt H. Lovatt (wounded), Surgeon F. Pocock, MC, RN, Lt & Qr-Mr F. Hore (w.), Lt B. Claudet, Lt D. Broadwood, Lt R. Stanton (died of wounds), Lt G. Underhill, Lt H. de Berry, Lt S.H. Inskip (killed). *Middle rank:* Capt. J. Palmer, DSC (PoW), Lt C. Lamplough, Lt J. Jackson (k.), 2nd Lt A. Norris, Lt W. Dollery (k.), Lt T. Cooke (w.), Lt W. Sillitoe (k.), 2nd Lt W. Bloxsom (w.), 2nd Lt W. Boxall, Capt. C. Tuckey (missing, later confirmed k.). *Front rank:* Capt. C. Conybeare (w.), Capt. R. del Strother (w.), Maj. C. Eagles, DSO (k.), Maj. A. Cordner (k.), Lt Col. B. Elliot, DSO (k.), Capt. & Adjt A. Chater, Maj. B. Weller, DSC, Capt. E. Bamford, DSO, Surgeon H. Colson RN. Away at the time of the photograph were Capt. Dallas-Brookes (k.) & Lt Rigby.

Capt. Arthur Chater RMLI, Adjutant of the Chatham Bn RND for some months in Gallipoli and of the 4th Bn RM for the Zeebrugge raid, for which he was awarded the DSO.

Sgt Harry Wright, captured at Zeebrugge, as a prisoner of war.

Zeebrugge. The brows aboard HMS *Vindictive*, of which so many were damaged before the platoons could climb ashore. Note the gym shoes, worn to make getting over the brows easier.

'A shambles.' Sorting out the mess of equipment back at Dover, after the Zeebrugge raid. The bodies had been collected and removed, but the tangle of boots, webbing and assorted gear speaks volumes.

Life on Active Service

Maj. Norman Burge RMLI, Commanding
Officer of Nelson Bn RND.

Maj. Charles Jerram at his ablutions in
Gallipoli. Shaving was a luxury to be revelled
in, at least when the enemy were not lobbing
high explosives into the camp.

'Decided to give a dinner party in honour of the new Mess so made most elaborate
arrangements ...' *Romano's without the bill* – the Cyclist Coy Officers' Mess at Gallipoli,
where Norman Burge held his dinner party.

Aftermath

Capt. Christopher Andrews RMLI, killed age 34 on 11 May 1915.

Lt Jack Barnes, of the same battalion, killed aged 19 a few hours later.

The grave where both Capt. Andrews and Lt Barnes were buried. This photograph is all that remains of it. At the end of the war the grave could not be found and so both are commemorated on the Helles Memorial to those with no known grave.

Pte Vickers RMLI, No. 1 Coy Ply. Bn, 26 April 1915

During the lull we cleaned our rifles, got fresh supplies and
had what we called breakfast. We sat down on our 'packs'
(taking turns at sentry), and soon began to 'nod' when the
order to retire was passed from the right of the line. We retired
to the extreme edge of the cliffs but as we were short of both
stretchers and bearers some of our wounded were left in the
trench. We made a counter attack, driving back their snipers.
On regaining our trenches we found they had bayoneted our
wounded. Three Scotties near me were in a state of semi-
consciousness through loss of blood. They had all been
bayoneted through the chest. We got all the wounded away,
and not a second too soon, for a large body of Turks made their
appearance a few hundred yards away. Our Company acted as
rearguard and we retired with very few losses. We were taken
aboard HMS *Goliath* in a thoroughly exhausted condition.
Here many touching scenes took place for we all sought our
chums and I felt very relieved to find my chums E. Morris and
J. Matthews aboard unscratched. It was very touching to hear
men asking for their chums and to be told by others 'I saw him
killed'.

Charles Lamplough, having helped in the recapture of the lost trench,
also found himself covering the withdrawal.

Lt Lamplough RMLI, No. 4 Coy Ply. Bn, 26 April 1915

After we had recaptured the trench we took up a new and
smaller position round the head of the gully as we were going
to retire, so we once more dug in and some snipers had a go at
us but we soon disposed of them and when all the wounded
were taken down to the beach we went down and took to the
boats and were all put on board the *Goliath* soaking wet, as we
had to practically swim to the boats, but we got some food and
we were all simply dead tired. Out of 2,000 our casualties were
about 700. We [No. 4 Company] had one officer [Lt May, who
had led the patrol into the fort at Kum Kale on 4 March] and a
sergeant major killed and six wounded and 210 were
casualties in our Battalion so it gave us a nasty smack and we
lost a terrible lot of gear and ammunition.

James Thompson had to organize his own transport from the beach, and was very glad to be a signaller.

Pte Thompson RMLI, No. 2 Coy Ply. Bn, 26 April 1915

We remained in our hiding place until daylight when along the sea shore came about the most motley crowd I have ever seen. About thirty-five in number, these were Marines, KOSBs, SWB and wounded of all sorts. One poor beggar had his tongue shot out of his mouth.

Our position was dangerous, as they had practically no ammunition and with the Turks on each side of the cliffs above, and all my signal gear gone. One chap volunteered to swim off to the ships and ask for boats.

In the meantime I tied my red handkerchief on a stick and a white handkerchief on another piece and stood on a rock semaphoring. To our joy, after twenty minutes HMS *Blenheim* answered with her searchlight so when we told how we were situated she sent boats for us and took us all aboard. The ship's company gave us plenty to eat and hot tea to drink. We remained there until evening when we were all transferred to the *Ansonia* where we re-organized and mustered our losses. Were found to be 197, 43 in one Company. KOSBs losses being 270.

Lieutenant Charles Conybeare concludes his description of the action with a touch of bitterness, for the small force of Royal Marines, King's Own Scottish Borderers and South Wales Borderers were given little credit for a hard fight. He also makes no mention of the fact that he was wounded in the course of the action.

Lt Conybeare RMLI, No. 3 Coy Ply. Bn, *Globe & Laurel*, April, May 1919

The last man off the beach was Col. Matthews, and the last two companies were Royal Marine Companies, No. 1 (Capt. Tetley) and No. 4 (Capt. Andrews), *not* as was stated in Sir Ian Hamilton's, something about 'had it not been for the heroic devotion of a band of KOS Borderers, who did rearguard, the force would never have got off.' They had no casualties coming off, the *Goliath* had closed in to what appeared to be about 600 yards from shore, and if any Turk showed himself on the skyline, he was sniped with a 12-pounder or 6-inch gun.

As stated before we were told we might expect to be on our own for six hours; when we left we had been there nearer thirty hours, and there was still no sign of our own troops; in fact, this spot on the coast was not reached for several more days, so it was just as well we left when we did, as reinforcements were asked for, but refused, there being no troops to spare, and we could not have stuck another night like the first.

Undoubtedly the action at Y Beach counts as an 'if only' incident, but war is full of such. If the orders had been written, clearly and with room to exploit advantage, if Hunter-Weston had shown any ability to think on his feet, or indeed had shown any interest at all in what was occurring at the most northerly British landing, pressure could have been brought to bear on the Turkish forces at Cape Helles. In reality the landing force at Y Beach was wasted. The final number of casualties for the action, as ascertained for Blumberg's *Britain's Sea Soldiers: A History of the Royal Marines 1914–1919,* was 14 officers and 317 NCOs and men killed or wounded in the Plymouth Battalion RMLI, and 296 King's Own Scottish Borderers, plus nearly all their officers, 8 of whom were killed. A memorial service was held aboard ship for the dead left on shore. A piper from the KOSB played a lament and the chaplain of that battalion, who was conducting the service, had to stop on several occasions because he was overcome by emotion.

This was only the beginning of the Royal Marines' activity on the Gallipoli Peninsula. The Plymouth Battalion itself was landed at Cape Helles on 28 April. On the same day, part of the Royal Marines Brigade, consisting of Brigade Headquarters, the Chatham and Portsmouth Battalions, No. 1 Field Company, Divisional Engineers, Royal Marines, and stretcher bearers of the 3rd Field Ambulance, landed at Anzac Cove, under the 1st Australian Division. They were expected to be there for two days, and were therefore landed without stores or kit. Yet again such judgements were found to be ridiculously wide of the mark. The Brigade, joined by Deal and Nelson Battalions on 29 April, remained for 14 days. During this time they were well appreciated by the Australians, alongside whom they fought. They were involved in holding and improving the trenches, and in several major attacks.

The nature of warfare on the peninsula was such that there were no real breaks from action, as 'Rest' camps and bivouacs were always within shelling distance and casualties occurred daily. Major attacks frequently ended up without gain, and an increasing number of casualties arose from disease, especially dysentery. The terrain was difficult to dig into, whether for defensive positions or attempts to bury

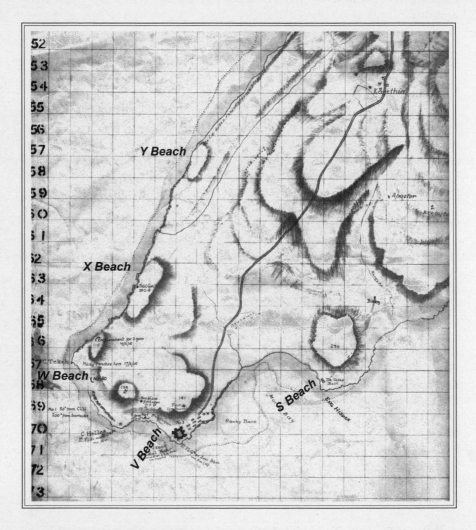

Landing beaches at Gallipoli, 25 April 1915.
Original map drawn by Maj. Sinclair RMLI of HMS *Inflexible*,
additional annotations by author.

the fast putrefying dead; the days were hot and the nights unbearably cold, and the pressure unremitting. Arthur Chater found himself Adjutant of his Battalion, Chatham, within a few days of landing at Anzac Cove, and the Battalion Diary gives a clear indication of how the fortnight at Anzac was spent. It is a strictly accurate but unemotional account.

Lt Arthur Chater RMLI, Chatham Bn, Battalion Diary, 28 April 1915

At noon on April 28th the transports of the Royal Naval Division arrived off Gaba Tepe, where the Australian Army Corps under General Sir W. R. Birdwood had effected a landing on April 25th. At 3.30 p.m. the Chatham and Portsmouth Bns, RM Brigade, were ordered to land for a period of roughly 48 hours and relieve the Australians in the centre who had been in the trenches since the landing.

The Brigade landed and relieved the trenches on the SE side of the main gully forming the position during the night – the Chatham Bn being on the left.

The sector allotted to the Chatham Bn was rather extended and for the first two days it was impossible to relieve all the Australians in the centre trench on this account.

The order of Companies from Left to Right was D, B, A and C, the MGs were employed on the right and left of B Company and Bn HQ was in rear of B Coy.

Lieutenant Sydney Hope Inskip, known as Hope, a subaltern in B Company of the Deal Battalion, landed on the 29th, and in a letter home describes his first few days on the peninsula. He carefully leaves blanks for the name of the ships and transports, conscious of the censor's pen.

Lt Hope Inskip RMLI, B Coy Deal Bn, letter dated 30 June 1915

We were lying off Gaba Tepe on the transport '———' and a destroyer came round saying we were to get ready to move in an hour's time. You can imagine our excitement, and as I had just had the mail with your enclosure of my 'gazetting' as 1st lieutenant, I had plenty to think about. Punctually at 7.15 p.m. the destroyer '———' came round for us and we all scrambled on board heaped like sardines! It was quite dark and as we neared the beach we could see all the Australian bivouac fires, also heard the crackle of rifle fire and the screech of shrapnel. It was very weird and impressive and as the majority of us were all going into action for the first time, we got our first taste of reality when some stray bullets came onto our deck and wounded one or two of the fellows. We had as our rendezvous a valley since named 'Shrapnel Valley', a very fitting name too, as it was everywhere.

Well, we moved off about 2 miles and reached the support trenches – more shrapnel and bullets – we were the last company up so did not go into the firing line straight away but bivouacked for the night. It was worth all the risks in the world to see the pleased and thankful look on the faces of the Australians whom we relieved. You see they had been going it hard ever since 25 April when they made their landing, which in everyone's opinion will rank amongst the finest feats ever performed by an army in the world's history. They scaled absolute precipices with nothing but their bayonets, and opposed by hundreds of Turkish machine guns and thousands of rifles.

To continue, the following morning I had to go with my platoon and deepen a communication trench. It was tricky work, as you were more or less in full view of the Turks' trenches, 400 yards distant or so. We got it nearly done and continued it the following night. Our company was the fatigue company and had to get all the rations and things up to the firing line and a very risky job [it was].

The Companies of the Chatham Battalion would almost certainly have been glad to swap duties.

Lt Chater RMLI, Chatham Battalion Diary, 30 April 1915

On the 30th D Coy was relieved from the position on the left by New Zealanders. In the evening B Company's Trenches were lost to the Turks and Capt. Hatton was killed in the attempt to retake them, which was effected during the night – B Company being reinforced by D Company in the centre and the Australians on the flanks. During this attack 2nd Lt Watts in command of the MGs on the left was wounded whilst bringing one of the guns from the trench. The centre trench was also heavily attacked and Lt Herford, in command, was wounded. This trench was reinforced by Marines and Australians and made secure.

The position was again attacked at dawn on the 1st May, but without result. Lieut. Curtin was killed while repelling this attack. B Coy was relieved from the trenches and went into bivouac in rear of Bn HQ which were that day moved to a position in rear of A Coy. A. F. Hayward, Bn Sgt Major who had been promoted to the rank of 2nd Lieut. and posted to D Company, was wounded [he died later] during an attack on the evening of May 1st.

In his personal diary, Company Sergeant Major G. Bramley, of D Company, puts some 'flesh' on the bones of Chater's Battalion Diary.

CSM G. Bramley RMLI, D Coy Chat. Bn, Saturday 1 May 1915

Were relieved by the Australians again to give us a rest, so we retired to bottom of gully, to have a wash and a good feed. I had just had a wash and was just going to have a nice drink of tea, as I had only had water to drink since landing (Wed.), when the Turks made a determined attack to gain the ridge, where B Company were, so we had to rush up the hill to reinforce them, and we had our first bayonet charge. We lost about 60 men from B Company, also their Captain [Hatton], but we drove them back, didn't they run, so instead of having our rest they sent B Company down. The casualties of our Company were about 11 killed and 20 wounded.

Nothing happened except sniping so we [were] relieved by the 4th Bn Australians and rested during the day and at night marched to our headquarters and joined up with our Battalion again.

A Marine called Albert (his diary does not reveal his surname) of the Deal Battalion, having landed at Anzac Cove on 29 April and fought off numerous Turkish attacks on the 30th, wrote of the attack by the Chatham and Portsmouth Battalions on 1 May.

Pte 'Albert' RMLI, Deal Bn, 1 May 1915

Chatham and Portsmouth Marines made a charge and slaughtered a good number of Turks. That caused them to ask for an armistice to bury their dead, but enemy was seen bringing machine guns and ammunition up on stretchers. Of course we let them have it again. It was because of that little piece of treachery Australians swore never to take prisoners.

In reality, it was the killing of their wounded that ensured that the 'Diggers' decided that Turks would not be taken alive, but all instances of Turkish 'perfidy' were swiftly passed among the troops, and the attitude to 'Johnny Turk' hardened considerably from that of the Plymouth companies at Kum Kale and Sedd ul Bahr.

Lt Chater RMLI, Chatham Battalion Diary, 2 May 1915

On May 2nd the remaining three Coys and MGs were relieved by Australians and whole battalion bivouacked near new Bn HQ. Capt. Graham was wounded whilst returning to bivouac.

It was decided that the Royal Marines would provide support for the Anzacs engaged in an attack on the feature known as Baby 700.

Lt Chater RMLI, Chatham Battalion Diary, 3 May 1915

During the night May 2/3 the 4th Bde made an attack on a ridge to the east of the main gully, which remained in Turkish hands, and made fire and support trenches over the ridge. At dawn the Chatham Bn was ordered to advance and support these trenches, which were being enfiladed from the left and right rear by MG fire. Three Companies advanced up the minor gullies leading off. Captain Richards, the adjutant, led a charge up the steep slopes, coming under Maxim and rifle fire from front and both rear flanks. On gaining the ridge the supporting trenches were gained and held for a time. Captain Richards was himself killed before reaching the trenches. On the left a machine gun under QMS White was brought into position on a projecting part of the ridge, and did considerable damage. After holding onto the trenches for about two hours it was found that, owing to the withdrawal of the troops occupying the position on our left, the trenches were being enfiladed from that flank and it was found necessary to evacuate them. This evacuation was completed during the night – A Company had been ordered to support a post held by Australians at commencement of this action and so had been separated from the remainder of the battalion. Other casualties in this action were Lieut. Grinling killed and Lieut. Thorneley wounded.

Arthur Chater recorded it as 'a black day for the Chatham Battalion'. CSM Bramley's Company had suffered badly, but morale was boosted by the thought of the number of enemy casualties in comparison. Bramley makes special mention of the death of Captain Richards. The fact that – in a situation where most of the dead had to be left – men went out to bring back the Captain's body says a great deal about how highly he was regarded by the Battalion. The place where he was killed became known as Dead Man's Ridge because of the corpses that could not be brought in.

CSM G. Bramley RMLI, D Coy Chat. Bn, Sunday 2 May 1915

. . . at night the whole Battalion advanced in the attack to take another hill, the highest point. 4th Batt. of Australians lost nearly every man – as they had machine guns everywhere our losses are very heavy. I don't know what they are yet, we lost nearly all our officers, in my company we lost all the officers and about half our men. We have not got the ridge yet but have cleared all the Turks to the other side except the snipers, and it is almost impossible to find them but when we do they don't live long.

We stopped advance about 11 a.m. Monday and took up our positions. We are still here Tuesday morning. There is not much firing and we have got all our wounded back but our dead are still out there. We shall bury them in the next advance. The health of the troops and their spirits are excellent and owing to the ground and us doing the attacking we are making very good progress, and although our losses are heavy, the Turks' losses are about 3 times as great as ours. Our Adjutant was the first in our Battalion and the first to be killed, we were very sorry to lose him as he was so popular owing to the way he acted in Antwerp, so we sent a party out and fetched him in. Tuesday resumed – We started again in the afternoon to attack, as in the meantime the artillery shelled their positions, doing splendid work. Our observers stated about 2,000 casualties from artillery clearing the trenches, so never had much opposition to gain the ridge, but snipers are still about, we continued on and off all night.

Private Robert Pottinger in A Company had been having an arduous time, apparently doing a 'Grand old Duke of York' in support of the Australians.

Pte Robert Pottinger RMLI, A Coy Chat. Bn, 3–5 May 1915

At about 3 a.m. we were roused and ordered to support the Australians. On our march we were passed by a continual stream of wounded – we prepared for a bayonet charge uphill. The Australians however secured their position and we retired into the valley. A bayonet charge by A Coy to clear the Turkish trenches was arranged for the evening but had to be abandoned as the Turks had evidently discovered our plan.

We were aroused at 1 a.m. by a terrific fusillade in the trenches above and prepared to move. The excitement however subsided and the morning was occupied in digging a communication trench across the valley. In the afternoon the trenches on the right flank were broken by hand grenades and a stiff fight followed. A Coy had once again to advance uphill with bayonets fixed but once again our assistance was not needed. In the evening we advanced to relieve the terrible trenches on the right. We bivouacked below the ridge and went into the trench at 9 p.m. on Wednesday 5th May. The day passed in comparative quietness. I received a slight knock on the head from a bullet which broke my bayonet. We were relieved at about 6 a.m. and once again bivouacked just below the ridge. The night was intensely cold and a hellish fusillade, which was maintained all night, made sleep impossible.

Lieutenant Arthur Chater continued with the Battalion War Diary, matter of fact as always.

Lt Chater RMLI, Chatham Battalion Diary, 4–6 May 1915

The battalion now went into bivouac in the gully and assisted in holding the main position until on May 6 a definite scheme of defence came into operation, by which time Chatham and Portsmouth Bns RMLI and 4th Bde AIF [Australian Infantry Forces], the whole being under command of Brig. Gen. Trotman RMLI, were allotted a sector of the defensive lines comprising three main posts, being from left to right POPE'S, QUINN'S and COURTNEY'S.

Albert, with the Deal Battalion, and in a less than congenial position, was forward as a scout and was not as sanguine.

Pte 'Albert' RMLI, Deal Bn, 1 May 1915

Dug advanced firing line. Myself and five others acting as scouts taking cover in bushes 50 yds in front of trench. This in case enemy crept up under cover of bushes. Enemy must have observed our movements and turned MG on us. We lay flat while the bullets were clipping the branches off the bushes all about us. It was lucky that only one fellow was hit. We were glad when darkness came and we could go back to [the] firing line. For the next two days things were quiet except for shell fire and we amused ourselves potting at the enemy when they were blown out of their trenches by our ships' shells. Our casualties were up till then 22 officers and about 60 men.

Company Sergeant Major Bramley was still finding it difficult to cope with the corpses, which became one of the most unpleasant features of the campaign. Such situations, where putrefaction set in quickly, did occur on the Western Front in summer, but in Gallipoli it was especially bad, and was not helped by the mutual distrust reducing the number of truces for the dead to be collected and interred.

CSM G. Bramley RMLI, D Coy Chat. Bn, 9 & 10 May 1915

Sunday we marched down to our camp at 5 a.m. as we are doing 24 hours on and the same time off, but didn't get much rest owing to the rifle fire and big gun fire. Never had a night's rest as we stood to at 12 and marched up to reinforce the 16th Battalion Australian Regiment who took another line of trenches, but it was awful the number of dead Turks lying about. They had been lying about for days and the stink was unbearable, there must have been hundreds of them. So we marched back to our camp about 9.30 a.m., remained in camp until 8.30 p.m. when I had to take 50 men to help the artillery to get a gun in position, but never finished it as the ground was too rough, so left it there at 1 a.m. Tuesday and I had a sleep till 3.30 a.m. when I had to go out again in the firing line. They did not come too near, although we were sniping and throwing bombs all day and had about 20 casualties. We shall get the gun up tonight and then we might be able to do more.

It is awful to see the dead lying about in hundreds, where we are now there is about 200 of our chaps buried and a lot more we can't get owing to snipers. They stink awful and over the ridge you could not count the Turkish dead. There is not much fighting going on, only sniping and [it] was very quiet Tuesday night, but it has started to rain, it is coming down heavy and we are wet through and cannot get shelter.

On 12 May the RM Brigade was relieved by the Light Horse Brigade and embarked about midnight in the *Cawdor Castle*, after being ashore for 14 days.

Within a few hours they would be landed again, but CSM Bramley and Private Pottinger both recorded how good it was to rest properly. Lieutenant Hope Inskip echoed their feelings.

Lt Inskip RMLI, B Coy Deal Bn, letter dated 30 June 1915

. . . we got a hot meal at 1 o'clock after being worked to death and on rations for a fortnight. You cannot imagine the restful time we had for one night; the chief thing of all was the beer and ginger ale which was a little different from the incessant water. I slept in a hammock that night, never so happy before, as we all came to the conclusion that we had been through a 'living hell'!

The Royal Marines steamed south to Cape Helles and landed at W Beach, now called Lancashire Landing, but the 'living hell' was much the same. There they found the Plymouth Battalion, which had landed two days after their evacuation from Y Beach. Lieutenant Charles Lamplough, back ashore on 28 April, felt the Battalion had not been rested or fully reorganized.

Lt Lamplough, No. 4 Coy, Ply. Bn, 28 April 1915

We had breakfast at 4 a.m. and landed at 5 a.m. on W beach, we are going to do working party on the beach, landing stores for a bit as we are very disorganized and cut up and want a rest. We were given our camp lines and we dug our holes for our bivouac and then went down to do fatigues. It was frightfully cold at night and [we] could not possibly sleep as we had to walk about to keep warm so were jolly glad when morning came.

Sergeant Will Meatyard was clearly not impressed by the 'holes'.

Sgt Meatyard RMLI, HQ Coy Ply. Bn, 26 [28] April 1916

. . . [We] took up station just below the ridge of the high ground, which sloped down towards the sea. We made ourselves as comfortable as possible by digging hollows with our entrenching tools, just enough to allow our forms to be protected from the cutting wind.

Nor was there improvement next day, Thursday, as the weather broke, and the men found themselves not only cold but wet.

Lt Lamplough RMLI, No. 4 Coy Ply. Bn, 29 April 1915

Fatigues again today. It is lovely in the daytime and hot but at night it is terribly cold as we have nothing to put over us, but hope to get blankets soon. The Turks shelled our camp with shrapnel twice today but did not do much damage. The firing line is only about 2 miles away. Were working till 11.30 p.m. in the pouring rain and consequently we had to turn in in wet clothes and of course that along with the cold was pretty bad as once more we did not get any sleep.

The duties of providing the supplies for the line were not as obviously dangerous as holding the front line, but were far from a 'cushy number'.

Sgt Meatyard RMLI, HQ Coy Ply. Bn, 26 [28] April 1916

Now we started to do what I call 'Hard work', for several months, under shell fire all the time, also many casualties from bullets, although we were termed to be 'Resting' behind the lines. We started off by unloading lighters, and hauling the guns up the sandy beach. For the latter job we were soon making roads. With this kind of work we kept hard at it day and night (all hands in), with a few shells to liven us up.

Bandsman John Allen, acting as part of the stretcher party for Drake Battalion RND, would have relished the chance to dig for the sake of self-preservation.

Bandsman J. Allen, Royal Marine Band att'd Drake Bn, 27 April 1915

At this time we had no cover against shrapnel or shell at all, for orders were passed, no one was to dig in for fear of digging up the dead. Dead men were strewn all over the cliffs and a little inland. I noticed 9 men (Dead) together laying on the ground.

Major Norman Ormsby Burge landed with the Cyclist Company on 3 May, from the *Franconia*. He describes the situation at the beachhead.

Maj. Norman Burge RMLI, Cyclist Coy RND, 3–4 May 1915

Landed from *Franconia* with D, E and F Platoons – both Curtis and Puckle. Very hot. Landed at W beach and bivouacked on high ground N of beach next door to Drake Bn and close to a 60 pr [pounder] battery. No wonder no one else wanted that particular bit of ground as enemy were going to find it. Started digging in at once, successive lines of trenches 2' wide and about 3' deep – but one strikes water about that depth which is a great nuisance. Some slight shelling near us in evening but only small stuff. Anyway, everyone delighted to be on shore at last, the original landing under fire must have been ghastly – a small bit of beach 200 yards long, commanded on all three sides (it's a bay) by small cliffs stiff with trenches and maxims in holes in the cliffs, barbed wire everywhere and even in the water. No wonder many boats were towed in whose occupants were all killed before touching the beach.

Mostly digging all day. French [OC Cyclist Company] and the rest of the Coy turned up – but they couldn't get lighters. Everything frightfully busy – hundreds of mules ashore pulling heavy loads up the sandy hill. Quite a small town of tents and boxes on the beach. German aeroplane came over during forenoon and dropped 3 bombs on transports but only

hit sea. Also one over hospital which missed. Went to see
Cyclist Coy of 29th Div. They've got all their bikes on shore.
Another Taube dropped a bomb not far from me which luckily
just went over cliff.

The Second Battle of Krithia began on 6 May – not, as suggested by the
Commander-in-Chief, at night, but in daylight. This was the decision of
Hunter-Weston, who was wary of night attacks after problems at
Anzac Cove. At Cape Helles the ground was a lot easier to cover, but
Hunter-Weston still opted for a daylight frontal assault. The orders
were issued late, and the bombardment would last only half an hour
and be of shrapnel, because the British artillery had no high explosive
with which to destroy the Turkish trenches. The Royal Marine Battalions were fortunate not to be in the thick of this 'battle', which cost
well over 6,000 Allied losses for a few hundred yards' advance.

Major Norman Burge and Lieutenant Charles Lamplough were
involved in the follow-up to the action of 6 to 8 May, holding the new
line and fending off Turkish counter-attacks. Burge, at least, was glad
to get into the front line.

Maj. Burge RMLI, Cyclist Coy RND, 10–12 May 1915

Very hot still and nights very cold though, with only a blanket
and waterproof sheet. Hear we are to go to the advanced
trenches tonight for a short spell. Jolly good thing – it's not our
job of course, but we don't want to be always in reserve and it's
just as well to get the youngsters 'blooded' a bit – it teaches
them more than French and I can. Start off about 7.30 p.m. as
of course you can't get near the trenches in daylight and all
reliefs and supplies have to go up by night. So off we go in the
dark, soon leave the road and get into a narrow path and go
stumbling up a gully in single file. Very slow and interminable
short halts getting over ditches and dodging barbed wire not
yet completely cleared away etc. We vary the proceedings by
dropping flat on our tummies every now and again when a star
shell or rocket lights up everything. We extend the line to the
Right of the Hood Bn, then on our Right are the Ansons and to
their Right again are the French [troops] who seem a bit
nervy. Anyway they are continually firing. On arrival our bit
of trench allocated will only hold ½ our men – so the other ½
have to start digging a new trench about 10 yards in rear. As it
will be light at 4 a.m. the men do not need to be told to 'dig like
blazes' 'cos by now they know jolly well what happens if you

are <u>not</u> well dug in. So the shovels are plied right speedily withal. I take 1st watch till 1.30 a.m.

Tuesday 11th May. Smallish night attack by the Turks about 2 a.m. just after I'd gone to sleep but about 15 rounds per man <u>and</u> the Maxim guns put a stop to that all right. No one hit with us. At 7 a.m. got an order to withdraw ½ our lot to a ruined cottage about 300 yards in rear. A rotten time to get such an order as it's extremely unhealthy to leave the trenches in daylight. I go back with A, C and D platoons – a few men at a time – 2 men hit getting back – Artis in both legs (a fair shot) and Hill the neck (from a sniper). Get back to our new position and find one is fired at more or less continuously by shrapnel (deliberately at you) and rifle fire which misses the trenches in front and comes to us instead. Also one poisonous beast of a sniper we can't locate. Whilst we are digging to improve existing dug-outs we get a shrapnel into us – hitting Cpl Harrison badly (3 in back and one in arm). Foote has a near squeak. Shrapnel through his pack – tin plate – waterproof sheet and shirt when it stopped. Several pick and shovel handles splintered by bullets so we've got off mighty lucky. Our shoemaker hurls himself into dug-out hearing shell coming and doesn't see me in the way. Result, I'm sort of felled by him and am jammed in the corner with his arms tightly clasped round my neck. Remained on floor of our dug-outs, scraping out more earth with our entrenching tools till we feel a bit safer.

About 10 p.m. the E. Lancs Brigade come up to relieve the Naval Battns and ourselves. They arrive in single file and announce their presence by treading on us. They are full of delight at coming up but appear a bit staggered when we tell 'em the advanced trench is only about 300 yards further on. Seemed to sort of think it was too abrupt and ought to have been broken a bit more gently to them. I am <u>not</u> pleased at hearing shots from 2 snipers commencing from nasty dark gully, down which we've presently got to go.

Wed. May 12th. Just at midnight enter French and other ½ Coy. As we are under fire we postpone conversation about beauty of the night and I tactfully refrain from mentioning about the snipers as we can't go looking for them in the dark anyway. Off we stumble again, but downhill this time and make a very good pace 'cos we don't like the bullets overhead. They're not meant for us in the least but the fact remains that we're too close to be pleasant and also we're tired (practically no sleep for 2 nights and living in heavy marching order all the time with a blanket and 2 days' rations as well.)

Charles Lamplough had not been having a very good time with regard to trenches either, and had also been digging in under heavy fire.

Lt Lamplough RMLI, No. 4 Coy Ply. Bn, 8–11 May 1915

Well, about 5 o'clock in the afternoon the Turks started to fire on us with their artillery and then we started because they were getting up reinforcements and there was an awful artillery duel and also a lot of rifle fire, so we had to stand by to move and about 8.30 p.m. we left our trenches to take up some new ones and we had to advance in lines shoulder to shoulder under very heavy fire and had several casualties, but finally got there and had to dig most of the night and we were dead tired.

Sunday May 9th . . . We have found the direction of our trench at last and it is quite the worst we could possibly be in – we are enfiladed all the time with rifle and shell fire so we had a lot of digging to do to make ourselves comfortable. Nothing much happened today, just firing and shelling. We had a few casualties.

Monday May 10th – Still the same old game being enfiladed like blazes from both sides and cannot do anything, they had an attack at night but our front line attacked like blazes in the morning. They started bombarding about 11 o'clock and gave the village and hill hell. The last two or three days we have advanced quite a bit, Tetley and Carpenter got wounded . . .

Tuesday May 11th – Another attack by our people but otherwise nothing doing, and it got quiet about midday. Andrews had been writing some letters in the morning and he went out of his dug-out to give them to the Colonel to be sent back and he got a bullet in the stomach and died poor chap. We are all awfully fed up as he was awfully popular with the men. Then we were told we were going to be relieved, thought of going back for a rest so we were jolly bucked, but they started to shell us like blazes and poor old Barnes got killed, shrapnel through the head, so now we have lost 17 officers and there are only the Colonel and adjutant and 6 of us subs left.

Lamplough was very glad of a few days in less dangerous surroundings, which enabled sea bathing and attendance at a Sunday Service. He was also given temporary command of No. 1 Company, due to the dearth of senior officers, and much to his surprise because there were two subalterns with greater seniority. This period of command lasted only a few days, because the much depleted battalion was reorganized into two companies.

Lt Lamplough RMLI, No. 4 Coy Ply. Bn, Wednesday 19 May 1915

Well, we are reorganizing the Battn. into two companies, Edwards having one and Richards the other. We heard by wire that Stuart has been made Lieut. in place of May [killed at Y Beach], so I was very annoyed because he would be senior, but I have just received a letter from H saying I have been promoted Lieut. . . . I am awfully bucked.

On 21 May Lieutenants Francis Law and Charles Conybeare returned to the Plymouth Battalion, having recovered from their wounds sustained at Y Beach, but that same day two officers were wounded and so numbers were not increased. One of the casualties was Charles Lamplough.

Lt Lamplough RMLI, No. 4 Coy Ply. Bn, for 21 May 1915

I am writing this up a few days later . . . The Colonel, Lough, Conybeare, Edwards and myself were standing having a talk about 6.30 p.m. and one of their high-velocity shells came over – got Edwards in the foot and me in the arm and also killed one and wounded about ten men, so that was a nice finish to a quiet day. Edwards and I lay in a trench and got our wounds dressed. Of course they kept the fire up till dark . . . We then went to the 2nd Field Ambulance and then started off on 1½ mile walk to the Cas. [Casualty] Clearing Station, arriving about 10 p.m. They put us on stretchers and we tried to sleep.

Charles Lamplough was evacuated to hospital in Cairo and his diary for Gallipoli ends.

Arthur Chater, however, was still with his battalion and keeping up the War Diary.

Lt Chater RMLI, Chatham Battalian War Diary, 25–28 May 1915

On the night of May 25–26 the Royal Marine Brigade relieved the 1st Royal Naval Brigade in the RND Sector of Defence.

This section was on the extreme right of the British Lines –
having a front of about 800 yards – right rested on the French
left and on the right of the 42nd (East Lancashire Territorial)
Division. The Sector was divided into three and held from left
to right respectively by Plymouth, Portsmouth and Chatham
Bns. (The Chatham Bn being supplemented by the RND
Cyclist Company under Major French RMLI.) The Deal Bn
being in Reserve. The Chatham Bn relieved the Drake Bn
(Cmdr Campbell).

The trenches were on the whole good and had it not been for
a cloudburst about 5 p.m. in the evening all would have been
very comfortable, but the trenches were flooded in parts and
thus much discomfort and delay was caused. The enemy
trenches were about 500 yards to our front, with a strong
loophole redoubt to our right front.

Private Pottinger, Sergeant Meatyard and Company Sergeant Major
Bramley all suffered in the wet, and wrote of the appalling conditions.
There were times in the campaign when cloudbursts caused such
destruction that friend and foe alike had to abandon trenches and sit
on the parapet, and many men and mules were drowned in the floods
down the nullahs. Whilst this particular storm was not as dangerous, it
was extremely unpleasant.

Pte Pottinger RMLI, A Coy Chat. Bn, Tuesday 25 May 1915

9 p.m. Fell in and marched to trenches. The country was
every[where] under water as a result of the rain of the
previous few days. The long struggle through the flooded
communication trenches knee deep in mud and water, I shall
never forget.

Sgt Meatyard RMLI, HQ Coy Ply. Bn, 25 May 1915

At midnight we advanced to the firing line, the mud was well
over our knees, and up over our thighs in places, where we
were able to use trenches.

CSM G. Bramley RMLI, D Coy Chat. Bn, 26 May 1915

Our battalion relieved East Lancashires in the firing line,
after the most awful march. They had a cloudburst and it filled

all the trenches and swamped the valley. We had about 2 miles march through communication trenches up to our waist in water and mud. We were covered in mud up to our chests and wet through, and got there 1 a.m. Wednesday and then had to start draining our trenches and get them dry.

Despite the severity of the storm it was clearly localized, for Major Norman Burge felt little of its effect, until he too had to go up to the front line.

Maj. Burge RMLI, Cyclist Coy RND, 25–26 May 1915

Heavy thunderstorm on our front lines in the afternoon – but just missed our camp 'cept for some drops as big as pennies. Must have been a cloudburst as about 7 p.m. a regular river was rushing past our camp, and a lot of camps were flooded out. We just escaped it by a foot. Fell in 10 p.m. to go to trenches.

Got up to our place about midnight after a poisonous march. Very muddy first of all and then had to go in single file through about $3/4$ mile of communication trenches which were nearly up to the knee in muddy water and frightfully slippery.

Sergeant Will Meatyard managed to get himself cleaned up, but in vain.

Sgt Meatyard RMLI, HQ Coy Ply. Bn, 25 May 1915

When the sun came out we took off our puttees, to allow for drying, after digging off the thick of the mud with our clasp knives. Our QMS, Bamfield, got sniped in the head whilst using the field glasses and died instantly. Having got my legs and puttees free from some of the mud, it was just getting dark when I received a message that I was to take charge of a telephone station just in a trench in rear. This undone all the drying I had done, as I had to pass through a trench again that was deep with mud and water, what a life, but if there was nothing worse than this one would say that war is a pleasure.

During the night our Battalion advanced 250 yards without the Turks finding out, a good feat as the picks and shovels had to be used quickly and quietly. The RND Engineers pegged out

the trench plan with white pegs previously, which made it
easy for our men to dig without much explanation or guidance.
Whether there was anything moving at night or not the Turks
were continually firing casual rounds, with occasional bursts
of machine gun fire, and it was due to this that we had 4 killed
and 12 wounded, light considering the task that had been
achieved.

The Royal Marines were held in reserve for the Third Battle of Krithia,
which began on 4 June, but Major Burge wrote about how much his
men were sent back and forth during the first days of the battle.

Maj. Burge RMLI, Cyclist Coy RND, for 4 June 1915

Have to write this up from memory as we have been in the
trenches till last night (Monday 7th). We fell in at 3.15 a.m.
and moved off to 4th line trench – the Drakes being behind us
– Collingwoods and Ansons in front. I went to act as observer
and keep an eye on the French to the hill on our right – by [a]
redoubt they had made. At 8.30 a.m. the artillery
bombardment of certain strong points commenced. Not very
exciting as not many guns were firing and those only slowly.
At 11 a.m. however, the bombardment of the enemy's trench
line began – which was magnificent and at 12 noon exactly the
Infantry advanced. I could see them take the 1st Turkish
trench and then go beyond. An enormous fire was poured into
them, so it looked as if the Artillery hadn't done them much
harm – which was the case. The French seemed to be sticking
a bit, so I left my place (which was a very hot bit) to go back to
report this. At about 1.30 p.m. we got the order to go up to the
1st line – so up we went and found it almost impassable. The
front trench was crammed with men and there were also a
great many dead and wounded in it. We were really only in the
way and it seemed that we were being continually sent to
trenches already occupied – a bad bit of Brigade Staff work.
Eventually we were put in the Support Trench and from there
back to our original trench for the night.

Saturday 5th June. Called up once or twice during the night
to go to trenches that were already occupied and began to get
very sick of this booming about. A perfectly beastly
forenoon . . . hundreds of desponding rumours about
yesterday's show. Of course we know now that we didn't
achieve anything like what we wanted to – but my idea is that

the objective was far too ambitious, that the opposition was very much underestimated and too much reliance placed on the Artillery preparation. I'm sure the Turks are too strong for a general advance all along the line, as unless it's successful everywhere, a success here is neutralized by a failure elsewhere . . . Sent Bowen and his platoon to Garrison Redoubt near my observation post. You get a ripping view from there and can see the Turks in the various gullies round KRITHIA and also their communication trenches. Carruthers was wounded here – graze in head. It's all right with N wind – but the approach to the redoubt is pretty dreadful – hold your nose and dash. There are a good many Turks lying about just here – two of them are snipers the Coy bagged the first time we were up in the trenches. You can't bury 'em by day of course, and whenever we're going to at night we get moved off somewhere else.

Norman Burge was having a trying time, neither achieving much nor having his men rested.

Maj. Burge RMLI, Cyclist Coy RND, for Sunday 6 June 1915

. . . We've now been more or less continuously under shell fire for over a month and always exposed to it. It's not like France, where you can get your rest out of range of the enemy, and even on days when I don't mention shelling there's always some.

Sergeant Will Meatyard, who heard that many trenches and prisoners had been taken on the 4th, went up to the firing line on 7 June, and, like Burge, had to cope with the problem of the unpleasant and unhealthy presence of the dead, but at least had more hopeful news.

Sgt Meatyard RMLI, HQ Coy Ply. Bn, 7 June 1915

Advanced to firing line at 1 p.m., cheers were heard at 7.30 p.m. and it was learnt that a line of trenches had been taken by the British. It was fairly quiet the next day. There were many dead bodies lying about in front of the trenches, and at night time parties in reliefs were sent out to bury them, which generally meant digging a shallow hole alongside the body and rolling the body in – most of them would not bear lifting, the hot climate had the effect of decomposing them very quickly, and they soon turned quite black in colour, and the stench was almost unbearable. During this work, which was generally undertaken at night, casualties were frequent.

Private Pottinger, with A Company, Chatham Battalion, did not share Sergeant Meatyard's belief in success, and he was nearer the action.

Pte Pottinger RMLI, A Coy Chat. Bn, Monday 7 June 1915

In the evening moved out and up gulley in readiness to support C and D Companies if necessary in proposed attack. Everything went wrong. C and more so D Company suffered heavily.

CSM Bramley was one of the wounded, and his diary gives only brief detail of what happened.

CSM G. Bramley RMLI, D Coy Chat. Bn, 7 June 1915

7 p.m. started charge, Marines led, our company was on left, we got right into close quarters with them. Finish diary for a time as I am wounded in leg so shall have to rest for a little while but the worst part was I walked all the way to the beach after I had been dressed and did not get there till 10 p.m. but I had the help of two more who were wounded, they got it in both arms, so I put one hand on each shoulder.

CSM Bramley was evacuated, with about 600 other wounded, to the Royal Naval Hospital, Bighi, Malta, and his diary closes.

Major Norman Burge's cyclists came out of the line that evening, but did not have an easy march back into their 'home' trenches.

Maj. Burge RMLI, Cyclist Coy RND, 7 June 1915

The Collingwoods have suffered very badly in Friday's [4th] show – also the Ansons. The latter have only two officers left. We are to be relieved by the RM Bde this evening, which is good news – as out of the last 12 days we've been 8 in the trenches, and although one doesn't want to grumble – it's more than our fair share for Divisional troops. But I'm afraid we'll never be more than ordinary infantry, at any rate till we get well on. We get away at 7 p.m. – still daylight and soon after we've left a very heavy fire starts, which is annoying as such a lot of 'overs' [shell rounds incorrectly ranged, passing beyond target] are due down our path. So we scoot it down the path pretty rapidly and arrive home like bits of chewed string at 8 p.m. I put my head into a bucket of water and therefore do not hear a shrapnel coming – everybody else did and got to their dugouts. The ground was quite laced up with the beasts' bullets all round me, so I had what was a d—d lucky escape. Shan't put my head into a bucket again – at any rate not in the open.

There followed a comparatively 'quiet' time for the Royal Marines. Burge was boosted by getting down to W Beach for a bathe, shave and change of clothes, and the company of a chap who had served in the *Victorious* with him and had three bottles of beer to spare! On 26 June he was sent in temporary command of the Howe Battalion. The climate, flies and disease, however, were beginning to take a heavy toll, and although he stayed in the line Burge was afflicted as others were. Despite this, the continued shortage of high-explosive artillery ammunition exercised his mind more than his own personal discomfort.

Maj. Burge RMLI, OC Howe Bn, Monday 28 June 1915

Just my blooming luck to feel very seedy – inside all wrong and headache – but I can't grumble as I've done jolly well to be practically free from what is an almost universal complaint. There is a hell of a battle going on – the 29th Div and some Indians on our left – a ship is out, escorted by destroyers and is enfilading the Turkish trenches with high explosive. Thank 'Eaven the Navy is not starved for ammunition like we are – only 2 rounds per gun per day are we allowed, and shrapnel at that, which is useless against trenches.

The sick list grew daily. The trenches which the Chatham Battalion took over early in July were particularly unhealthy, and were commented upon by Arthur Chater in the War Diary.

Lt Chater RMLI, Chatham Battalion Diary, 16 July 1915

The condition of the trenches which were now being held were
very bad and great difficulty was found in obtaining food and
water. During the time that the battalion occupied these
trenches they were much improved as regards to defence and
sanitation – the lack of food and unsanitary conditions caused
a large number of men to go sick and placed the general health
of the battalion in a condition from which it took a long time to
recover.

Sergeant Will Meatyard, highlighting an advance by Royal Marines,
illustrated how seriously they took the risk from the putrefying bodies
of the Turks.

Sgt Meatyard RMLI, HQ Coy Ply. Bn, 14 July 1915

I forgot to mention an important incident that happened on
the 13th. After the Scots had retired, Major Sketchley, who
was on the spot, collected a few Royal Marines who were round
about in the trench, and leading them over the parapet,
himself carrying a fly wisp [whisk], retook the trench that the
Scots had retired from. The trenches we were now in smelt
awful, so many Turks lying at the bottom of the trench half
buried, and also in between the sandbags on the parapets.
Those that had handkerchiefs tied them around their mouths.
At 5 p.m. our guns opened up again, and Portsmouth,
Chatham, and Nelson Battalions attacked, taking several
trenches, 2 machine guns, others having been destroyed by
gunfire, and 422 prisoners. We dug a new trench and had
several casualties from Turkish bombs while doing so. This
new trench was necessary to replace an old trench that had
been filled in without the numerous dead in it being removed.

Norman Burge was already considering the problems of remaining in
the peninsula as autumn and winter approached, which seem to have
been put to one side by those not 'at the sharp end'.

Maj. Burge RMLI, OC Howe Bn, Tuesday 29 June 1915

Piping hot again – no wind and they say it will be hotter still
next month. It will be dreadful if we have the autumn and

123

winter here – howling gales and lashings of rain. Besides, if we are in the same spot, ½ of it is flooded in winter.

His fears were to prove well founded, but first he was to move from Howe Battalion, whose CO returned fit for duty, to take command of Nelson Battalion, who had lost their Colonel and five officers killed, and eleven officers wounded, in an attack on Achi Baba Nullah. Norman Burge continued his diary until early August, when he became too busy. He finally admitted it could not continue at the end of August, when, after writing nothing for three weeks, he scrawled his final entry.

Maj. Burge RMLI, OC Nelson Bn, Monday 9 August 1915

Quite impossible to go on with diary. New draft would occupy remainder of this book.
Undersized, untrained, weedy youths of 14–17. Dreadfull!!!

At the end of July the Royal Marine Brigade was reduced to two full battalions, by combining the Portsmouth and Plymouth battalions and the Chatham and Deal battalions, each old battalion providing two companies of the new. This is indicative of the attrition rate, increasingly from disease, and within the new brigade it was common for a subaltern to command a company. Arthur Chater was given command of 'A' Chatham Company and handed over the writing of the War Diary, and later he too joined the ranks of those invalided from the peninsula.

Disease or wounds were fast diminishing the diarists of the Royal Marines. Private Pottinger, after bouts of sickness, was evacuated to Alexandria in early August, suffering from dysentery. Sergeant Meatyard was still there, as was Bandsman John Allen of the Royal Marines Band, serving as part of the Drake Battalion stretcher party. Both men recorded the arrival of fresh troops in early October, and the fatal results of their orderly advance.

Sgt Meatyard RMLI, HQ Coy Ply. Bn, 14 October 1915

. . . The 2/2 City of London Regt arrive. Being new to the conditions they marched their fatigue parties in fours very close to the front line, and suffered in consequence. The Turks spotting them opened fire with artillery and killed about 50 in no time.

Several days later the new troops had apparently not yet learned their lesson.

Bandsman J. Allen, RM Band att'd Drake Bn, 20 October 1915

Turks have got a fresh supply of ammunition this last few days and they use it liberally for all sizes of guns. New troops (City of London Fusiliers) advancing by Platoons to trenches on 20th and got shelled – several casualties. I visited our Machine Gunners in 'Mac Turk Alley' last time up where there was dead of both sides all around, the Chief and I too eager to see all got rather exposed, were sniped at. Result Dip Quick before he had time to fire again. Saw a skeleton with Bandage still round its skull.

The autumn saw the Royal Marines in the reserve, though of course still taking casualties. The campaign was in stalemate, and with no sign of change. The idea of breaking through to Constantinople seemed laughable in the face of Turkish determination and, even more damning, lack of reinforcements from the West.

In truth, the whole campaign had only one end from mid August, when the response to the request for 95,000 men by Sir Ian Hamilton, the Commander-in-Chief, was a grudging allowance of 13,000 reinforcements and 12,000 fresh troops, some of whom Meatyard and Allen saw in October. Those seeking the concentration of force on the Western Front were in the ascendant, both in Britain and in France, where General Joffre was especially keen on his autumn offensive. This was at odds with the view of the French government, which still retained faith in the Gallipoli campaign. It even appeared that the French might prove Hamilton's best hope, when, disappointed by the failure to break out at Suvla Bay, the French offered two divisions to boost their men on the Asiatic side. Hamilton's expectations were dashed, however, when it became clear that Joffre would only consider sending these troops in late September, after his autumn offensive. It was clear that whatever hopes the French government entertained, Joffre had his eyes firmly focussed on the Western Front.

Hamilton, clinging to the idea that capturing the Narrows and moving on to Constantinople was still achievable, found that instead of gaining fresh divisions he was to lose them. Bulgaria's entry into the war, on the side of Germany and Austria-Hungary, saw Serbia pleading for assistance from the Greeks, who in turn requested manpower from France and Britain. One French and one British division were therefore to be removed from Gallipoli and sent instead to Salonika. No more assistance could be expected from home, where the losses of the autumn offensive had mounted to almost 250,000 French and British casualties. Another division, the 2nd Mounted Division, had to be evacuated because too many men had fallen sick, and Hamilton bemoaned the fact that of the 100,000 men on the peninsula half were unfit.

London broached the obvious course on 11 October, and asked Hamilton how many men he thought would be lost in an evacuation of Gallipoli. Hamilton's reply was that he expected such a withdrawal, which he was firmly against, could mean the loss of half his men. A week later, Hamilton was taking his leave of his Staff, having been replaced by Sir Charles Munro, who was in favour of all available troops being used in France and Flanders. Hamilton was not entirely to blame for the failure of the campaign, but was an obvious scapegoat.

On 30 October, having visited his corps and divisional commands, Munro telegraphed Kitchener, recommending evacuation of the peninsula. Kitchener, with Hamilton's doom-laden forecast of 50 per cent losses still in mind, was sent to see the situation in Gallipoli for himself. Ringing in his ears was the understandable veto of the First Sea Lord of a revived plan for the Royal Navy to try and force the Narrows without military support. He had also decided to move Munro to Salonika and leave General Birdwood in command of any withdrawal from Gallipoli. He arrived at Mudros on 9 November. He spent three days with Birdwood, inspecting the positions on the peninsula, and came to the same conclusion as Munro, but sought to lessen the obvious failure that would be proved by a total evacuation. He therefore telegraphed the War Committee on 22 November that he recommended that the forces should remain at Cape Helles but be withdrawn from Anzac Cove and Suvla Bay.

Back in London, the War Committee was more in favour of a complete withdrawal, without the 'figleaf' that Helles would provide, but dithered over making the final decision. In the meantime the weather in Gallipoli turned for the worse in a sudden and catastrophic fashion. The temperature plummeted and a torrential storm broke on 26 November, drowning many and forcing friend and foe alike to sleep on top of their parapets. Then the snow and hail began. Many of the mules drowned during the bad weather – this brought a silver lining for some of the troops, in the form of mule stew.

Before the final decision to evacuate Anzac Cove and Suvla Bay, though not Cape Helles, was made on 8 December, the commanders in the field were already organizing a three-phase withdrawal. A joint naval and military committee met under the chairmanship of Sir Charles Munro, who had been made Commander-in-Chief of Mediterranean Forces (excluding Egypt), and agreed that the preliminary phase of withdrawal should begin at once. This was the evacuation of all men, livestock and stores not required for the winter defence. Throughout all phases the priority would be to save men, even at the expense of materiel, and it was imperative that the withdrawal be kept secret from the enemy.

The troops on the ground heard of the evacuation around 16 December. The preliminary phase had already been completed, and the intermediate stage involved a considerable degree of subterfuge. The positions were maintained with fewer and fewer men, whilst every effort was made to give the appearance of normality. Fires were lit, empty tents left standing and the usual transports came up the line 'delivering' stores which did not exist. Rifles were rigged with string and tins of trickling sand to provide sporadic daytime fire. The troops gave up firing during the night, unless attacked, and the Turks began to accept this silence as normal. The final phase of evacuation at Anzac and Suvla took place on the nights of 18 and 19 December, and were a resounding success. Even the guns were brought off, though not all the stores, and over 83,000 men had left the peninsula without a single man succumbing to enemy fire.

The men at Cape Helles were told of the successful withdrawal of their fellows; they were informed that they were to remain, without the French infantry. Even this position changed when a new Chief of the Imperial General Staff was appointed on 23 December. Lieutenant General Sir William Robertson had no qualms about ordering the remaining troops from Gallipoli. It was the only sensible thing to do, and it was good news for the troops at Helles, where the Royal Naval Division were holding the former French part of the line. There was even dressing up involved to deceive the Turks.

Pte 'Albert' RMLI, Deal Bn, 31 December 1915

Relieved French on extreme right in valley of 'Kereves Dere'. They then left the peninsula for Salonika. Most curious place on whole of Gallipoli. We were not allowed to fire at enemy and they not at us. We dressed in French uniforms to get enemy to believe there were still some Frenchmen left. We had to keep strict silence and wore sacking over our boots to deaden the sound. This all came in to help the evacuation.

The Turks had moved south after the evacuations up the coast, and were putting increasing pressure on those remaining, with heavy artillery fire.

Withdrawal was planned in a similar way to that from the other sectors, with men in their muffled boots, no lights being shown, and no night firing. The Turks at first assumed the same ploy meant that the withdrawal was taking place and that they could advance, but their probing of British positions proved that there was still an enemy presence, and thereafter they were much more cautious.

Lieutenant Colonel Norman Burge, returned to the command of Nelson Battalion after being wounded, was conscious that the withdrawal at Cape Helles was not as easy as at Anzac Cove, because his men were a lot further from the beaches, and the communication trenches permitted only single file most of the way down. He was detached from his battalion to help organize, as Officer in Command Rendezvous, the final withdrawal of the RND from V Beach, set for the night of 8/9 January. The vestiges of the Division filtered back according to a highly choreographed plan.

RND Order No. 26, 4 January 1916, copy No. 19 sent to Lt Col. Norman Burge (extracts)

WITHDRAWAL FROM THE FRONT TRENCHES: 4. The Guards in the Front Line will come through those in Support Line with the Special Parties, halt until the Barricades have been closed and mines connected, and then proceed with Support Line Guards. The same procedure will be followed through all the Lines.

EMBARKATION: 5. Troops will be embarked in Motor Lighters each of which takes 400 men. The Senior Officer in each Lighter will take charge of the unloading of the Lighter into the troop carrier. This must be done as expeditiously as possible.

The Senior Officer of the 1st Lighter to come alongside any ship will act as Staff Officer to the Ship.

DESTRUCTION OF STORES: 7. All stores and material which cannot be evacuated will be destroyed in accordance with previous instructions. Arrangements must be made for stores which are to be burnt after evacuation to be set alight by means of candles at 0500 on the morning following the Final Withdrawal.

Preparations will be made to bury the blankets of men who

are holding the Section on the last day unless they can carry them on their persons, but they must not be carried by hand.

All mess kettles will be evacuated on the 1st night of the final period, and must be carried by men embarking.

All serviceable spare cable will be reeled up and returned together with spare instruments forthwith.

ARTILLERY: 8. The F.O.Os [Forward Observation Officers] will be withdrawn at dusk on the last day, but a few guns will continue to fire for an hour after dark.

STRAGGLERS: 9. Every precaution must be taken to avoid straggling. On no account will there be any delay if parties are not complete.

Destroyers will be stationed off all beaches in use for embarkation as well as off DE TOTT'S BATTERY and 'Y' Beach, and will endeavour to take off any stragglers who may find their way down to the shore.

It was a tense time for Albert of the Deal Battalion RMLI, as he was one of the last of his battalion to withdraw.

Pte 'Albert' RMLI, Deal Bn, 8 January 1916

The main body of British troops left. There was only 12 of us of our battalion manning 300 yds of firing line. For the last 4 hrs we were walking to and fro on guard. It was a nerve-wracking experience and had the enemy tumbled to our little game it would have been all up with us. We were in a valley and had a hill behind about 500 ft high to get over. At 12 o'clock the evacuation of the whole line started. We marched steadily down to the beach, a distance of 4 miles, passing Po[rtsmouth] and Ply[mouth] Marines who were entrenched in the last line to cover our retreat. We waited on the beach for about 2 hours and then went aboard the destroyer *Bulldog*. The enemy had not rumbled so far.

One of Norman Burge's old unit, the Royal Marine Cyclists, was also rearguard.

Pte W. Corbett-Williamson RMLI, at Lancashire Landing

When Major J. E. F. d'Apice, our DAA [Deputy Assistant
Adjutant] and QMG [Quartermaster General], now also acting
as Camp Commandant, told me that he would require only
two orderlies for the last lap, I chose myself and my second-in-
command to stay on to the end. After smashing their bicycles
under my supervision, the other six orderlies left that night.
The two of us who remained spent the last hours of the 8th
January, 1916, and the first hour or two of the 9th taking
signals from the signal office, about twenty yards away, to the
office of the GOC Embarkation, Major-General the Hon.
H. A. Lawrence, who with Brig-Gen. H. E. Street (Corps Chief
of Staff), Major d'Apice, and Gen. Lawrence's own staff-officer,
sat around a bridge-table on which there was a candle stuck in
a bottle for light, as all electrical equipment had been
destroyed or removed.

In some ways the scene might have been taking place on
manoeuvres in peace time; I myself came smartly to attention
as I handed each signal to the GOC Embarkation, who read it
in silence and passed it round to the other three officers, who
also read it in silence before I was dismissed. And yet I had the
feeling that a desperate game was being played for very high
stakes. The sense of drama was heightened by what I saw
outside. In the darkness, thirty feet below me, I could just
make out infantry battalions marching silently round the cliff
to 'W' Beach where they would embark in lighters.

Very early in the morning of the 9th January, I handed what
turned out to be the last signal to Gen. Lawrence, who read it
in silence and passed it round. Our Corps Chief-of-Staff broke
the silence. 'I think it is time for us to go,' said Gen. Street.
Gen. Lawrence and his staff-officer left at once, while Gen.
Street handed me two fairly heavy suitcases containing
papers. We hurried out of the office, and, seeing my rifle
leaning against a wall, Gen. Street picked it up and led the
way down the zig-zag path to the track between the cliff and
the sea.

At a nearby wooden jetty, put up on the previous afternoon,
a ship's boat was waiting for us, so Gen. Street, Major d'Apice,
another staff-officer who had just joined us, and we two
orderlies, were rowed out in a rising sea to Admiral de
Robeck's yacht, *Triad*. After hot drinks and biscuits had been
given to us, we two orderlies settled down in a cabin and had
just got off to sleep when a terrific explosion shook the *Triad*:
it was the shore magazine going up. Lord Kitchener had said,

'You will slip away in the dark, and the Turks won't even know you've gone.' He was dead right, and the explosion was our 'Goodbye'.

Corbett-Williamson went on to win the Military Cross as a lieutenant in 1918.

In all the months since the Fleet had arrived nearly a year before, this, the withdrawal, was the only aspect of the campaign which went to plan. The withdrawal from Cape Helles was as slick and well executed as those from Anzac Cove and Suvla Bay; a model of how a withdrawal should be both planned and executed. Only during the final minutes did the Turks realise what was happening, and by then the beaches were nearly deserted, except for the last men to leave. The men were glad to see the back of the peninsula, glad to live to fight another day, but the shadow cast by Gallipoli was long. The challenge of the future would be to make a landing as successful as a departure.

The Royal Marines of the Royal Naval Division left many of their number behind in Gallipoli and the surrounding waters. Among the officers who survived, hardly any of them had not been wounded or invalided from the peninsula from disease, at some point in the eight-and-a-bit months of the land campaign. As an example, Charles Lamplough, wounded on 21 May and sent by hospital ship to Alexandria, suffered persistent bouts of dysentery whilst he recovered from his wound. This kept him from the front and he was sent home to England on 12 October. After service at sea, he joined the 4th Battalion that was sent to Zeebrugge in 1918.

Despite all their attempts to work up the Gallipoli Peninsula towards the Narrows, and eventually the prize of Constantinople, the Allies had been held back. Their failure was due to a variety of reasons – the terrain, the determination of the Turks, rampant disease, their General Officers – but not lack of effort from the men themselves. When the first men waded ashore it was, perhaps, already too late for success anyway.

After a period in Salonika, the Royal Marines headed west in May 1916, back to where the war would be won, the Western Front, and the push that was meant to bring that victory closer – the Battle of the Somme.

4

The Somme

The series of battles that make up the Battle of the Somme began on 1 July 1916. The French had put immense pressure on the British to do something on a large scale that would distract German attention from the nightmare that was Verdun, and quickly. The commander of the Fourth Army, Sir Henry Rawlinson, had grave doubts about the execution of the plan, especially with regard to the length of bombardment and the idea of a breakthrough which would be exploited by cavalry. In addition, Sir Douglas Haig, commander of the British Expeditionary Force since December 1915, had told his French counterpart that he might not be ready for a major offensive until August. The French persisted, despite Haig's remonstrations. None of this boded well for the offensive. The losses on 1 July were enormous – 57,470 British dead and wounded. It was, however, only the beginning of the painfully slow advance of the Allies that year on the Western Front. The final battle took place in the rain and mud of November, when weather conditions put a stop to further major offensive action. On a front roughly 60 miles long, a gain of a few miles had been achieved. This gain had cost approximately 630,000 Allied casualties.

The British area of the Western Front actually stopped a few miles north of the river Somme itself, which came under the French Sixth Army. The 63rd Royal Naval Division – part of the Reserve Army, redesignated the Fifth Army, under General Sir Hubert Gough, on 30 October 1916 – were in the vicinity of the river Ancre, about halfway between Fonquevillers, at the north of the sector, and Mametz to the south. The final chapter of the Somme has the official title of the Battle of the Ancre. By the end of September, the Allies had taken Thiepval but the village of Beaumont-Hamel, an objective of that first day's battle, was still holding out after four and a half months, and the village of Beaucourt remained in German hands. After a period of appalling wet weather a major push was finally set for 13 November and the 63rd Royal Naval Division were to play an important part. Their objective was Beaucourt, what remained of it.

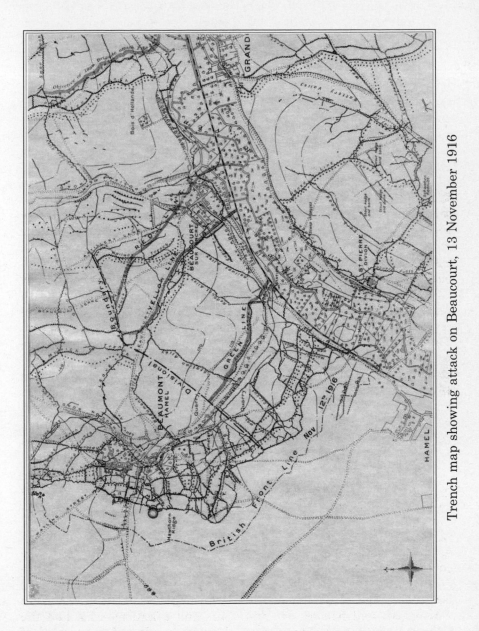

Trench map showing attack on Beaucourt, 13 November 1916

The 63rd Royal Naval Division had been formed after the withdrawal from Gallipoli and was made up of many survivors of the peninsula, boosted with new drafts. Having been put through training and a tour of duty in a fairly quiet sector, the Royal Naval Division (RND) arrived in the back areas of the Somme battlefield in October 1916. The RND consisted of 188th, 189th and 190th Brigades. The first two brigades were made up of the naval battalions Hawke, Howe, Nelson, Anson, Drake and Hood, which consisted of Royal Marine and Royal Navy officers and seamen, and two Royal Marine battalions, which were themselves amalgamations: the 1st Battalion RMLI combined the old Portsmouth and Deal battalions; the 2nd Battalion RMLI was an amalgamation of the Plymouth and Chatham battalions. After their training they were fit and fresh and ready to be used in a major assault.

The 190th Brigade consisted of units other than Royal Navy and Royal Marines, although Royal Marines were serving in the Machine Gun Company. The Brigade Headquarters were also provided by the Royal Marines, although they had just lost their Royal Marines Brigadier. Charles Jerram was Brigade Major of 190th Brigade and later recalled its varied personnel.

Maj. Jerram RMLI, 190th Brigade RND

They were a mixed lot. The HAC [Honourable Artillery Company] had been employed as GHQ troops and Officers Training Corps and were delighted to get back into the war, whilst the Royal Fusiliers and Bedfords were both Militia Battalions, an almost forgotten organization now. The Royal Dublin Fusiliers were a New Army battalion. And finally the Brigade Staff were all Marines until just before the battle, when the Brigadier, Trotman, was invalided. On the whole we were a great deal more raw than the Marines and Naval Battalions which had served all through Gallipoli, and it was our first battle other than for Brigade HQ, which was the old Royal Marines HQ transferred to 190th Brigade.

Major Jerram omitted to mention the 'leavening' of Royals in the Machine Gun Company of 190th Brigade, which included Private William Brown and his officer, Lieutenant Goldingham. William Brown had returned to a Royal Marine unit after service aboard a hospital ship, and had been trained as a machine gunner for the 190th Brigade. He recalled the inclement weather that preceded the RND's first battle in France, and how pleased he was that the Division was next in line to the 51st Highland Division.

Pte William Brown RMLI, Machine Gun Coy 190th Bde RND

Each time we went in the line we had the 51st Highland Division on our left. We had as deep a respect for them as they had for us. It is very comforting to know you have neighbours on either side who can be relied upon to give a good account of themselves, should the need arise.

Autumn had set in and we had a lot of rain, and the trenches and land had become a quagmire. To make matters worse it had turned bitterly cold. From now on we were invariably soaked to the skin, and often up to our waists in mud and water for hours on end. It is most amazing that anyone could possibly survive such conditions. Early in November rumours began to get around that something was afoot. We came out of the line about the first weekend in November and marched back to billets in Puchevillers, about 12 kilometres back from the line. During the early part of the week the Divisional Commander, General Paris, went up the line with his staff for a final reconnaissance, and a shell blast blew off one of his legs.

In the evening of Wednesday [8 November], every gun behind the front for miles each side of us opened as one. The din was so terrific and the air vibrations burst your eardrums, and if you touched the wall of a house or anything solid it felt like a mild electric shock. This barrage was kept up without a break till the Sunday night, November 12th, when every gun ceased firing at once. After four whole days and nights of that racket, the silence was uncanny, almost unbearable.

Before the guns stopped we were on our way up the line for the assault on Beaumont Hamel. We reached Hamel village and spent the night in a long cellar under a row of what had been cottages. About four in the morning, I had to draw the rum ration for my gun crew, and was just about to issue it when the order came to take up our positions in the trenches, from where we were going over. I tipped the water from my water bottle and put the rum in, to issue it when an opportunity occurred.

Sergeant Will Meatyard was now the Signal Sergeant of 2nd Battalion RMLI. He also commences the battle with details of 'going up the line' to the front-line trenches on the eve of the assault, and had more luck in issuing the rum ration.

Sgt Meatyard RMLI, HQ Coy 2nd Bn RMLI

Hearing that we were about to move, I handed money and a letter to the safe custody of a corporal who was stopping behind, in case of accidents. At 2 p.m. we moved. It was very heavy going in the deep mud – arrived at the trenches at 4.30 p.m. after a struggle. Passed numerous batteries in forward temporary positions all ready for the attack. We had not proceeded very far up the trenches before we came to a stop. The trenches were packed with troops, so we had to sit down in the mud until there was a move ahead. The Huns seemed to get the wind up about something, and sent over quite a number of heavy shells. These smashed in the trenches, causing many casualties. Our trenches (communications) being end on to the enemy's artillery, our position was rather unfortunate – being jammed in as we were and with shells dropping all round, but not actually in the trench. When we did move, several heaps of earth, where the trenches had been blown in, had to be surmounted and crossed. I passed one spot where many were buried, and one of the lads was shouting for his chum who was buried, 'Are you there Bill?' It was dark when we arrived at the dugout told off for Headquarters, which was packed when we got inside. Here the night was spent. Although we knew it was life or death for some of us the next morning, we spent a very cheerful night, chiefly due to the successful efforts of Jerry Dunn, our Cook Sgt. I forgot to mention one other important item of stores I was responsible for – a jar of rum. Each man was to be served out with a tot of rum before going over in the morning. The Colonel, Adjutant, Doctor, orderlies and other details were in this dugout. After we had been squatted smoking and yarning for some time, Jerry called me over. I guessed something was in the wind and he suggested that as he was making cocoa for the morning, I might get permission from the Adjutant to serve out 'the bubbly' right away. The Adjutant consented and I gave Jerry the job, as he had a VERY steady hand. Some did not drink rum, so Jerry returned this to the jar, which was taken in the morning.

The Corps History makes special note of Cook-Sergeant Dunn, commenting that 'the well known Cook-Sergeant Jerry Dunn, of the 2nd

Battalion, saw to it, with his yarns, that they passed a cheerful night, and gave them hot cocoa before they started in the morning'. The alcoholic addition to that cocoa, and its 'cheering' effects, were not noted.

Someone else who was concerned with rum at that time was Captain Lionel Montagu RMLI, Commander of D Company, Hood Battalion. The Honourable Lionel Montagu was the son of Baron Swaythling, and in more peaceful times was interested in breeding racehorses. In a letter to his mother, after the battle, he notes the arrangements that he had to make.

Capt. the Hon. Lionel Montagu RMLI, D Coy Hood Bn RND

You have no idea what a lot of arranging and issuing of stores has to be organized. There is a lot of work for a Company Commander – he has to arrange how the bombs, grenades, picks, shovels, spare ammunition, wire-cutters, wire gloves, Very lights and roman candles, and last but no means least, the rum, is to be carried and used . . .

The plan was for the battalions to leapfrog each other as they advanced, giving each a chance to rest and reorganize. The first objective was called the Dotted Green Line. The 1st Battalion RMLI, with Hawke, Howe and Hood battalions, were to attack and take this. The 2nd Battalion RMLI, with Anson, Nelson and Drake battalions, were to pass through and take the second objective, called the Green Line. The move would then be repeated through the Yellow Line and final objective, the Red Line. This was on the far side of Beaucourt itself. The plan was clear enough on paper, but in practice it became muddled, as all plans were, as various units came across unexpectedly strong enemy opposition whilst others found the going less difficult than envisaged. Captain Lionel Montagu certainly had a clear idea of his objectives.

Capt. Montagu RMLI, D Coy Hood Bn RND

All our plans had of course been fixed. The Hood Bn were to advance, helped by a company of the HAC, with the railway and the River Ancre on our right. We were to move off first and take the first three lines of trenches and reorganize in the third trench. The Drake Bn were then to go through us and take the line [the Green Line] just above the road, called

Station Road, which runs down to the railway station and river. We were then to go through Drake and take a line called Yellow Line, just this side of Beaucourt, and then another brigade were to come through and take us to Beaucourt. You will see from what I am going to tell you that the units got hopelessly mixed up and that Hood, under Col. Freyburg [Montagu uses this spelling: it should be Freyberg], with various units of other battalions, took all these objectives, including the village of Beaucourt.

Private William Brown was part of the brigade that was intended to relieve Hood Battalion, and was formed up in a similar position, but to the rear, ready to push through when the initial objectives were taken.

Pte Brown RMLI, Machine Gun Coy 190th Bde RND

I don't know what the strategy was in the other sectors, [but] in ours, the 188th and 189th brigades carried out the initial attack and my brigade, the 190th, was in reserve. The two brigades had to advance and take certain objectives, then hold on and consolidate. The 190th brigade then had to carry on through them and advance till they could go no further, then hang on to what they had won at all cost till help and reinforcements could reach them. The right of our line was on the brow of the hill, which formed the north bank of the valley; at the bottom of which was the River Ancre. From the brow of the hill along which we were advancing, down the slope to the river, it was a quagmire and unoccupied. The hill on the other side of the river was Thiepval Ridge, the scene of very heavy fighting in the early days of the Somme battles.

Evidently, all ranks had a clear idea of the plan of attack, even if the reality was to make a travesty of this plan. Captain Lionel Montagu took his company to the assembly point and awaited zero hour.

Capt. Montagu RMLI, D Coy Hood Bn RND

On the night of the 12th we got into our assembly positions and spent one night there. It was of course very cold. We arranged our companies in waves, in depth by platoons, about 10 yds apart. Everyone had a definite job. The first two waves were to get straight ahead as close to our barrage as possible and to take the third line of the enemy trenches. The third and fourth waves were to clear up the second and first lines respectively and then rejoin on the third line. I decided to go with the third wave as being most likely to give me control of my company.

Away to the left of the Hood Battalion and the 190th Brigade, Sergeant Will Meatyard and the rest of 2nd Battalion RMLI were getting into position. They would actually advance 15 minutes after the first battalions.

Sgt Meatyard RMLI, HQ Coy 2nd Bn RMLI

About 3 a.m. on the morning of the 13th, certain platoons crawled out in No Man's Land and got close up to the Germans' barbed wire – there lying flat and still, patiently waiting for zero. At 5.45 a.m. we were ready and waiting, the morning light just beginning to show itself. All watches had been synchronized. At five minutes to six the CO announced five minutes to go. What a time it seemed going. There was not a sound to be heard. The question was (and our success depended on it), was Fritz in the know – as it was nothing new for him to get wind of an attack and the time it was coming off – but this time he was apparently taken by surprise. Each morning at dawn for the last few days our guns had been giving him pepper, and no infantry attack took place . . . I expect he got fed up with these alarms.

By this time Captain Lionel Montagu had begun his advance into the morning mist.

Capt. Montagu RMLI, D Coy Hood Bn RND

The time was fixed for 5.45 a.m. and we all advanced in the pitch darkness, which was accentuated by a dense Scotch mist. It was a weird sight seeing the dim figures of the men advancing in waves through the mist with little bursts of flame coming among them and lighting up the fixed bayonets. I speedily found myself with about 60 men and about two platoons of Drake Bn too far ahead, having gone over the three lines without seeing them, though we had bombed some dugouts. We were right in our own barrage and suffered a few casualties from it. I felt rather lost but fortunately recognized the station and Station Road which I had made a mental note of when we had gone across to the other side of the river (Schwaben Redoubt) to study the ground on this side, over which we were to advance. This stood me in good stead now. I knew that I had got too far ahead but did not like to bring them back as nothing could be more demoralizing. I brought them back in two moves of 20 yards to get more behind our barrage. My servant, Wright, was hit here in the leg by our own artillery, just by me. I wrote to my CO [Lt Col. Bernard Freyberg] saying where I was and that I would wait till he came up. I saw him soon afterwards on the line above Station Road and it began at last to grow lighter. After this all was plain sailing as he immediately took charge of everybody and ran the whole show. He immediately reorganized us giving me the right, and, watch in hand, waited for our barrage to move. At the exact moment we moved on again about 20 or 30 yards above our barrage, Freyburg in front with Arblaster, Hill and myself in close attendance.

It may have been 'plain sailing' for Montagu's group, but elsewhere the RND were suffering heavy casualties. Half the casualties of the two RMLI Battalions occurred before they reached the first German line, over the muddy shell-pocked slope. Most of these were caused by German heavy machine-gun fire. Before the Dotted Green Line had been reached, all the Company Commanders in 1st Battalion RMLI had been killed. Drake Battalion, on the extreme right, had lost heavily in the barrage. Amongst the casualties was Lieutenant Colonel Tetley, their commanding officer, who had been mortally wounded. Arthur Tetley had been Private Vickers' Company Commander in Gallipoli. Hawke and Howe Battalions came up against an enemy strongpoint, a redoubt between the first and second German lines, which had been missed by the artillery barrage. Small parties of the Hawke Battalion reached the Dotted Green Line, having had their commanding officer wounded. The Nelson Battalion pushed through the Hawke, and came against the same withering German fire. Many of them fell around the enemy position, including their commanding officer, Lieutenant Colonel Norman Burge. The survivors struggled on to the Dotted Green Line. Parties of the Anson Battalion, likewise without their commanding officer, passed through the Nelson Battalion and got to the Green Line. As usual, what appeared clear-cut and achievable on paper had swiftly descended into a shambles. Charles Jerram accepted that this is what happened to 190th Brigade.

Maj. Jerram RMLI, 190th Bde RND

The Honourable Artillery Company were magnificent and never got sufficient credit . . . The rest of 190th Brigade was I'm afraid in a mess, as they got thoroughly mixed up with the Forward Brigades hung up round the Strongpoint.

One of the major factors in the 'fog of war' was limited communication. Without the benefit of radio, messages could only be passed by written notes and field telephone. Each Company had 'runners', but their chance of getting the message through was limited. The more desperate the situation the more likely the runner was to be killed or wounded on his journey. Thus messages were never received and units were frequently unaware of the position of their neighbours. In the case of telephone communications, the telephone line would be laid as the advance was made, and would lead back to Brigade and then Divisional level. Sergeant Will Meatyard and his signallers had to advance under the enemy fire unrolling great coils of telephone wire as they went. Even if they managed to keep up unhurt, the chances were that shell fire would break the cable and parties would have to keep going back to repair it.

Sgt Meatyard RMLI, HQ Coy 2nd Bn RMLI

Receiving a certain codeword the CO, Adjutant and our Headquarters Staff went over amidst not many shells but plenty of spitting bullets, and arrived at a German trench. Under previous arrangement this was now the advanced telephone station. From here I received orders to lay a wire to a certain position ahead and with Pte Peach, or 'Pippy' Peach as he was called, proceeded to lay the wire forward. We unreeled it as we went along. Almost everything had been hit by shells, and it was one continual mass of debris and mud pools. Some were half filled with water and many had badly wounded men lying helpless in them – ghastly sights. First aid had been rendered to them in most cases. Eventually reaching the position I connected up and got through to Headquarters. Many around me were getting sniped. As the CO came along I gave him the necessary tip to keep very low, which he did. The Adjutant, Capt. Farquharson, was wounded here, and whilst getting back was wounded again. Capt. Muntz, Adjutant of the 1st Bn RMLI, was also sniped here. He was shot in the head and died. The German trench we were now in was in a chronic state, once you took a step you had a job to get your leg out, the mud being so deep and sticky. Wounded Germans and our own men were lying about all over the place; what had been dugouts were now partly closed by the muddy landslides that had taken place as the result of our gun fire and choked the entrances. The telephone was working well and I was in communication with Brigade. German prisoners were now coming in in large numbers holding up their hands and saying 'Finny' [*fini*].

Private William Brown, with the machine guns of 190th Brigade, had reached a point at which he was meant to halt for an hour.

Pte Brown RMLI, Machine Gun Coy 190th Bde RND

About two hours after the start of the engagement our instructions were to take cover and stop for one hour to enable the 188th and 189th Brigades to mop up and consolidate before continuing the advance. We had then been struggling on for about two hours, so I shared a shell hole with two or three mates. We had suffered pretty heavily by this time but the attack was going very well all along the line. We had reached a point just south of the ruins of Beaumont Hamel [Beaucourt] railway station by this time; the other two brigades were some distance ahead of us.

At 7.30 a.m. the advance to the Yellow Line was timed to begin, and a barrage commenced. Hood Battalion and the remnants of Drake Battalion reached their part of that line without much difficulty, and parties of Anson Battalion and details from the 1st and 2nd Battalions RMLI also made it to the objective. William Brown set off behind them, but did not get far.

Pte Brown RMLI, Machine Gun Coy 190th Bde RND

When we got the order to advance I heaved my gun up on my shoulder and climbed out of the shell hole, pulling myself up with my right hand. As I put my hand on the rim to get on top, I had a bullet through it. I stopped and had a look at it; then had a good mutter, as it didn't look like enough to go back with; yet it would be darned inconvenient to carry on with.

The bullet had gone through my knuckles in front of my

142

little finger, and it appeared to have split the top of my thumb.
I picked the gun up and started off again, got about half a mile
and was held up, so I had another look at my hand. The two
middle fingers were hanging down [and] there was a gaping
hole through the palm, I could have poked four fingers
through. Instead of my thumb being split, it was gone, and
when I lifted it up for a better view, the two fingers hung down
the back of my wrist and a slab of meat flopped down the front
of my wrist from where my thumb had been. I lifted the fingers
up and over into the palm, and slipped my fingers under the
slab and pushed it back up over the stump of my thumb and
held it in place. I passed word along to the section commander,
Lt Goldingham, that I had been hit. He came along in a few
minutes, and said 'Damn. All right, you had better make your
way back. Good luck.' I whistled to a Red Cross man I spotted,
and he came over and fixed my field dressing. I dumped my
equipment, but retained my revolver and bottle of rum,
handed over to Beresford of the HAC my gun as instructed
beforehand, and started off. A shell burst just as I started and
I looked back, and when the smoke cleared both gun and
Beresford had vanished.

Meanwhile, Lieutenant Colonel Freyberg, commanding the Hood
Battalion, was increasingly frustrated. Having had a comparatively
easy advance, he wanted to exploit his advantage and carry on into
Beaucourt, but was told to wait because other units had not even
managed to get to the Green Line, and the line of the brigades was
ragged and insecure.

Capt. Montagu RMLI, D Coy Hood Bn RND

We then got to our next objective, a line just this side of
Beaucourt. Here we captured German mail and a dump of
German rations. We opened their parcels and smoked their
cigars. We found lots of good things to eat, including sausages
and cakes, as well as socks etc. From the letters we discovered
it was the 2nd Guards Reserve Regiment against us.
    Here Freyburg told us to dig two lines of trenches. Picks and
shovels were scarce but the men dug splendidly with their
entrenching tools. Our doctor joined us here, having dressed
and evacuated nearly all our wounded under heavy fire. We
got news here also that Kelly, Edmondson and Gealer had

been killed, also one of our clearing parties had captured a major, five other officers and about six hundred men.

Sergeant Will Meatyard and the rest of the 2nd Battalion RMLI were still on their way to the Station Road.

Sgt Meatyard RMLI, HQ Coy 2nd Bn RMLI

The CO, waving his cap above his head, said 'Come on Royal Marines', and over they went to the next trench. Leaving a signaller of the RFA [Royal Field Artillery] with this telephone, I joined on another reel of wire. Having passed a stick through the centre hole of the reel and slung my own telephone, I ran forward and the reel unwound as I went along the surface of the ground. I apparently drew the attention of machine-gunners at the strongpoint, and also some snipers who were lurking in that direction. At about every fifteen yards I dropped into a shell hole and took a breather. Then I got my legs free from the mud and made the wire ready to unreel easily. Then I made another dash and so on. As I did so each time, the machine guns opened up, but each time I dropped I think it rather deceived them, as they did not know whether I was hit or not. By this means I escaped all their bullets and got to the point that I was aiming at . . .

Having arrived at the new trench I connected up again and found that communication was still good. I told one of my men at the intermediate stations to bring on the aeroplane shutter. It was getting dark now and I knew that in the morning the 'Communication Plane' would be over to find out our exact position, and that we should want to communicate with it.

During the night the cable was often broken, but Sergeant Meatyard and his signallers managed to find and repair the breaks. In the morning the 2nd Battalion RMLI was the only battalion that was able to communicate with the communication plane by means of the shutter device. On that morning, Tuesday 14 November, the Royal Naval Division received assistance in the form of some tanks, which took the troublesome strongpoint. At this stage tanks were still very much a rarity – and a novelty. The groups that had reached the Yellow Line, except those with Freyberg, pulled back to the Green Line, where the battalions consolidated. Over to the left the 51st Highland Division had managed to take Beaumont-Hamel after very heavy fighting.

Within the Royal Marine battalions of the Royal Naval Division, casualties had been very high. The commanding officer of the 1st Battalion RMLI had only one officer remaining fit for duty, and the CO of the 2nd Battalion RMLI had two.

On the far right, Captain Lionel Montagu had spent the afternoon of the 13th digging in, as German snipers and machine-gunners in Beaucourt became more active. Besides the Colonel, there were eight officers of the Hood Battalion left in action, out of 23, including Montagu and the medical officer. The remnants of Drake Battalion had the medical officer and three other officers. After a very cold night in the open, the troops under Freyberg prepared to take Beaucourt itself.

Capt. Montagu RMLI, D Coy Hood Bn RND

Freyburg soon had things organized. I was to lead the second wave in support of him from the second trench. The prospect seemed to me to be very doubtful. The snipers and machine guns were so active that it was dangerous to show your head, even for an instant, and we were to attack at 7.45 a.m. By this time the trench of which I had command had become packed by the people (HAC etc.) jumping in and taking cover. I passed down the word for everyone to clear his rifle and be ready to start at 7.45 a.m. I had always heard that it was impossible to advance against hostile machine guns unless our artillery had first knocked them out. These and the snipers were quite unaffected by our barrage, which seemed feeble. Such were my doubts that I sent a message to Freyburg at 7.15 a.m. to ask him if he intended to attack, by means of one of my runners (Tucker). He never got the message as the runner was killed, but he told me that he had exactly the same doubts and nearly called it off . . . At 7.45 a.m. our barrage became a little more intense but nothing like enough to stop the snipers and machine guns. I saw Freyburg jump out of the trench and wave the men on. Three men followed from my trench and I got out with my runner, with bullets raining past us (one through my sleeve). The first wave stopped three times. Freyburg was knocked clean over by a bullet which hit his helmet, but he got up again. I and my runner dived into a shell hole and waited about half a minute. I said I would go back and get more men out of the trench and crawled about ten yards back to do so. Then about a dozen men came out and I got up and waved the rest on. They all followed. We soon got into Beaucourt (of course absolute ruins) and found that the Germans could not face our men and were surrendering in hundreds. It was an amazing sight – they came out of their holes, tearing off their equipment. I myself rounded up at least fifty, waving my revolver at them and shouting 'Schnell'.

Despite some patches of German resistance and problems from snipers, Freyberg's force set about consolidating their newly won position. A battalion HQ was formed and a telephone message sent down the line. Freyberg, who had been wounded again but was still on his feet, was in the HQ with Montagu.

Capt. Montagu RMLI, D Coy Hood Bn RND

I had had many talks with Freyburg during the previous day, how sorry he was about Kelly and Edmondson etc., now we had a long talk here . . . How splendidly the Battalion had done in attacking and carrying the three objectives including the strong village of Beaucourt, consolidating two lines and taking over 1,000 prisoners, besides machine-guns and vast quantity of stores . . . I told him that if I got out of it alright I would call a racehorse 'Beaucourt' . . . Suddenly it started, such heavy shelling as I'd never experienced. Not in ones or twos but in dozens and all big 5.9 howitzers. The house telephone, SOS rockets etc. were blown to pieces . . . Freyburg said, 'They are ranging on this house,' and he and I took cover in the shallow trench where the HAC were. Here we lay for about half an hour. I don't want to exaggerate, but I am sure that thirty of these big shells fell within twenty yards of us. During the shelling we discussed the situation and agreed that it probably meant that the 'Boche' were to attack. I now expected to see them on top of us at any moment. We passed the word to the HAC to look to their rifles. I remember Freyburg commenting on the fact that a few shells were dud. We feared gas shells and took out our gas helmets. We did not put them on but continued to sniff. There was something comforting in what I usually thought was an unpleasant smell. Two or three times we were half buried by bits of house, earth and stones. One in particular I remember hit the bricks and smothered us with a bright pink dust . . . One shell fell a bit closer than the others. I felt something hit me in the small of the back but it did not seem to hurt at all. I heard Freyburg say 'Goodbye Montagu' and then 'Steady Hood' and I saw he was hit and was going a very bad colour. He asked me if I had any morphia. I gave him a quarter grain [an apothecary's

measure: 10 grains equates to 1 gram] and labelled him to say
I had done so, I then dressed his wound with my field dressing
(he had none) as best I could. There was a hole in his neck
which was bleeding rather profusely. He lay there for about
ten minutes and I thought he was going to die.

Rather to Montagu's surprise, Freyberg later became quite alert and
asked if Montagu could walk him to the dressing station. Montagu
helped Freyberg back the 300 yards or so to the Regimental Medical
Officer, over the mass of shell holes and still under enemy fire. The
command of the battalion was handed to Montagu and it was he who
led the Hood Battalion out of the front-line trenches when they were
relieved in Beaucourt early next morning, Wednesday 15th. Charles
Jerram recalled the two Royal Marines Battalions marching out of the
line, unnaturally smart.

Maj. Jerram RMLI, 190th Bde RND

When the Division pulled out, the remnants of our two [Royal
Marines] Battalions marched out past the Divisional
Commander, every man perfectly turned out in a clean
uniform brought up by their QMS during the night. And on
passing through a village were booed by the inhabitants who
thought they were running away without fighting! Perhaps
one of the best compliments we've ever had.

Bernard Freyberg won the Victoria Cross for his leadership and
bravery at Beaucourt. Lionel Montagu received the DSO. He survived
the war and did indeed name a horse 'Beaucourt'. It was a bay colt and
in 1918 it ran in the 2,000 Guineas at Gatwick racecourse, where it was
unplaced. It later won a race at Gatwick – long before there was an
airport there.

Sergeant Will Meatyard did not escape unscathed. During the
morning of 14 November, he was hit in the head and arm and began
the journey to the rear. His description is typically understated when it
comes to his injuries and the pain and discomfort he endured.

Sgt Meatyard RMLI, HQ Coy 2nd Bn RMLI

When I woke up I found myself in a dugout, head and arm
bound up. Hadn't the slightest idea how I got there. One of the

stretcher bearers of the Howe Battalion had bound me up. After a while I thought I could walk and with the assistance of one of the staff I was taken to the rear. With two other walking wounded we toddled off all together. An incident I remember was, as we passed a battery of artillery, one of the crew came up with a basin of hot cocoa and asked us to partake of it. It was a Godsend, and showed the kindness one can get at the hands of a soldier . . . We arrived at the First Field Dressing Station, and entered therein. They soon got to work. I had several pieces of shell extracted from my arm, and the head wound dressed – I can't recommend the razor that was used to get the hair off!

Will Meatyard was told that if he would go as a 'walking' case he could get down the line more quickly, so he stood in the motor ambulance all the way to the Casualty Clearing Station. Here he was fed and placed in an Ambulance Train.

Sgt Meatyard RMLI, HQ Coy 2nd Bn RMLI

Placed in train, and after fourteen hours of agony, reached the 1st Canadian Hospital at Etaples. Here I underwent an operation by a very clever doctor. I think it was due to him being such an expert that I kept my arm.

Will Meatyard may have been lucky to keep his arm, but it still kept him in hospital in Cambridge and then in a convalescent home until April the next year. He was not sent back to France and survived the war. For his steadiness and calm action at Beaucourt, he was awarded the Military Medal.

Private William Brown, with his wounded hand, had an equally difficult journey to the rear as a 'walking' case.

Pte Brown RMLI, Machine Gun Coy 190th Bde RND

When I got back to the German front line, a dressing station had been established at the bottom of the bank, our side of it. The German front line had run along the top of a bank about 30 to 50 feet above a depression about 100 yards wide; our front line had run along the opposite bank. This bank was only about 10 feet high. The 51st Highland Division named this depression after the battle.

On reaching the dressing station at the bottom of the bank, I hung about for a bit with a view to getting my hand dressed. Then Jerry dropped about half a dozen shells on the edge of the bank above us, so I thought I would try and find my way back to a dressing station in Hamel village. When I got there it was gone – it had followed us up, and was the one at the bottom of the bank. I began to feel pretty groggy by this time, so I took a good swig out of my rum bottle and in a few minutes I could have taken on the entire German army single-handed! I seemed to have tramped miles without finding a dressing station, stopping for a rest and another swig oftener and oftener. Meeting a padre, he stopped and sat by the side of the road and had a chat. He told me there was a station about a quarter of a mile down the road, so off I went again. When I got there I found three or four of my gun crew who had been wounded. I gave them the remainder of my rum (there wasn't much anyway), poked my head round the entrance to the station, saw a table and a form so I went in and sat on the form and promptly passed out. When I came round my hand had been dressed, a label tied to my tunic and the MO [medical officer] was at a table. He turned round and had a syringe in his hand as big as a sizeable oil gun, with a spike on the end like a six-inch nail. I was about to partake of my anti-tetanus injection. He stuck the spike in, just above my left wrist, and shoved it right up to my elbow, gave the handle a shove and a lump came up at the end as big as a hen's egg. He then pulled this abomination out two or three inches, left it hanging, and kneaded the lump till it went flat, [then] gave me another squirt and repeated the process all the way down, by which time he had emptied the contraption. I was then given tea, cigarettes and tobacco, and told to wait. After a few minutes an orderly came out with an officer with a leg wound, and told me to give him a hand to walk to the next dressing station about a mile down the road. On reaching it we were given more tea, then put on one of the open-top London buses. [London buses had given sterling service in transporting troops to and from forward areas, and a contingent of London Transport personnel still marches proudly in the parade past the Cenotaph on Remembrance Sunday in recognition of their efforts.] On our way back we stopped at a big field dressing station, [where] some of us had another anti-tetanus injection. On reaching Varennes I got a fresh dressing and was taken to an army bell tent with camp beds and told to make myself comfortable. This was impossible as my hand had come round from the first numbing shock and was giving me considerable pain. No one came in to me all day. About midnight an orderly came calling out my name and number. When I answered I was bundled into an army truck and taken to another dressing station about a mile distant. Here there was a railhead . . .

After about two and a half days we reached Boulogne and I went into hospital there. On the Thursday following the Monday I was wounded, I was taken to the docks and put on a boat that landed us at Dover. We got off the boat and walked up into a long shed where trains were waiting. The walking cases had to walk up and start filling from the front. At 4 a.m. Friday morning we pulled in at St Leonard's railway station and were taken by ambulance to various hospitals.

William Brown saw no further action. He certainly avoided tetanus, but his wound became gangrenous and took many months to heal, though he was fortunate not to lose his hand. In July 1917 he was discharged from the Royal Marines and took up employment in civilian life.

The action at Beaucourt was successful in that the Somme battles concluded with the British in control of Beaumont-Hamel and Beaucourt itself, but during the winter the German Command decided to withdraw some seven miles and make a new line of fortified villages and strongpoints to be attacked in 1917. The area around Beaucourt and Beaumont-Hamel became a quiet backwater of the war until the Germans recaptured it during their advance in March 1918. That advance was the last major success of the German army. Overstretched, their advance was halted in April and from then on the Allies pushed the Germans ever backwards until the conclusion of the war.

The name of Beaumont-Hamel is well known; Beaucourt rather less so, although A. P. Herbert, who was an officer in the RND, wrote a poem entitled 'Beaucourt Revisited' which still appears in anthologies. With the passing of those who fought there, only this poem, the cemeteries and recorded memories of that generation are left to remind us that Beaucourt was more than a village near a railway halt in northern France.

III

ON LAND AND SEA

5

Zeebrugge

The attack on Zeebrugge on 23 April 1918, St George's Day, shows the Royal Marines very much as their motto says: Per Mare Per Terram – By Sea and By Land. It was a combined operation with the Royal Navy, including a handful of men from the Royal Australian Navy, and some small French vessels. Of those who were to land on the mole at Zeebrugge harbour, two thirds were Royal Marines, both Royal Marine Light Infantry and Royal Marine Artillery. The others were sailors, most of whom had served on the Western Front with the Royal Naval Division.

The 'triangle' of Belgian ship canals linking the inland town of Bruges with Zeebrugge and Ostend on the coast was captured by German forces by mid October 1914. It soon became an important outlet for German destroyers, submarines and minesweepers docked in Bruges. Without Zeebrugge and Ostend, German vessels would have had to work from Germany itself, thus limiting the area small craft could cover and their ability to respond to events. They would therefore be a less serious threat to the vital Channel traffic. Everything for the Western Front had to cross the English Channel, whether it was men, pack animals, ammunition, or food supplies. On the return trip were men going on leave and the wounded. In the course of the war over 1 million wounded passed through Dover, besides those to other coastal ports such as Southampton.

The idea of hitting the Germans at Zeebrugge had been put forward as early as 1914, but for various reasons it had been shelved. Rear Admiral Tyrwhitt had proposed a plan in November 1916, and it had been raised yet again in the autumn of 1917, when unrestricted U-boat action put British supply routes in great jeopardy. At that time, however, there were hopes that success inland at Passchendaele would allow Zeebrugge to be used by British forces, following an anticipated German withdrawal. As that dream disappeared in the mud of the wettest early autumn for years, the idea of disrupting German access to the Channel, and cutting local maritime losses by up to 30 per cent,

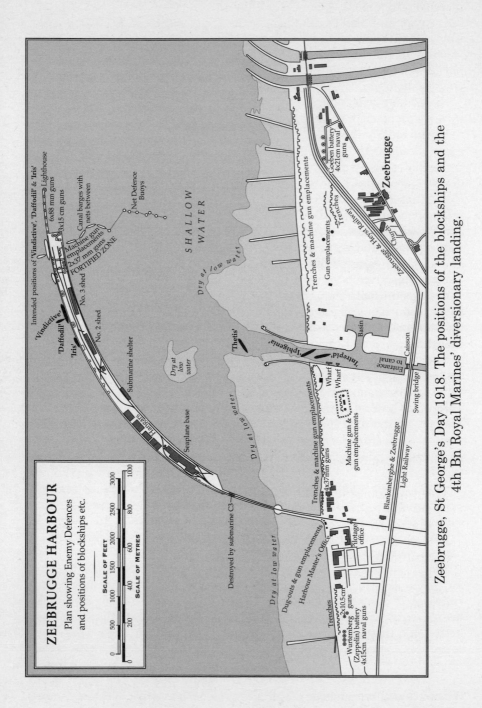

Zeebrugge, St George's Day 1918. The positions of the blockships and the 4th Bn Royal Marines' diversionary landing.

increased in appeal. A new and vociferous advocate for action against Zeebrugge and also Ostend appeared: Rear Admiral Sir Roger Keyes. Keyes took command of the Dover Patrol with a plan ready to put forward to the Admiralty. This plan, already in a high state of preparation following underlying acceptance at the end of December 1917, was finally given the go-ahead on 24 February 1918.

Keyes' plan was to block the canal mouths at Zeebrugge and Ostend, by sinking blockships across them. At Zeebrugge the blockships were to be the elderly light cruisers *Thetis*, *Iphigenia* and *Intrepid*, specially adapted and with concrete in their keels. The German defenders were to be distracted from destroying the blockships as they passed by a diversionary attack on the Zeebrugge Mole, which would make them think that the destruction of its gun batteries and defences was the main objective. The 4th Battalion of the Royal Marines was to be formed for this task. The defenders of the mole itself were to be denied reinforcements by the blowing up of the elderly British submarine C3, and originally also C1, among the girders of the viaduct connecting the mole to the shore.

Lieutenant Charles Lamplough joined the 4th Battalion on 22 February, via Plymouth Headquarters, from HMS *Revenge*, bringing with him his batman, Private Deed, and Sergeant Radford. They were to report for 'Special Service' and were to return to the *Revenge* on completion of that service. His notes on the training period are short and to the point. The Plymouth Division provided C Company; B Company, from the Portsmouth Division, would arrive on the afternoon of the 23rd, and A Company, from the Chatham Division, on the 25th.

Lt Charles Lamplough RMLI, No. 9 Platoon, C Coy 4th Bn RM

Training took place on Freedown, where the Mole had been taped out, but there was a cover plan for the purposes of secrecy. The ground was supposed to represent part of a canal bed in France that had been drained and used as an advance ammunition dump and store depot etc.

Training was carried out by day and by night and the attack was carried out under every possible combination of circumstances.

Training included a great deal of PT [Physical Training] and bayonet and commando type training, such as disarming sentries etc.

Within this short passage much is left unsaid, but it covers three vital aspects of the build-up to Zeebrugge; the maintenance of secrecy, the intense training and preparation for the exact manoeuvres, and the degree of general fitness and military discipline honed to a peak. This latter caused much friction and grousing among the old sweats, not about the 'commando type' training, but the time spent at drill on the square. Sergeant Harry Wright wrote to his wife in a far from joyous mood.

Sgt Harry Wright RMLI, No. 10 Platoon, C Coy 4th Bn RM

We fell in at 9 o'clock this forenoon, half the time was spent at physical drill and the rest bayonet fighting and turning to the right etc. The NCOs have to drill with the men and on the whole we are entirely turned over to the depot staff who have been skulking down here for ages and now using to the best of their ability all the sarcs they can bring forth. This to men who have fought in France etc, etc, result is after only a forenoon's work the men are fed up and soured so you see dear what we are up against. I thought I had quite finished with Left, Right, etc. I had a tummy full of that at Plymouth, and came here to learn tactical schemes.

The resentment of drill was clearly exacerbated by the fact that the instructors were not the sort to have seen recent action. A more serious result of this was the refusal of No. 7 Platoon to fall in on parade on 15 March. This 'collective insubordination' was taken extremely seriously. There was no indication of an unwillingness to prosecute the war, no undercurrent of dreaded 'Bolshevik tendencies', but the authorities were perturbed. Courts of Inquiry were assembled within days. It was decided that much of the blame lay with the officers and NCOs who had not nipped the problem in the bud. Four days later the major in charge of B Company, and three subalterns, were withdrawn from the battalion and returned to their divisions. Captain Bamford was put in charge of the company and new subalterns brought in, not all from the Portsmouth Division. The NCOs and men of No. 7 Platoon were returned to Forton Barracks, Gosport, having been given a dressing-down by Brigadier Neville-White, who 'Told them what I thought of them'. He recommended that 'should it be found impossible to deal drastically with any of these NC Officers or men for mutiny, I would strongly urge that they be subjected to a vigorous course of close drill for a month or two in order to discipline them.'

Despite the problems, many of the battalion were extremely happy in their unit. Private Ernest Tracey, a 17-year-old who had lied about his age, was clearly pleased with his lot. He made one of Lieutenant Hope Inskip's No. 1 Platoon, A Company.

Pte Ernest Tracey RMLI, No. 1 Platoon, A Coy 4th Bn RM

We were of the very best, and word soon got around that the other units were similar, as though the officers had been picked for a team job. They bought mouth organs for use on the march, and they made themselves interested in a man with his affairs at home, etc. On parade, it was On Parade, but even so at times when on the march the officers would move along the unit and come out with a cheery 'Everybody happy' or something like it.

Off parade, it was Off Parade; Lieutenant Inskip would often come out with something like: 'How are you today, are you short in any way, can I help you at all?'

I would say every man was 100% content within his unit, and would not want to leave that high degree of contentment.

Private Tracey obviously had not spoken to No. 7 Platoon, or Sergeant Harry Wright.

It may appear as though there was insufficient thought concerning the training of the battalion, but this is a misconception. In fact, great attention had been paid to what the battalion should 'learn', and there would be plenty of 'tactical' work for Harry Wright. A list of suggestions for training was sent by the Assistant Adjutant General, Royal Marines, Herbert Blumberg. It is couched in suitably positive terms.

Enclosure to RMO Confidential Circular No. 20923/17, 10 Feb. 1918

The object of the training is to get the men physically fit, full of dash and accustomed to short sharp raids by night, equipped in the lightest order.

The Company must therefore be worked up in Bayonet, Bombing, Rapid Shooting at short range, Snap Shooting (especially standing), and Trench fighting.

Heavy marching is not required. Marches should be from 5 to 10 miles without packs, to get men in condition only. Wrestling, football, running, boxing (when gloves are available) and such games as Prisoners' Base, can be easily carried out during instruction hours. (These sort of games now form a great feature of army instruction.)

Practice in trench fighting is essential. Lewis Gunners and Bombers must be thoroughly trained. They must be exercised respectively with Ball Ammunition, and Live Bombs at night.

Lewis Gunners are not required to be mechanical experts, but men who can get into Action quickly, keep their gun going and instinctively remedy stoppages. Similarly the Bombers are required to be skilful throwers of the Mills Grenade, and not to know details of construction of a variety of Grenades.

All the Company should be put through a Musketry Course with mark VII Ammunition, the practices being framed to develop rapid shooting at short ranges, and snap shooting.

Practice in Night firing is essential.

It is suggested that in the daily programme should be included:

- 1 hour, Bayonet and Trench Fighting (not necessarily continuous).
- ½ hour Swedish [a system of physical training].
- ½ hour Games at odd times, and running.
- 1 hour Section, Platoon, or Company Training.
- ½ hour Musketry Instruction, chiefly on rapid snapping, with marches of from 5 to 10 miles without packs.

Practice in night work, even if this can only be carried out in a very elementary way, is essential.

Digging is not required, but men should be practised in quickly passing up filled sandbags.

Open warfare tactics are not required, and should only be occasionally carried out as a change.

Officers should practise with the Revolver.

These suggestions emerged as detailed and concentrated work programmes for the battalion as the example from the Battalion Orders of one day, 26 February, indicates.

Routine tomorrow:

8.30 a.m.	'B' Coy to Rifle Range.
	MG Section to 30 yards Range.
9.0	'A' Coy to Gymnasium.
	'C' Coy to Infantry Drill.
10.15	'A' Coy to Infantry Drill.
	'C' Coy to Gymnasium.
11.0	'A' Coy to 30 yards Range.

11.30	'C' Coy has use of Trenches. MG Section, TM [Trench Mortar] Section, and HQ details to Gymnasium.
3.0 p.m.	All Subaltern Officers to Gymnasium. 'B' Coy to Gymnasium.

'A' Coy will carry out Night Firing. 'C' Coy and MG Section will carry out Night Training. OC Coys will arrange details.

The degree to which the battalion's training was planned presages that of a Second World War raid. This was not the gathering together of a motley crowd and flinging them at the enemy in a hopeful, and probably hopeless, gesture. This was thought through at all levels, and the men who set forth for Zeebrugge were well prepared physically and mentally. The aspect that had not, and could not be covered, was that casualties would be so high before they ever got ashore to put the training into effect.

Of course, one of the problems with such a planned operation was the maintenance of security. At a local level, the men remained in ignorance of their real destination until they moved to the *Hindustan* and *Vindictive* on 6 April, expecting to undertake the operation on the night of the 11th to 12th. They then had to remain incommunicado, because of weather delays, until the night of the 22nd to 23rd. At a higher level, subterfuge rather than ignorance was required. It was accepted that security in France was very good, but that in London 'loose talk' was a real problem. Despite great efforts to track down enemy agents, there was less success in curtailing the gossip on the social circuit, from which an horrendous amount of knowledge could be gleaned. This was certainly part of the reason for an extraordinary missive of 22 February, from the Adjutant General, Royal Marines, Major General Sir David Mercer. This letter, marked Confidential, purported to detail the 4th Battalion's taking over of a sector in France, thus relieving an RNVR Battalion. In fact, the Battalion was only intended to be on foreign soil for a few hours.

Maj. Gen. Sir David Mercer, Adj. Gen. RM, 22 February 1918

On arrival in France the 4th RM Battalion will be attached to the 188th Brigade of the RN Division replacing temporarily one of the RNVR Battalions and forming a Royal Marine Brigade. All transport and transport personnel will be provided by the RND on arrival in France.

2. With reference to para 1 of RMO Circular No. 2477/17 of

6th Nov. 1917, and para 4 of RMO Circ. 3477/17 of 9th Feb. 1918.

The men are to be fitted with puttees and not leggings.

The gymnasium shoes will not now be required but are to be taken on charge by the 2nd Quartermaster for issue to Superintendent of Physical Training for use in the gymnasium as necessary.

3. Shrapnel helmets and Box Respirators will be issued as soon as received at Deal, and men are to be trained in their use. They [the men] will be put through the Gas Chamber in France.

4. The necessary arrangements for billets, food, etc., are being made by the GOC RN Division who will communicate in due course with the OC Battalion who is to at once comply with any instructions he may receive.

5. The RMA Trench Mortar detachment will be told off to the 63rd Trench Mortar Battery on arrival in France.

6. Instructions will be issued later as to the date on which Officers and Men will be transferred to books of RM Brigade.

This document is annotated '6 copies'. It is a cover story for the presence of all the training around Deal, down to the use of Trench Mortars and a mention of the gym shoes, which would be of more use than boots on ropes and perilous brows. The Divisional Commander in France must have been warned of this false trail, otherwise he would have found himself making impossible plans for the RND. Likewise, Lieutenant Colonel Elliot, commanding the 4th Battalion, knew the accurate plan. The obvious answer is that this was concocted at a time when security was paramount but likely to be compromised by incautious tongues in the corridors and salons of power. There is also the possibility that it was feared that those who opposed Keyes and his 'schemes', might, even at this late date, have sought to 'tamper' with it.

Whether this was a necessary subterfuge in face of a known threat, or Rear Admiral Keyes and his planners being somewhat paranoid, is not yet clear. In the event, secrecy was certainly maintained.

The Royal Marines and sailors were also fed false information, lest any hint of the objective be revealed, as Ernest Tracey remembered.

Pte Tracey RMLI, No. 1 Platoon, A Coy 4th Bn RM

We were mustered one day in the Globe Theatre [within the Barracks] and our battalion commander, Lieutenant-Colonel Elliot, gave us the story that the objective was somewhere around Calais (this was a blind!) where at that time the German offensive was forcing the Allied troops back towards the coast.

The tactical training was made as realistic as possible, and this was not without risk. The use of live ammunition meant that there was always a degree of risk, and on 1 April there was a major incident with a Stokes Gun of the Trench Mortar Section at Freedown. Five members of the Royal Marine Artillery lost their lives. At the ensuing Court of Inquiry it was discovered that a 3-inch mortar round had exploded in the gun, with lethal effect. The cause of this 'prem' [premature explosion] could have been human error, but Captain Brooks-Short RMLI, a Stokes Gun Instructor from the Royal Marine Depot, Deal, thought this 'most unlikely, in view of the state of efficiency of the gun's crew'. His belief was that the accident had been caused by a defect in the shell that would not usually be apparent at time of firing. The Court's conclusion was that the cause of the premature explosion could be narrowed down to one of four, but it was impossible to determine which with any certainty. Whatever the cause, it meant the battalion turning out for funerals before ever getting wind of the enemy.

On the Saturday, 6 April, the battalion left Deal, even at this stage amidst deception. It looked as though the battalion was leaving for France, as the Transport *King Edward*, which had been a River Clyde ferry steamer, took them out of Dover harbour. Yet once over the horizon, the ship headed round the Kent coastline and transhipped the men to the *Daffodil* at the Mouse lightship before transferring them again at the Swin to *Hindustan* and *Vindictive*.

When the men boarded the *Hindustan* and *Vindictive*, their real objective was made clear and the reason for all their hard work and training explained. Private Philip Hodgson reveals a further attempt at misinformation, this time to be given up 'reluctantly' if captured.

Pte Philip Hodgson RMLI, No. 12 Platoon, C Coy 4th Bn RM

During the first days on board *Vindictive* we were shown the detailed model of Zeebrugge Mole and received further instructions showing how our training at Tavistock and Deal fitted in with the projected raid. Among other things, we were told what to say if by chance we were taken prisoner by the Germans, at first to say nothing but when pressed to admit that all British ships had a device with which underwater submarines could be heard fifteen miles away. On hearing this, a cry of 'Tell that to the Marines' went up, but when quiet had been restored and I said it could be done they all turned on me and threatened to throw me overboard.

The men were now cooped up and ready to go. Hopes that the operation would take place on the 9th and then 10th were foiled by bad weather, but on the 11th everything looked hopeful. The men were transferred to the appropriate craft and set out across the Channel. The decision was taken to abort the attempt, however, because the wind was directly against them, and so back to the Swin they went. This was very trying for all concerned, as Lieutenant Charles Lamplough noted.

Lt Lamplough RMLI, No. 9 Platoon, C Coy 4th Bn RM

These disappointments and the strain were very trying, especially as the men had been trained to such a pitch and then left to wait on board the ships. Everything possible was done in the way of amusements and games but there could be no communication with the shore.

The waiting became ever more tedious. Only on 22 April could another attempt be made, and by now the men had been stuck aboard ship, with limited opportunity to maintain fitness, for 17 days. They were heartily glad to 'get on with the job', whatever the dangers.

This time there was no hitch and at one minute past midnight, the very beginning of St George's Day, HMS *Vindictive* came alongside the mole at Zeebrugge and was held in place by the Mersey ferries *Daffodil* and *Iris*. The old *Vindictive* had been specially altered for her role, with a strengthened port side, extra guns, protection against blast and 14 gangways for the men to get down onto the mole. She went to Zeebrugge ungainly and odd looking, and returned a mass of twisted metal and debris. In the smoke and under heavy fire the *Vindictive* actually came alongside the mole some 400 yards nearer the shore than intended. This made the task even more difficult. The Royal Marines should have been set to attack the fortified zones approximately 120 yards from the seaward end of the mole, but this had to be left to the naval storming party during the initial stages, as the Marines were faced with securing the landward side from the German defenders. The casualties sustained in coming alongside, and the difficulty in getting the party from the *Iris* ashore, meant that there were not enough men to take both objectives. Only when the landward end of the mole was secure could the Royal Marines launch an attack to help the naval storming party, and the recall sounded before this had been fully developed.

The recall was sounded at 12.50 a.m., as the blockships were safely on their way to the inner harbour and heading for the canal mouth. Fifteen minutes later the *Vindictive* and her companions, *Daffodil* and *Iris*, headed slowly for home.

The events on Zeebrugge Mole that night were recorded by the Adjutant, Captain Arthur Chater, Lieutenant Charles Lamplough, commanding No. 9 Platoon, and Sergeant Harry Wright of Lieutenant Stanton's No. 10 Platoon. Private Bill Scorey, of Lieutenant Theo Cooke's No. 5 Platoon, wrote a vivid account of the landing to his sister and brother-in-law a few days after the battle, and other accounts come from Private Philip Hodgson of Lieutenant Underhill's No. 12 Platoon and a Private, who by deduction is Private James Feeney of Lieutenant de Berry's No. 7 Platoon. His account was published anonymously in the *Globe & Laurel* in April 1919, but by a process of elimination amongst his platoon, from the account and from records, he is the only man who fits as the author.

Private Feeney wrote a short entry in his diary on 22 April, after the order had been passed that the operation was to go ahead that night.

Pte James Feeney RMLI, No. 7 Platoon, B Coy 4th Bn RM, 22 April 1918

Stunt to come off tonight. Stowed hammock, packed up our packs, and went on board the *Vindictive*. We brought our dinners with us, cooked in the mess-tins; also all the bread, sugar and tea we had in the mess. We are doubtful that it will come off, but we all hope that it will.

We have taken up our stations and had tea, and we are on the way to the Mole. Everything seems certain as the wind is holding favourable. I do wish that it comes off, as the suspense is awful.

At 7 p.m. I can count 57 vessels all going the same way home. We get tea at 8 p.m., and are to get our usual rum ration at 10 p.m. If the wind is right at 10.30 p.m. we are to see it through tonight, no matter what happens. Going down now for a short sleep before the landing starts. I hope it won't be my last short one on this planet. All the boys are quite pleased now that it is to take place tonight. I hope we make a good show and have a decent slice of luck. It would be rotten to strike a mine, or have a collision with another of our ships. This finishes before the 'Scrap'. I hope I shall be able to finish about the battle.

At 11 p.m. the battalion went to action stations. Harry Wright was in the cramped Sergeants' Mess when the order came down.

Sgt Wright RMLI, No. 10 Platoon, C Coy 4th Bn RM

Our little Sergeants' Mess was crowded. We hastily shook hands and then went out to get our men up on to the upper deck, into the darkness. Rifles were loaded and bayonets fixed. The sea was beginning to get rough, and the *Vindictive* was moving very slowly. The Destroyers went on ahead and put up a dense smoke screen. No lights were showing on any of the ships and everyone spoke in whispers. Our nerves were strained almost to breaking point. Would we get alongside the Mole without the Germans seeing us. There we stood, shoulder to shoulder, rifles in hand ready for the dash forward – not a movement, hardly a whisper, and only the noise of the propellers breaking the silence. Would we ever get there. 'Ah, what is that?' A star shell floating just over the ship and lighting it up as if it were day. No sooner had that light died down than another went up. 'They've seen us,' someone whispered, for the lights had been fired from the Mole.

Then the silence was broken by a terrific bang followed by a crash as the fragments of shell fell among us, killing and maiming the brave fellows as they stood to their arms, crowded together as thick as bees. The Mole was just in sight, we could see it off our port quarter, but it was too late. Our gunners replied to their fire but could not silence that terrible battery of 5-inch guns firing into our ship at a range of less than 100 yds and from behind concrete walls.

A very powerful searchlight was now turned on us from the sand-dunes at Zeebrugge and their powerful batteries fired on us. The slaughter was terrible, Colonel Elliot and Major Cordner was both killed with the same shell while in an exposed position on the bridge, waiting to give the order 'Advance'.

Captain Arthur Chater was on that exposed bridge and saw his two seniors fall.

Capt. Arthur Chater RMLI, Adjutant 4th Bn RM

On the way up to my station beside the Battalion Commander on the bridge I met Major Cordner, the Second in Command.

We stopped and talked for a minute or two on the built-up deck. Although I cannot remember the matter having been previously discussed, I had always assumed that Major Cordner's station would be somewhere near the after end of the built-up deck. At the end of our talk I remarked, 'And now you are going aft?' To my surprise he replied, 'No, I must be with the CO until the ship is alongside and then I will go aft,' since the CO and Second in Command should not have been together. We went up to the bridge and joined the CO. The three of us stood together on the port side of the bridge. The remainder of Battalion Headquarters were below us on the lower bridge. I hung my fleece-lined Burberry on the chart house door, where I later found it badly torn by shell splinters.

As the ship approached the harbour we heard the sound of shell fire ahead. Star shell started coming over us and we realized how well we were being concealed by our smoke. Then the wind changed, and the smoke suddenly drifted away. On the port bow we saw the Mole, about which, for the past two months, we had thought so much. A moment later there was a burst of shell fire and shells came whistling round us.

Breast-high splinter-proof mattresses had been placed around the bridge. Although only 22 years old, I probably had a far more intimate experience of shell fire than either the CO or the Second in Command. At Antwerp in 1914 I had quite unnecessarily put my head up over the parapet of a trench and been wounded for my stupidity. At Gallipoli I had been hit in the back by a shrapnel ball. We were still some distance from the Mole and now instinct told me to keep my head down. I suggested that my two seniors should do the same, but they either did not hear me or they did not agree with me. Anyway, they took no notice. A moment later, a shell appeared to hit the front part of the lower bridge beneath us. My two seniors dropped to the deck on either side of me. I grasped hold of them and spoke to them in turn, but neither of them answered me. I then made my way across the bridge and down the starboard ladder to the starboard waist, and called out for Major Weller, Commander of C Company and the next senior officer in the Battalion.

The *Vindictive* had originally had 14 gangways or 'brows' that were to be used for the landing parties to get onto the Mole, but the heavy fire had destroyed all but two of them. Many of the landing parties therefore had to shin down ropes under fire or crowd over the brows. Captain Chater saw that Nos 10 and 11 Platoons, which were to have gone over first, were greatly reduced in numbers, so he ordered Lieutenant Theo Cooke and No. 5 Platoon to lead the way. Private Scorey was thus one of the first to land.

Pte Bill Scorey RMLI, No. 5 Platoon, B Coy 4th Bn RM

. . . How I escaped God knows, for the first shell that hit the *Vindictive*, which our Coy was on, killed dozens and set them all aflame, all the lads round me were blown to bits and I was flung between her funnels, my tin hat was shattered and so was my rifle, but I soon found some more.

We then had the order, 'Steady Pompey Company'. We were just going alongside the Mole, our section was the first to land, what there was left of us, and we were very lucky too, for no sooner were we on top of the wall, than the German machine gunners had the range, and were playing hell with us, then the heavy guns fired point blank into us, but we still advanced and soon silenced them.

Meanwhile, Sergeant Harry Wright, one of the remnant of No. 10 Platoon which had joined what was left of No. 9 Platoon, had scrambled onto the Mole. He seems not to have known that No. 5 Platoon had preceded them.

Sgt Wright RMLI, No. 10 Platoon, C Coy 4th Bn RM

As the *Vindictive* approached the Mole in the darkness we stood by ready to land. We were packed tight in five ranks, Lieutenant Stanton in front with me, as Platoon Sgt, in the rear. The two rear ranks were standing directly underneath one of the *Vindictive*'s Cutters.

It is usual, of course, when boats are hoisted inboard, for the plug to be removed for the water to drain. This had not been done and the Cutter was half full of water.

The first shell exploded inboard, fired from the Battery at the sea end of the Mole, exploded directly overhead and some thirty members of my Platoon were killed. Those of us standing under the Cutter escaped unhurt, the water in the boat breaking the force of the fragments of the shell.

Lying mortally wounded on the deck of the *Vindictive* was my young Officer, Lieutenant Stanton. As I knelt beside him he had just time to whisper 'Carry on, Wright', before he died.

And so died a gallant young Officer who thought more of his duty than himself. He was well liked in the Platoon.

. . . the order to advance was given by Major Weller who had now assumed command. The Remnants of Nos 9 and 10 Platoons now lead the way up the ramp. My officer, Lieutenant Stanton, having been fatally wounded, I had the honour of leading No. 10 Platoon on shore.

Up the ramp we dashed, carrying our ladders and ropes, passing our dead and wounded [who were] lying everywhere and big gaps made in the ship's decks by shell fire, finally crossing the two remaining gangways which were only just hanging together. We jumped on to the concrete wall only to find it swept with machine-gun fire.

Our casualties were so great before landing that out of a platoon of 45 men only 12 landed. No. 9 Platoon, led by Lieutenant Lamplough, had also about the same number.

Surgeon Commander McCutcheon, aboard the *Vindictive*, later commented on finding Lieutenant Stanton that 'one of the most pathetic incidents of the engagement was when I found Lt Stanton lying on the mess deck side by side with his servant [Pte Davies]. Stanton was unconscious due to a dangerous wound of the skull. His servant, who was severely wounded in the right arm and scalp, had his left arm round his master's neck and shoulders. He informed me that he was alright, but that Mr Stanton was very bad, and he was trying to keep the heat in him.' Robert Stanton died of his wound at 6.50 a.m. on the morning of 28 April at Dover Military Hospital.

Charles Lamplough did not realize that *Vindictive* was not in the intended position until he was on one of the brows with his few remaining men.

Lt Lamplough RMLI, No. 9 Platoon, C Coy 4th Bn RM

In the original plan, my platoon, with No. 10 Platoon, was to capture an anti-aircraft gun position and strong point on the Mole and then advance to the shore end of No. 3 shed. The Portsmouth Company would then pass through my position and continue the advance up the Mole. Nos 11 and 12 Platoons were to turn left and capture the important battery at the sea end of the Mole so as to ensure the safe entry of the blockships.

On arrival at the brows I realized for the first time that the ship was berthed in the wrong position and we were abreast the centre of No. 3 Shed and close to my objective.

The ship was rolling quite heavily and the brows were at a considerable incline. We jumped down and onto the path inside the sea wall and then down ropes that had been secured to the railings to assist us to negotiate the 16 ft drop onto the floor of the Mole.

I took my Platoon to the shore end of No. 3 Shed and established my position there before deciding what to do. During my landing there had been a tremendous amount of firing of every sort and the noise was terrific, but the most encouraging, until unfortunately knocked out, was the firing of the pom-poms from the foretop of *Vindictive*. We also saw the explosion of the submarine C3 at about this moment.

After these platoons had landed, No. 7 Platoon prepared to go over the brows. Private Feeney formed part of that second wave and followed Captain Bamford, who organized the support of the desperate naval party which, though it could not knock out the seaward end guns with its few men, managed to kill enough of the guns' crews to prevent the 4.1-inch guns opening fire on the vital blockships.

Pte Feeney RMLI, No. 7 Platoon, B Coy 4th Bn RM

We got down two gangways, and Plymouth section went over before us. The sailors were going over individually before that. Sgt Brady gave us the order to go up and over. The fire main had been perforated by shrapnel and we had to pass under it. We got something to keep us cool; down my back I got a shower. The sergeant stood very near it. He was trying to hide the bodies of three of the pom-pom gun's crew from us when we got on a level with the hinge of our gangway. The battalion Sergeant Major and the adjutant were superintending the getting over of the ladders. Well, it was not like anything I ever saw on parade, except that these two were just as cool. I offered to give a hand with the ladders when I was passing up the gangway, but Sergeant Major told me to go over.

Private Philip Hodgson, who was part of No. 12 Platoon's Lewis Gun team, helped the Sergeant Major with a ladder.

Pte Hodgson RMLI, No. 12 Platoon, C Coy 4th Bn RM

Loaded as I was with full equipment, small arms, ammunition, rifle and two panniers, each with four trays of Lewis gun bullets, it was not easy but somehow I scrambled over and dropped off the parapet wall, almost alongside RSM Thatcher. He was attempting single-handed to lift a heavy wooden ladder, which had been brought in *Vindictive* over the iron railing, along the inner side of the footway to enable us to get down on to the main part of the Mole. 'Give me a hand lad,' he shouted, so I dropped my rifle and the panniers and together we soon had the ladder over. 'Now off you go, it is safer down there,' so picking up my things I was soon down on the main part of the Mole. Moments later, the RSM was badly wounded, was got back on board *Vindictive*, but had to have a leg amputated.

Whether RSM [Regimental Sergeant Major] Thatcher did actually lose a leg seems debatable. He was fit enough to be married in September 1918, and appears in uniform in several later group photographs of Royal Marines.

Meanwhile, Private Feeney was making his way onto the Mole.

Pte Feeney RMLI, No. 7 Platoon, B Coy 4th Bn RM

I walked up very carefully, and in the anxiety to keep my balance on the see-saw of the gangway, I forgot about the rain of lead, and I really felt comfortable when I put my foot on the concrete . . .

Sgt Besant got on the ladder, and shouted for No. 1 Section. As we were No. 2 we did not go. We waited for Corporal Smith, but as things seemed a bit mixed I asked McDowell to come along and we went. Captain Bamford came up just then from the left side of us and we went down immediately after him. I had arranged with Lightbown that we would stick together, but in the confusion of getting over on to the ladders I lost him, so McDowell and I hung on together . . .

I ran across to the dump-house opposite the ship, and took cover by lying on the ground. The ground floor of the dump-house was raised about two and a half feet over the roadway, and had a pathway like as if carts were loaded there, like at a railway goods store. We had a grand chance of chucking bombs in the doors of this dump-house, as we had splendid cover.

Whilst amusing myself here, a portion of concrete was removed out of the Mole by the explosion of the submarine [Sandford's C3] that was stuck in the piles. I could not attempt to describe what this operation sounded like. It was about the very last word in noise.

When we got back we were told that the dump-house was to be blown up now, so we went away on the left, and I could see no one to fire at. I felt rotten to hear the rattle of the shells striking the funnels, and could do nothing just then. Captain Bamford came up and said, quite cool, 'Fall in, B Company.' I fell in with McDowell, and Sergeant Brady took charge of us. There were only 16 there, and Captain Bamford was leading us along, when he looked back to see how many of us he had, and apparently he thought we were insufficient, as he told the Sergeant to retire to the ship. The sirens had gone over 10 minutes then, and we retired in twos to the ladders; it was running the gauntlet over that fire-swept zone. I went with McDowell, and we got up together on the two ladders.

When I climbed over the railing at the top I nearly fell back, as my rifle was slipping off my shoulder. The gangways were heaving up and down now, and the hail of shell was awful. Then for the first time it occurred to me that I might get hurt if I hung around much longer, so I was getting careful at last. I made a jump at the gangway, and got over, and threw my rifle in. I scrambled down as best I could, picked up my rifle, and went over to the starboard side. It was terrible here, and I was mad with myself. I was getting nervous and funky from looking at the dead and listening to the dying. I threw off my equipment and gasmask, and sat down next to poor Tubby Smith; he had one leg clean knocked off, and was talking bravely. There were some deeds done that night that make words seem light and not able to touch on the thought you wish to express.

In fact Captain Bamford was responding to the recall, otherwise his small force would have been left. Retiring was more easily said than done, as Private Scorey found out.

Pte Scorey RMLI, No. 5 Platoon, B Coy 4th Bn RM

We then had the order to retire, but the devils started to come on the wall at us, but few got away. One fired point blank with his revolver at one of our lads, but he paid dearly for it, for our

Captain [Bamford] crowned him with his loaded stick. We then tried to board a Destroyer which was lying alongside the wall, but she sent out oil fumes at us, and we replied with liquid fire, she couldn't put to sea because the blockships had played their part, and blocked the harbour. We then had to come aboard owing to the tide, but had to climb up the wall again by ladders, which was about 15 to 20 feet high so it was no easy job. No sooner were we on the top than a shrapnel shell came and scattered us, some got blown back on the Mole and some in the water. I went in the water myself, but managed to get on board by a rope which was flung to me, she then pushed off leaving some men behind. I think I was the last man aboard.

Lieutenant Charles Lamplough and his group of Nos 9 and 10 Platoons, including Sergeant Harry Wright, had been bombing some German dugouts and then turned their attention to a German destroyer.

Lt Lamplough RMLI, No. 9 Platoon, C Coy 4th Bn RM

During the period we were on the Mole we did what we could to harass a destroyer alongside with such weapons as we had available and also dealt with a few Germans who came down the Mole close to the sea wall as if in an attempt to interfere with our scaling ladders.

The whole time we were there German coast defence guns bombarded the *Vindictive* and Mole and a considerable number of shells burst at the base of the wall alongside the ship, not an encouraging prospect for our retirement.

At about 12.50 a.m. the recall was sounded and units commenced to retire, taking their wounded with them. My position being nearest to the shore end of the Mole, it was my duty to cover the retirement, and we left, only when, as far as I could see, none of our troops remained.

When we got back to the wall, fortunately and to my great surprise, one of the scaling ladders remained, also one of the brows to the ship. On arrival on board I reported to the Captain that as far as I knew we were the last to leave.

Unfortunately we learnt later that Captain Palmer, 3 NCOs and 10 Privates failed to return and were taken prisoner.

One of those left behind was Sergeant Harry Wright.

Sgt Wright RMLI, No. 10 Platoon, C Coy 4th Bn RM

A shell had struck the *Vindictive*'s siren, so that she could not make the retire signal, but another ship was ordered to do so. The signal to retire should have been a succession of short blasts, instead of which the other ship made a succession of long and short blasts. We took it however for the signal to retire and commenced doing so when the order was passed that it was not the retire signal and we were ordered back to our posts. We obeyed the order, and very shortly afterwards we had the terrible ordeal of seeing our only means of escape slowly move away.

Harry Wright and his companions spent the rest of the war in German prison camps, in a state of semi-starvation, as Germany was desperately short of foodstuffs.

When the ships set off for home the full extent of the losses and damage could be assessed. In the *Iris* the CO of the Royal Marines aboard, Major Eagles, had been killed, and shell blast had smashed the platoons drawn up on her deck. One shell hit a group of 56, killed 49 and wounded the others. *Vindictive* looked like a cross between a slaughterhouse and a scrapheap.

Pte Feeney RMLI, No. 7 Platoon, B Coy 4th Bn RM

Then we saw the cost of our landing, one thing was evident – it cost a great deal of blood. I shall never forget the sight of the mess-decks; dead and dying lying on the decks and tables where, but a few hours before, they ate, drank and played cards. In the light of day it was a shambles.

The admiral's flagship passed and greeted us warmly. We never got our rum ration that morning, although I got a mouthful of 'neat' about 2.30 a.m. from an officer who was doing the Good Samaritan with a jug in one hand and the nickel-plated end of a half-pint flask in the other. We had all the bodies collected up together at one end of the ship. I had a last look at Corporal Smith and Rolfe [Private Frank Rolfe RMLI, aged 19].

'Shambles' was also the word Charles Lamplough used about the decks.

Lt Lamplough RMLI, No. 9 Platoon, C Coy 4th Bn RM

The ship was a shambles both on the upper deck and below, with doctors and every available individual doing their best for the wounded. Fortunately *Vindictive* was not hit again and she steamed, probably as she had never steamed before, but HMS *Iris*, with the Chatham Company on board, was badly hit and suffered heavy casualties, including her Captain and the Commanding Officer of the RM Company, Major Eagles, both of whom were killed . . .

My impression of the operation was that as far as our objectives were concerned, i.e. capture of the battery at the seaward end of the Mole and the damage to material on the Mole, the operation was a failure.

His reasoning seemed sound enough, according to the Operation Orders he had received. Paragraph 7 of the RM Operation Order stated: 'It must be firmly impressed on all ranks that the capture of the fortified zone at the seaward end of the Mole is the first essential to ensure the success of the entire enterprise.'

Whatever else they had achieved amidst the mayhem they had not captured that fortified zone and it was therefore quite natural to be conscious of failure. This feeling was shared by others, including Arthur Chater and Captain Bamford.

Capt. Chater RMLI, Adjutant 4th Bn RM

I discussed the operation with Bamford. We had failed to gain any of the objectives which had been laid down in our orders. We felt that our part of the operation had been a complete failure. We had lost many good men with what seemed to us no result. We felt extremely despondent. We did not then know that, although our part of the operation had not gone according to plan, the attack on the Mole had created the necessary diversion to enable the blockships to enter the canal.

It is clear from this that the purely diversionary role that the landing parties were to take had not been passed down the chain of command. The most senior officers engaged on the operation that night were dead. It is possible that they knew the overall importance of the landing on the Mole, but it had obviously been decided that it would impinge on the effectiveness and morale of the landing force to let them know the degree to which they were purely a distraction to allow the blockships the safest passage to the canal mouth. Thus, even the Adjutant was conscious only of failure, and was only relieved of that impression at Dover.

Capt. Chater RMLI, Adjutant 4th Bn RM

Vindictive reached Dover at 8 a.m., and went alongside the Admiralty Pier. On landing, I met Admiral Keyes. He told me that aeroplanes had been over Zeebrugge that morning, and had reported the canal entrances blocked. He said that the operation had been a great success. I told him how we felt, and asked him to tell the men. The Battalion was falling in on the Pier to entrain for Deal. Before we commenced to entrain, the Admiral came and told us his good news.

When the men got to Deal they presented a ragged sight to the few people who saw them arrive.

Pte Feeney RMLI, No. 7 Platoon, B Coy 4th Bn RM

We had all the wounded that could walk with us, and some that could not. Motors took down the latter to the hospital. We could not keep the step on account of the heels and toe-plates being off our boots, and we made no sound when marching through the town. We attempted three times to sing 'take me back to dear old Blighty', but we could never finish it . . .

At dinner we were spoken to by the Acting Commandant, and from his remarks I gather we have had the honour of being associated with a deed that is on a par with any in the past, great and glorious as they no doubt have been. Everyone knows we got leave, and the newspapers said it was very good, and asked us to repeat the dose often. Those blessed quill-drivers, I should like to see them on a stunt like that, and to be told before they have got their wind to repeat the dose!

Feeney's attitude to those who were very keen to see someone else engaged in dangerous enterprises was that of all the fighting forces, who had no time for 'armchair warriors'.

The final realization of the losses sustained hit Bill Scorey when he returned to Deal, and a near empty barrack room.

Pte Scorey RMLI, No. 5 Platoon, B Coy 4th Bn RM

It seems so strange in the room here now, only five left out of 23, and only me and the Cpl without a scratch.

The men engaged on the raid on Zeebrugge were certainly greeted as heroes, especially at a time when the German offensive had pushed the Allies back from costly and hard-won gains and threatened defeat. This boost to morale was much needed. When a unit showed outstanding courage to a degree where it was difficult to select one man especially for the Victoria Cross, provision was made for the unit to select the recipient themselves, by means of ballot. Two Victoria Crosses were awarded in this way to the 4th Battalion, one going to Captain Bamford and the other to Sergeant Norman Finch RMA, who had kept up the fire from a pom-pom gun in *Vindictive*'s fighting-top despite the crews having being put out of action and he himself being wounded. He only stopped when another shell wrecked the gun.

Many men received other awards for their actions that night. Of those mentioned here, Captain Arthur Chater received the Distinguished Service Order and promotion. Lieutenant Theodore Cooke was also awarded the DSO. Lieutenant Charles Lamplough and Lieutenant George Underhill received the Distinguished Service Cross, as did Sergeant Major C. J. Thatcher, who had done such sterling work at the brows. Sergeant Harry Wright was awarded the Distinguished Service Medal, but could not receive it until he was repatriated at the end of the war. He served again in the Second World War and died in 1976 aged 87.

The Royal Marines of the 4th Battalion sustained 366 casualties out of a total of 730 men. Of these 119 were killed, including 10 out of the 30 officers. A further six officers were wounded and one was captured. In honour of their courage and in respect of their casualties, it was decided that there would never be another 4th Battalion Royal Marines.

Debate continues as to the real success or failure of the attack on Zeebrugge. German propaganda minimized the effects and some later appraisals took this evaluation at almost face value. However, the raid did achieve its objective in successfully blocking the entrance of the Bruges–Zeebrugge canal. German traffic from the port was made virtually impossible and their heavier craft had to move elsewhere. Several submarines were actually found in the area when it was retaken by the Allies in October 1918, as detailed in a private report by Captain Benn of the Royal Navy.

The Royal Marines felt that they had failed because they did not gain their specific objectives. Whilst this was true, they succeeded in the greater objective of drawing the enemy's attention away from the blockships, as intended. Tactically they may have failed, but strategically they were very successful and fully justified Admiral Keyes' congratulations. Destroying the guns on the mole was never going to alleviate the submarine threat in the Channel, but blocking the canal might, and that strategic aim was achieved. Furthermore, the raid provided a model of planning, training and deception that could be built on, on a massive scale, within a generation.

6

Day-to-Day Life on Active Service

There is a well-known saying that life on active service is 99 per cent boredom and 1 per cent wishing you were bored. For all the moments of fear and excitement, when the adrenaline is high, there are the thousands when life is extremely humdrum. This book has looked at a few of the 'active' days. In order to give a real picture of the combatants' lives during the war, their everyday life should also be shown. Whether within the steel 'wall' of a ship or under canvas, occupying time could be difficult. The daily routine of duties, parades and cleaning provided only the backbone of existence.

Living in difficult conditions far from the comforts of home meant that certain aspects of normal life took on greater importance than usual. Two of the most important were, and still are, mail and food. Every effort was made to ensure that a man received mail from home as regularly as possible. Delay in getting it through was a guaranteed source of heartfelt grumbling. Letters were the link with the family at home, the 'other life', especially to men who had volunteered for war service after years as civilians. Some of them had never left their home village or town before. Nearly all had never left Britain.

Letters from the troops had to be censored by an officer, although sometimes special envelopes were issued which meant that only a sample number of letters enclosed in them would be censored at Base, and they would not be seen by a man's own senior officer. Censoring was not a job that was enjoyed, and a considerable number of letters, like the one Charles Lamplough wrote before his first action in Gallipoli, went home unblemished by the censor's pencil. At times the censor did not have to prevent men passing too much information, because they made their messages highly cryptic. Alternatively, the censor had to prevent them from sending back total fabrication. Major Gerald Rooney, aboard HMS *Queen Mary*, recounted the letter a sailor sent home after the Battle of Dogger Bank.

Maj. Rooney RMLI, HMS *Queen Mary*, 1 September 1915

An amusing report of a censored letter by one of our blue-jackets to his home, in consequence of the admonition that no details or intelligence, or reference to recent action should be made in writing, ran thus, 'For dinner yesterday – had "sausage and sauerkraut" and by gum we served 'em up hot.'

When Norman Burge was the Officer Commanding in the Cyclist Company of the RND at Gallipoli he came across the opposite problem, and his diary entry for 21 May 1915 illustrates this point.

Maj. Norman Burge RMLI, Cyclist Coy RND, 21 May 1915

There is a great rush on to secure early copies of General Orders. One paragraph of these was headed RABIES – PRECAUTIONS AGAINST, and went on to talk of destroying dogs etc. – but some copies were issued before they discovered a printer's error of a B instead of an R in the word 'rabies'. Guess the Staff will get their legs pulled. Talking of babies, one man writes home – 'the shelling is terrific and the streets are full of dead babies'. How they expect me to pass such stuff I don't know.

Needless to say there are no babies – and no streets to put 'em in either. They appear to love harrowing tales in their letters home – possibly this is expected of them.

There were other fabrications of a more praiseworthy nature. When a man was killed, his senior officer, at whatever level that was, would write to the family to offer sympathy and a few more details than the harsh telegram. The dead man's friends would also often send letters back to the family, people they had heard of but never seen. Everyone wanted to know how and where 'their boy' died and where he was buried. Few knew the grim realities, especially in the mud of France and Flanders. Death was certainly not always clean and quick. Many died lingering deaths in the shell holes of no-man's-land, or tangled in the wire where their friends could see them but not bring them in. Some literally disappeared in an explosion and left nothing to bury. Even if a body was buried, shelling frequently exhumed it. Men learned to live with their dead, and the dividing line between the two was stretched thin. Ghoulish humour, or simply ignoring the reminders of the recently departed, kept many sane. There was a hand sticking out from a trench wall, desiccated by the environment in Gallipoli, that it was considered lucky to shake on going up the line. Such horrors were carefully hidden from those at home. Phrases such as 'died instantly', 'felt no pain' and 'buried where he fell' were virtually in standard use to conceal the truth.

The Reverend Percy Hallding, a chaplain with the Royal Naval Division, wrote a typical letter to Mrs Jane Fowler of Tottenham, whose 19-year-old son, Archie, had been killed in Gallipoli.

Revd Percy Hallding, Chaplain RND, 22 September 1915

Dear Mrs Fowler,

I received your letter with its enquiry after your son who was killed out here and am now in a position to give you a little more definite news. The adjutant of his regiment informs me that your boy was killed by a shell which fell among a working party down at W beach on the 7th July. His death was instantaneous, which will be a great comfort to you – as so many men are frightfully injured and die in great pain. He was buried on the beach in our cemetery there.

I sympathise very deeply with you and all the mothers of England who have so bravely given their sons to the country in her time of need, and who are now mourning over lost ones. May God bless and comfort you all.

Yours sincerely,

Percy Hallding
Chaplain RND

In a similar vein, but on a more personal note, was the letter sent to Mrs Jane Heaton in Eastney, Portsmouth, from her husband's commanding officer on No. 11 Gun of the Howitzer Brigade.

Capt. R. C. S. Morrison-Scott RMA, No. 11 Gun Howitzer Bde, 24 September 1917

Dear Mrs Heaton,

It is with the greatest sorrow that I write to tell you that your husband, Sergt. Heaton, was killed today by enemy shellfire at the battery position while fighting the gun. He did not suffer, for he received a fragment of shell through the brain. Poor, poor, dear fellow, – we all – officers and men alike – regarded him with affection and high esteem. He is for me personally the greatest loss sustained.

I should not tell you, but I do so to show you how highly he was held in esteem – Sergt. Heaton was recommended just a few days ago for the Military Medal, and it will almost certainly be granted. This is of course no consolation, but I know you will like to know that his courage, cheerfulness and soldierly qualities were fully appreciated by his officers and comrades generally. God bless him and you, dear Mrs Heaton.

Yours very sincerely,

RCS Morrison-Scott
Capt. RM
OC RMA How. No. 11

P.S. There were unfortunately five other fatal casualties at the same time and they have all been buried together in the military cemetery. The exact place of burial you will be able to know in due time through the Graves Registration Commission.

The writing of letters to the bereaved was one of the least pleasant jobs performed by officers, especially in close-knit units. It was particularly difficult for young subalterns in their teens who had no experience. Details of burials were often not borne out by what could be discovered after the war, but in this particular case Jane Heaton did have a grave to visit. Sergeant Jonathan Heaton, aged 40, is buried a few kilometres west of Ypres, in Gwalia Cemetery, Row II, Grave C13.

Of course, it was also the case that friends of the deceased also wrote to the bereaved as soon as circumstances permitted. Alfred Logan was in the 2nd RM Battalion. He was wounded whilst a private at Ostend in 1914, but had recovered and risen to the rank of acting sergeant. On 26 October 1917, his luck ran out. His widowed mother, Bessie, was sent the usual 'Madam, It is my painful duty to inform you . . .', but also received letters from his friend, Sergeant Black, and his company commander, Captain Weekes. The comparison is interesting.

Sgt W. Black RMLI, A Coy 2nd Bn RM, 30 October 1917

Dear Mrs Logan,

I am trying to send you a few lines of sympathy in your great bereavement. It must have been a great blow to you as it was to us when we heard of your son's death. Paddy (that is what we all called him) died as he lived, a good and brave soldier. He got killed instantly so we have the consolation that he didn't suffer, he was leading his platoon into action at the time. He was always cheerful whether he was in the trenches or out. I have known him a long time but I have never had a better chum. Sgts Wetton, Stamp, Ferris, Hurrell and myself all send our deepest sympathy.

> Kindest regards from
> Sgt W. Black, A Coy, 2nd RM

The following letter from Captain Weekes corroborates Sergeant Black's version of the death, so perhaps in this case it was true. Captain Weekes describes Paddy Logan as 'your husband' instead of 'your son', but to read into this any lack of interest or care is dangerous, especially since Captain Weekes stresses how long he had known Sergeant Logan. Sergeant Black, who would have known many of the family backgrounds of his friends from the sharing of news and parcels when mail was brought up the line, probably only wrote to Mrs Logan on 30 October. In contrast, after an attack, Captain Weekes probably had all too many letters to write, in addition to his other tasks. His error was most likely that of a tired man who had written the last letter to a new widow.

Capt. B. W. Weekes RMLI, OC A Coy 2nd Bn RMLI, 31 Oct. 1917

Dear Mrs Logan,

The Coy and indeed the whole Corps has to mourn the death of another very gallant fellow in your husband, who was killed in action on Friday last (26th).

He was the life and soul of the Coy and was killed instantly by a sniper whilst leading a very gallant rush on an enemy strong-point.

There is little I can say to lighten your sorrow for you; but believe me, there is no one in the Bn who does not feel his loss very keenly, and I mean this. Particularly do I feel his loss, for he was one of the few NCOs left who served with me in Gallipoli.

I cannot tell you where he is buried for the condition of the ground was so appalling that it was impossible to get them in at the time and it is only in the last 24 hours that we have been able to move anyone.

With very sincere sympathy from every Officer and Man in the Coy.

> I am
> yours most sincerely
> B.W. Weekes
> Capt., OC 'A' Coy

There were periods when normal letters were not permitted at all. This was usually before an important and surprise attack. The only method of assuring your family of your safety was a Field Service Postcard. This had a pre-printed text from which men could delete inapplicable phrases and add the date of their last received letter, but no extra phrases could be added. On a happier note all units made efforts to issue their own Christmas cards – even hospitals. Those from units at the front were likely to be sketches or cartoons, and whilst some were merely reproduced outlines on thin paper, others were neat watercolours.

It is also worth mentioning that there could be a certain sorrow at the loss of an enemy. This was often felt among those at sea. For all the Anglo-German naval rivalry that had preceded the war, there had been visits between the navies, and there was a feeling of common bond with those who took on the 'enemy' of the ocean. Nobody liked leaving men in the water, and the sight of a ship in her death throes could appear indelicate, like watching a man cry. Major Rooney reported how one of the men reacted during the Battle of Heligoland Bight.

Maj. Rooney RMLI, HMS *Queen Mary*, 28 August 1915

Hanley [an 18-year-old Able Seaman] states that he distinctly saw her [*Köln*'s] rudder, and that her propeller was still slowly revolving. One had to turn away from the sight, as he did not quite like to witness it, and says the cheerfulness on the part of some of the men made him feel hurt, seeing what a gallant little ship it was; anything like a cheer would have disgusted him.

Major Rooney was also very aware of the coincidence that meant HMS *Birmingham* sank a German 'chummy ship'.

Maj. Rooney RMLI, HMS *Queen Mary*, 31 August 1915

Birmingham was the light cruiser which did so brilliantly, [and] by a strange quirk of fate, the vessel she sank happened to be her chummy ship of a month before, during the battle squadron visit to Kiel, and among the prisoners taken (some 8 or 9 officers) were their hosts of Kiel, all d—— good fellows, they were indeed a sad remnant.

Although death and injury had to be faced, for much of the time there were more mundane matters at the top of men's minds. The comforts of sleep, dry clothing and varied, palatable food were highly prized. Early in the war Rooney turned his mind to the first of these, and set out in his journal the problems of watch-keeping in conjunction with other tasks.

Maj. Rooney RMLI, HMS *Queen Mary*, 1 September 1914

There are a certain number of little inconveniences, as well as some major ones, which render life a little less pleasant; at least at present (1.9.14). I will say, a little less pleasant, because the novelty of war has by no means worn off during the last month, or let's say the first month! This is of course largely due to the sustaining knowledge of having fought a very successful little action; insignificant certainly – but successful and to this ship at all events it entailed but little inconvenience, and is looked upon as having been real good fun. It is important enough in this way, the Captain calls it 'having 'blooded' the men', one feels that one has been put in one's place, the ship's raison d'être assured, and there is tangible proof that the *Queen Mary* and her crew are of some consequence after all; and so there is a 'settling down to it', and a feeling of assurance that at any rate 'guns do go off' – and that there will be some tangible result. To review pinpricks however, I must approach them each in turn and describe and rend them to pieces, without making a mountain out of a molehill, or conveying an impression of pessimism or grousing. The first drawback appears to be, the want of sufficient sleep and rest.

At times one is rather badly 'had', and after the usual watch kept (we keep three watches) comes a spell of coaling; to take a recent case coaling and ammunitioning in close sequence. An officer or man, of say a certain watch, keeps a four-hour spell prior to anchoring, and comes off watch tired, to find he has to get out nets, and coal for maybe twelve or fourteen hours, in a recent case (30.8.14.) twelve hours at a stretch coaling, then two hours cleaning ship, followed by another two hours. This was immediately followed by twelve hours arduous shell hoist work, getting in ammunition, with a break to rest at 2 or 3 a.m. till 7.30 a.m., upon which the labour was renewed till 5 p.m. Cleaning ship was then imperative – followed by a four hours' watch at a gun, after this an 'alarm' and the necessity for instant action robbed the tired member of his well earned rest. This of course is an exceptional but an actual case in point, and shows a balance of four successive nights practically out of bed or hammock, during which time very severe labour was the order of the day; of course also, this is the rub of war; but it tends to tire men, and render them more or less inefficient for, let's hope, only the time being; but frequent repetition, such as occurs in the case of battle cruisers, involves strain.

Gerald Rooney was not one to pose a problem without considering a solution and therefore goes on to make some suggestions for improvements. Whether these were ever mooted beyond the pages of his journal is not known.

Maj. Rooney RMLI, HMS *Queen Mary*, 1 September 1914

Can this be obviated? The answer of course depends upon naval strategy, is it absolutely necessary to have our ships always out, and always on the move? The system one has been accustomed to work with, on paper, has allowed a margin for rest, and time in harbour to each ship or couple of ships in turn; in paper schemes we have allowed say a force of 8 vessels, to have two days in harbour out of eight, to a portion, say a quarter, of their force, in order to coal, and to give the men rest. So far this has been denied us, and I don't see any very urgent strategical reason. No sooner have we coaled than we are off to sea again, with our hands keeping watch at the guns in their dirty coaling rig, and in some cases, we have been still sticking it down with one watch, striving to clean ship with a second, and manning guns with a third. This is rather forcing matters, and taking reserve strength out of a crew on the eve of action.

The Japanese system of rest, as practised in the RJ [Russo-Japanese] War has no place in our routine. They had special gangs of shore labour to coal, which attended upon vessels coming in, and coaled their ships, whilst the crews slept, washed and refreshed themselves, usually in hulks alongside, while the operation was carried out. Surely a rich nation like England could afford to do likewise, and could easily provide hulks with suitable accommodation for resting crews etc. A squadron like a BCS [Battle Cruiser Squadron] must risk a good deal in the way of efficiency by requiring heavy labour from its crews twice a week, which we average at coaling, and then putting to sea with jaded men.

Rest from the Officer's point of view. The three-watch system works very satisfactorily so far as ordinary routine, not including operations of coaling and provisioning etc. but as regards officers, the executive do not reap the same benefit as the men for the following reasons. They are acting or working a double role, or in a double capacity, as (1) officers of a turret, as well as (2) belonging to their proper watch, Red, White or Blue, for night work or foggy weather; so that their men may get two watches below of a night or a day, while the officer may have to go from a duty turret watch, on to the succeeding Red or White watch for 4" defence, making an 8 hour spell of standing by.

System working in Sept. sometimes same officer on watch, 12 hours on the bridge out of the 24, this of course being necessary in thick weather. Thus, say for instance, J keeps

Mdt. to 4 a.m. – MIDDLE WATCH on bridge with his proper watch.

7 a.m. to 8 a.m. – Rig sub-calibre.

9 a.m. to noon. – Sub-calibre firing.

Noon to 4 p.m. – TURRET WATCH kept on bridge because submarines are about.

5 p.m. to 5.30 p.m. – Rig night control, test instruments in turret etc.

8 p.m. to Mdt. – FIRST WATCH on bridge with his proper watch on bridge.

Thus a total of say 16½ hours makes it a tiresome day, for a more or less routine day, not considering alarms etc. This apparently cannot be bettered very materially, though it could be improved by calling another officer to do such emergency work as the afternoon submarine watch entailed.

There is such a thing as making men too comfortable, for inst. voice pipe men on the bridge are cuddled up in a windproof shelter, where they invariably go to sleep if not rousted out periodically; their mates, the lookouts, are expected to stand the same four hours with a glass to their eye in wind and rain – How very much better it is in every way to equalize the duties, and roust them all out for an hour's lookout at a time, relieving the lookout proper; it works admirably; and yet – senior officers apparently ask – 'Why do that?' Well! Why not?

I should suggest that men on watch not actually standing by, or looking out, be allowed to make themselves as comfortable as possible for their hour or so, and play games, or musical instruments if they feel inclined – lately (6.10.14) such an attempt as a cigar box violin etc., gramophone in TS [Transmitting Station] have been sternly repressed. I should think it is very excellent way of passing a watch to all concerned, as long as it is carried out in moderation and to no one's annoyance.

The fact that everyone was so busy certainly indicates that these problems weighed heavily with Gerald Rooney, from the amount of time he obviously spent considering them. It also shows a man who was far from the hide-bound, stiff-collared image of the Edwardian officer for whom 'change' was anathema. Nor was he one whose diary consists of problems and complaints. He could be quite poetic about the weather in the North Sea.

Maj. Rooney RMLI, HMS *Queen Mary*, 3 September 1914

What a glorious night, a running sea and a full moon, with masses of cloud charging along. The evening star hanging like a lamp. A hundred sombre hulls gliding along, and a good thousand hungry gun muzzles pointing southward, to welcome the HSF [High Seas Fleet]. 'Cheers! and a bottle of rum' and the devil will take the hindmost.

Maj. Rooney RMLI, HMS *Queen Mary*, 21 September 1914

Somewhere to Westward of Sylt off Danish German coast, very rough and blowing fresh. The winter appears to have set in already, and 'A' turret in its exposed position is gradually becoming a hall of the winds and spray. It is very often necessary to batten down, closing all orifices, such as gun muzzles, sighting ports, sighting hood, rangefinder, inst. manhole floorplate lets in enough air and brine to last a consumption hospital for a year. It is gradually becoming a fine art to reach the isolated 'A' [turret] without wading, or the assistance of a boat, so!

Maj. Rooney RMLI, HMS *Queen Mary*, 23 October 1914

North Sea Middle Watch, very uneventful, although we expected to encounter many things. The wind roared over the bridge all night, a crescendo howl, every moment seeming louder and shriller; hard to speak to anybody or give an order. Dark as pitch at times, and occasional showers of what seemed like iron filings, but I suppose it was rain, so how Bob Ewart kept station through it all, upon the invisible *Lion*, I don't know; cos I had to keep my head down most of the time. The *Lion* showed about as much light as a dyspeptic glow-worm.

The men ashore in Gallipoli, and later in France, would have been grateful for the comfort of shipboard life, even with heavy seas and disturbed rest. The conditions were rarely pleasant: either too hot and plagued by flies or wet and cold. In Gallipoli there was also little shelter from shrapnel even in rear areas, and frequently men remained in the same clothing for days on end. Norman Burge describes the delights of a change of clothes and a decent place to sleep.

Maj. Burge RMLI, Cyclist Coy RND, Wednesday 12 May 1915

I spend all the forenoon down at 'W' beach unsuccessfully trying to steal mules to bring our travelling kitchen and carts with our valises up from the beach. Eventually I am reduced to borrowing them. Go over to our new bivvy alongside Div Hqtrs. Go to tea with the Staff. There's condensed milk! 1st milk since we landed. Our valises come up in the evening. Oh the joy of taking off one's boots and being able to waggle one's toes at night. Have a beastly headache from fatigue, no sleep and rain so go to bed in the valise at 6.30 p.m.

This clearly had the right effect on him, for he rose next day feeling much better.

Maj. Burge RMLI, Cyclist Coy RND, Thursday 13 May 1915

Get up at 7 a.m. after being in a sort of heavy swound for 12½ hours. Feel very fit and consume enormous quantities of ration bacon and tea for breakfast. Everyone spends a lovely forenoon in washing. First the shaving of the Royal Beard (10 days growth), a bit painful but well worth it. Then the bath! – a waterproof sheet in a hole in the ground and filled with water. All this in the most brilliant and warm sunshine. Then a complete change of clothes right through – everything except the cap. One does feel smart and superior.

Food, as has been touched upon, was also very important. Fresh vegetables, eggs and ordinary bread were delicacies. Jam was rationed and usually 'Plum and Apple'. Strawberry jam was greeted as a rarity. In France parcels arrived from home quite quickly, and cakes and sweets were often sent by mothers, wives and sweethearts. Some officers had Fortnum & Mason hampers sent over, but most still had to supplement the hard biscuits and Maconochie tinned stew that formed a basic part of the diet. Major Norman Burge, amidst the flies of Gallipoli, however, managed to arrange a 'feast' from available resources that amazed and impressed his guests.

Maj. Burge RMLI, Cyclist Coy RND, Sunday 23 May 1915

Decided to give a dinner party in honour of the new Mess so made most elaborate arrangements. First, got a tablecloth – a bit of canvas which was well scrubbed. Then a centrepiece consisting of an empty shrapnel shell filled with marguerites, some blue sort of flowers and three poppies to give a bit of colour. Then we anticipated our ration of jam for four days – sent J [Jameson] off with the jam, two tins of tobacco and some biscuits to do a bit of swapping in the French Lines. He came back with a tin of sardines, a bottle of pickles and three bottles of vin ordinaire. The camp cook went off with a lot of bacon fat and stuff and swapped it in the Indians' Camp for flour etc. The guests were Lathbury [Capt. G. P. Lathbury RMLI], Major Harrison RE [Royal Engineers], who has done a lot for us, and a nice feller called Binns, who is or was in business at

Constantinople and is now Tempy Lt RM and interpreter. The menu was:

Hors d'Oeuvres *(Pieces of bread and butter with half sardine and a bit of pickle)*
Soup *Tophole!*
Fish *(Fishcakes made out of tinned salmon)*
Cottage Pie *(With real potato)*
Beefsteak Pie *(With real pastry – a triumph!)*
Jam Tart *(More real pastry)*
Wines – Vin Ordinaire. Rum *(Nearly enough for one tot each)*

The guests were absolutely dumbfounded as course after course rolled on – we all tried to look as if this was an everyday occurrence – but the Jam Tart was a surprise on the part of the Cook. We didn't know it was coming. We shan't have any jam for four days but it was well worth it. Hot attack going on from 10 p.m.

Monday 24th May – Whit Monday and Empire Day – our dinner party is much talked about – the pastry and the wine were the absolute limit in the way of surprises in a place where everyone gets the same food every day – and our little Mess has been christened 'Romano's – without the bill'.

Even in the midst of action a discovery of enemy rations was worthy of note in diaries and letters written afterwards – capturing rations seems to give as much delight as taking prisoners. Lionel Montagu recorded that when the Hood Battalion reached the edge of Beaucourt in 1916, and captured a ration dump, 'we opened their parcels and smoked their cigars, and found lots of things to eat – including sausages and cakes.'

The items requested in letters home were not usually expensive or difficult to get, although Lieutenant Walter Wyon Ward wrote a letter to his parents saying that he had had a share of a parcel of plovers' eggs. He was serving in the Royal Marine Artillery Howitzer Brigade and part of his particular job was to be the 'OP' [Observation Post] officer. Those sent forward for the day to the observation post were unable to receive normal rations. In May 1916 Walter wrote home to Norfolk with the following simple request.

Lt Walter Wyon Ward RMA, No. 12 Gun Howitzer Bde, 14 May 1916

Could you send a few things like potted meats. I want them for taking up to my OP when I have to be up there all day and night, as I usually take bully-beef sandwiches, and I am getting rather fed up with them. Things for making sandwiches, and small pork pies or something like that. I should also like several packets of mustard and cress seeds and radishes, as we had one rather good crop of mustard and cress and it grows very easily.

Aboard ship, mail was as important as on land but the food situation was generally better, especially in the battleships and cruisers. Corporal Harold Cauchey of HMS *Iron Duke* was at Scapa Flow in the winter of 1915 and records organizing a party to take frozen meat down to the cold storage hold on 15 November. His diary for Christmas Day notes that, 'We didn't do bad as we had a turkey, a leg of mutton and a ham in my mess. Also cigars, nuts etc.'

Relatives did send food parcels to men afloat, but the time it took for the parcel to arrive could cause problems, as Private Percy Wyvill discovered.

Pte Wyvill RMLI, HMS *Lord Nelson*, Friday 12 March 1915

Received a parcel from wife today, it had been on the way since Feb. 15th but everything in it is quite alright. One of my messmates received a rabbit, which had been in the Post for a month, my word, when it was brought into the Mess four chaps fainted, the air became dense, and a volunteer was called for to throw it overboard. The man who did deserves the VC.

After the *Triumph* was torpedoed in 1915, Corporal Fred Brookes was sent to a gun battery defending the mouth of Mudros Harbour on Lemnos, and he obviously missed the advantages of shipboard life.

Cpl Brookes RMLI, Lemni Point, Mudros, summer 1915

Rations of food were supplied by water from our parent ship, HMS *Europa*. We never got the full naval ration nor the little delicacies from the canteen. We never got fresh beef but tins of bully-beef. We never got butter but tinned products from the Paymaster's stores. We did get bread and endless tins of jam. In fact we lived on bread and jam.

Fred Brookes obviously felt he was missing out, but it illustrates the fact that men at sea generally ate regularly and had a reasonable standard of food.

The routine in a warship was set by the time – there was less freedom than ashore. Sometimes there would be a 'make and mend' afternoon, when the men could write letters, sit and chat or play games such as 'Uckers' – a form of Ludo. Some men liked to listen to music, but this was not universally popular when taken to excess, as Percy Wyvill complained.

Pte Wyvill RMLI, HMS *Lord Nelson*, Thursday 7 January 1915

. . . Next Mess have got their gramophone going, sixteen hours a day without a rest, every day alike. If the Germans do send their Zeppelins I hope the first bomb they drop hits that fearful heart-rending instrument which our neighbours call a gramophone. Music hath charms – No.

Generally, however, every period of the day was organized, from 'All Hands' in the morning to 'Pipe Down' at night. Monotony was the danger, rather than a shortage of things to do. Some people were so busy, though, that they had no time to be bored.

Cpl Brookes RMLI, HMS *Triumph*, spring 1915

At this time I had my time fully occupied in the ship, for, apart from my action station as ammunition supply, my night action as NCO in charge of the two 14 pounders on the starboard side and added to my duties as Corporal in charge of a mess, I had several unusual jobs. I was in charge of the Gunner's Party that scoured the guns. I was the Bandmaster of the drum and fife band and a fretted instrument band that played for the Officers during the evening dinner. I was Acting Schoolmaster of the ship, with classes during the afternoon for 'Boys' and those desirous of sitting for Petty Officer Tests and Royal Marine Educational Certificates. I was also 'The Parson's Yeoman' i.e. I was a kind of Church Warden, Verger, Secular Guide and advisor to the Chaplain, who on this ship was a volunteer shore parson. In fact he was the Sub Dean of Shanghai Cathedral before volunteering to fill the gap. As the Chaplain was censor of the ship I was assigned the post of Assistant Censor. (I took the letters out of their unsealed

envelopes and passed them to the censor, who, after censoring
the same, passed them back to me to replace in their envelopes
and stick down.) I was also the ship's librarian which was
linked with the job of Schoolmaster . . .

With all these jobs my daily routine ran like this: Turned
out of my hammock at 'Guard and Steerage' (instead of earlier
with 'All Hands'). Had early breakfast and then played during
the men's breakfast hour. We then played the National
Anthem at the hoisting of 'Colours'. We played at 'divisions'
when all the ship's company were assembled and inspected. I
gave out the hymn cards before morning prayers. During the
forenoon the band went to practice. I slipped out occasionally
to see my Gunners Party were getting on with their job as
ordered each morning. Went to dinner at 11.30 a.m. (Seven
bells) and at 12.30 p.m. the band gave a session known as
'Sailor's Band' until 1 p.m. When the 'Hands' were detailed for
their afternoon work I got my orders from the Gunner and set
my party to it.

I then taught school for the boys of the ship until 3.30 p.m.
when I had another quick look at my Gunners' Party before
'Evening Quarters' at 4 p.m. From 5 p.m. to 7 p.m. I was the
schoolmaster again and taught those wishing to sit for the
Petty Officers Test and RM Educational Certificates. Supper
was at 7 p.m. and at 7.30 p.m. I mustered my 'fretted
instrument band' and we played on the half-deck whilst the
Wardroom were at dinner. This band was composed mainly of
mandolins backed by a banjo and piccolo. We also boasted two
cornet players.

Throughout the day I might be sent for when the Censor had
some work to do, which was fairly frequent. On Sunday
afternoons I opened the ship's library for the issue and receipt
of books. When Holy Communion was celebrated on board I
was responsible that the bread and wine were ready. On
Sunday evenings the Chaplain held a 'sing-song' on the upper
deck, when Sankey and Moodey [a popular evangelical gospel
hymnal] hymns were chosen and sung by those attending. The
Chaplain would seize the opportunity to say a few appropriate
words. On week-nights the Chaplain attended sing-song
concerts organized by the ship's company and he shut his ears
to many things not intended for his ears. At the end of the
concerts he would say, 'I have attended your sing-songs, and I
hope you will attend mine on Sunday night.' His appeal was
mainly successful.

It will thus be seen that my time was fully occupied, but I
revelled in it all and enjoyed every phase.

Fred Brookes was undoubtedly busy, but having so many 'phases' to his work kept up the interest.

The routine ashore was more varied, but when a detachment was in the same place for a length of time, either in rest camp or a quiet area, both mind and body needed exercise and variety. Soldiers' 'newspapers', often produced within the sound of the guns, and far more up to date than papers from England, poked fun at authority, and especially the 'armchair warriors' back home, and had a variety of contributors, some of whom were already known for their writing, and others who went on to become well known after the War. The RND offering was *The Mudhook*, and contained verses by A. P. Herbert, who was one of its officers. Whilst the advertisements and articles were tongue-in-cheek, there was frequently a streak of truth within them. The first issue of *The Dardanelles Driveller* (price: one drink) set out its aims in an editorial.

The Dardanelles Driveller, **Issue No. 1, 17 May 1915**

. . . we take this opportunity of outlining the course which it is proposed to pursue. Humble in disposition, our aim will not be high; it will be our endeavour merely to take the place, in the Dardanelles, of the paper which each of our readers may happen to prefer. All tastes will, to the best of our abilities, be catered for; the daily news will be from a more interesting and we hope not less reliable source than is at the disposal of our somewhat turgid contemporary; the literary supplement will be on a level never yet attained in Sedd el Barr; the poetry such as can only be inspired by the Aegean or the Plain of Troy. Such is our aim. It must be for us rather than our readers to say if it is attained. But if our paper is of any use at all to the troops in the field we shall be more than satisfied. In conclusion we would add that the editorial staff will always be glad to receive contributions to our columns, but that nothing calculated to bring the flush of shame to the cheek of a modest recruit can in any circumstances be published – unless we are paid for it.

The first edition also included a Meteorological Report – 'The forecast for today will, according to our usual custom, be given tomorrow,' and a 'To Let' notice – 'Several excellent houses in Sedd el Barr, specially recommended for those undergoing open air treatment.' The 'fillers' were often especially telling.

More formal reading material was also popular, and Walter Ward, with his large gun's crew of No. 12 Howitzer, founded a reading room.

Lt Ward RMA, No. 12 Gun Howitzer Bde, 9 December 1917

I have started a Reading room for my men, with a canteen attached. We built it up inside a ruined house with sandbags and tarpaulins, and I have bought them two hanging lamps and they have two fireplaces and tables and cards and we are gradually collecting a small library. If you have any old books we should be grateful for them. Will you also send a subscription for me to some newsagent to have the *Illustrated London News* and the *Tatler* sent out to me every week. The men are awfully pleased with it all.

The men who manned the gun came from a wide variety of civilian occupations, and many would have taken great delight in the chance to read. William Ward described them:

About one third have been clerks, besides that we have three or four farmers, carpenters, builders, gardeners, grocers, greengrocers, ironmongers, postmen, policemen, chauffeurs, licensed victuallers, skilled labourers of all sorts, engineers, butchers, bootmakers, in fact everything you can think of, including a Company Director.

Sport was also considered important, though there was less opportunity for large team games aboard ship. Deck hockey was ever popular, and whenever possible the men were landed ashore to enable them to play football or cricket. Boxing tournaments were an easier matter, and were arranged between messes, ships and squadrons. Sport was not only a way of keeping physically fit. It encouraged team spirit, 'esprit de corps', and it gave entertainment and achievement apart from that of defeating the enemy. Only entertainment could have been the reason behind Private Wvyill's favoured 'sport' of rollerskating, which he undertook with some messmates aboard *Lord Nelson*.

Pte Wyvill RMLI, HMS *Lord Nelson*, Wednesday 17 March 1915

Skating on the foc'sle this evening, grand display, tried to break records and my neck, nothing doing in record line, but scored a good many tries with regard to my neck.

More fun – I had a boxing match with Morley, on skates, falling over every hit, no serious injuries.

He did engage in more ordinary activities, however.

Pte Wyvill RMLI, HMS *Lord Nelson*, Saturday 29 May 1915

Great day today, we hold aquatic sports, obstacle races round the upper deck, high diving, walking the greasy pole and swimming races. Myself and Morley are very poor swimmers but we both entered for the 150 yards open. Well, they took us away from the ship in picket boat and we had to swim back to the ship – it looked more like 150 miles instead of yards, but I did the distance, so did Morley. Incidentally, we were a long way behind the other entries.

The seriousness of the sport often reflected the conditions under which it was played. Just behind the front line there were many makeshift games, and ad hoc cricket and football matches, but in the safer rest areas there were properly organized sports at levels right up to Corps and Army size. Again, Walter Ward was trying to keep his men entertained.

Lt Ward RMA, No. 12 Gun Howitzer Bde, 10 June 1917

We are making an effort to give the men some sports etc. to amuse them in the evenings. We used to be able to play football and cricket, but here you can't get enough ground for it, so we are starting things like tip and run and other sports which don't take up much room. Could you rake up any old cricket balls or hockey balls, and a few tennis balls, and an old cricket bat or two to send out to me.

The previous summer, a quiet period and suitable location had enabled the gun's crew to play cricket properly.

Lt Ward RMA, No. 12 Gun Howitzer Bde, 14 May 1916

We had a most exciting cricket match this afternoon. Officers
and NCOs versus the men. Four of us officers were playing.
We went in first and as the ground was very rough and we
hadn't played on it before, we were all out for 27. I made top
score with seven. The men went in and made 80, we then
made 101 and got the men out for 48 and had a draw. It was
frightfully exciting as we got the last six wickets for only ten
runs.

However 'exciting' the cricket, it could not have matched the football
match in which Sergeant Will Meatyard took part in in Gallipoli.

Sgt Will Meatyard RMLI, HQ Coy Ply. Bn, 11 October 1915

In the afternoon we played a 'League Match' with the Howe
Battalion, my position being centre half. We lost 4–1. During
the game we had to stop twice as enemy shells were dropping
on the pitch, a very rare experience for footballers.

Cricket and football were not the only competitive sports which went
on. Troops out of the front line had routine drill, parades, marches and
practices, but also the chance to enter in a variety of competitions,
including athletics, show jumping and gymkhanas. 'Doing well' was far
more important in these formal sports. *The Globe & Laurel* printed the
following report from the CO of the 1st Battalion RMLI in August
1917.

Commanding Officer, 1st Bn RMLI, *Globe & Laurel*, August 1917

We have been having a very nice quiet time lately and glorious
weather. There have been Brigade, Divisional, Corps and
Army Horse Shows during the last month. Our transport took
first prize in the Brigade and Divisional Shows for 'Transport
turnouts', which consisted of one cooker, one watercart, two
limbered GS [General Service] wagons and two pack ponies.
We also took the Divisional General's prize for the best
limbered GS wagon in the Division. In the Corps Show, which
we took part in through being first in the Divisional Show,
they were all out on 'spit and polish', pipeclay and varnish, and

we didn't have a look in. We called it a moral victory, as none
had horses or harness in better condition than ours.

The horse show events included a tug o' war. The RM
Battalion won the Brigade, Dublin Fusiliers the Divisional, a
Battalion of the HLI [Highland Light Infantry] the Corps, and
a team of Canadian Seaforth Highlanders merely picked up
the rope and walked away with every team they pulled against
at the Army Show.

In Gallipoli, Major Norman Burge organized sports for his men which
were far more unorthodox, but undoubtedly successful.

Maj. Burge RMLI, Cyclist Coy RND, Thursday 24 June 1915

Started the Sports in the evening. Shrapnel Race, Biscuit
Race, Tossing the Picket and Spy's Hoard Hunt. Shrapnel
races consist of five shrapnel bullets laid out one yard apart –
at the end of each line there is an empty shrapnel case and the
men, taking only one bullet per journey, have to scuffle 'em up
with a spoon and tip each bullet in the case. This went well
until a real shrapnel came along (although we were hidden by
some trees) and postponed things for a quarter of an hour. The
Biscuit Race was done in pairs. First man ate large Government
biscuit. When it had all disappeared into his mouth he had to
run 150 yds and whistle a tune to his partner, who had to
recognise it and run to Judge to give the name of tune. This
was highly amusing as, owing to laughter and biscuit, most of
them were totally incapable of whistling anything for some
time. When they could it was mostly biscuit which was
whistled at first. Tossing the Picket was a five-foot pole –
farthest throw to win. As nobody knew (the thrower least of
all) where it would go after being swung round the head a few
times, it was a very exciting contest. The Spy's Hoard Hunt
was simply hidden treasure – the clues being supplied in a
document supposed to have been found on the body of 'Abdul,
the Terrible Turk, a sniper'. No one's found it yet and some
went badly off the track, as two men were indignantly ejected
from the HQ Camp next door – they being found digging busily
at the back of the General's dugout and quite convinced they
were on the right scent . . . Treasure hunt just found by young
Foote – a private in the Company whose father is Fleet
Paymaster at DHQ.

Norman Burge was improvising according to geographical position and available equipment. Considering the circumstances, his prep school sports-style games were probably better received than the more regular variety. Sports also had a more serious motive than mere physical fitness, as this article from the *Peninsula Press*, official news printed by the Royal Engineers Printing Section at GHQ, testifies.

The Peninsula Press No. 28, Thursday 17 June 1915, Official News

The following is the programme of a competition at ANZAC:

Commencing at 3 p.m.
JUDGES: Major Row, Major Cribb, Capt. Griffiths.
TIMEKEEPERS: Capt. Jarvis, Lieut Robertson, Lieut Mead.
CONDITIONS: Each company will enter 8 teams of 8 men. Two trained NCOs [trained in bomb throwing] of each company to take 4 teams each and to act as observers with periscopes.

1st PRACTICE
2 Jam Tin Bombs – 5 second fuse.

2nd PRACTICE
2 Percussion Bombs.

3rd PRACTICE
1 Gun Cotton Bomb (Lotbiniere) 6 sec. fuse.

All competitors will throw from the trench.

POINTS: Hits (i.e. inside enemy's trench). 2 points for every direct hit, 1 point for each hit inside a space of 3 ft either in front or rear of enemy's trench.

EXPOSURE: Judges will rule out of action any thrower exposing any part of head or body. Teams completing practice with absolutely no exposure will have 1 point added to total score.

TIME: Timekeepers will stand in the rear of each thrower and record any bomb thrown after 'fuse time' has elapsed ruling out of action 2 men for every bomb so thrown.

TRAJECTORY: In practice No. 2 the Judges will, at their discretion, award points for trajectory.

PRIZES: 1st Prize – 20 packets of cigarettes and 1 tin Marmalade; 2nd Prize – 16 packets of cigarettes and 1 tin Marmalade; 3rd Prize – 12 packets cigarettes.

This page has been annotated by Norman Burge: 'Perfectly true. This is up at Kaba [Gaba] Tepe.'

The mail, food and sporting activities are merely examples of the important things in day-to-day living for the serviceman at war. The real 'game' was played all the time – survival. Casualties could be expected every day in the front line, even when there were no attacks, counter-attacks or raids. To a great degree life or death was a matter or chance, and the usual view was that 'Lady Luck' would always fail someone else. Occasionally though, even potentially fatal incidents could be related as humorous after the event, even if the humour was forced. Fred Brookes, promoted Sergeant, and serving with the 2nd Battalion RMLI in France, related one such.

Sgt Fred Brookes RMLI, 2nd Bn RMLI

On one occasion I was in charge of a post in the front line when an inspecting officer asked me where our latrine was. I showed him an excavation in the rear of the trench which had a stick arranged for us to sit over with a latrine bucket underneath. The Officer said, 'There are some box-latrines on that dump over there,' pointing out the dump, 'Send one of your men to get one.'

'Very good, Sir,' I replied and detailed a man to get a box-latrine from the dump and bring it back. He set off, and, to get to the dump, he had to jump three trenches on the way.

He duly arrived at the dump, secured the box-latrine and started to return. In returning, however, he slightly altered his direction and jumped three trenches, as he surmised, the same he had jumped on his outward journey. By altering his direction he missed one of the original three trenches and jumped the front line instead and wandered over No Man's Land and into 'Jerry's' front line. Jerry captured him, box-latrine and all.

We saw him wandering towards Jerry's line and shouted, but he failed to hear us. I met this individual a long time afterwards when he, as a returned prisoner of war, was passing the doctor of the RM Infirmary at Stonehouse. He came over to me and said, 'You're the b—— that sent me for the b—— latrine.' I told him that we saw him and had shouted to him but he had continued on into Jerry's line. We both laughed over the incident that had such dire consequences for him.

A second potentially fatal incident was recorded by Norman Burge in Gallipoli, May 1915.

Maj. Burge RMLI, Cyclist Coy RND, 12 May 1915

At about 2 a.m. we get back to our old bivvy to find it occupied by some of our troops. We didn't turn them out as we are going to move anyway, so move on to the place we had an eye on before – a small vineyard with vines about two feet high. I am a bit behind the rest of the Company (chivvying a couple of stragglers along) when I see a suspicious looking varlet in the shadow of a bush. He looks like I don't know what – so at once I'm quite convinced he's a sniper shifting billet in the dark. I get very close to him (my revolver still closer to him) and ask him who he is. He replies in Turkish – or what sounds like it so I grab his rifle and let out a yell for my Orderly who is about 30 ft in front of me. The sniper thereupon responds with a terrified yell of 'Guard turn out!' I then find he's a sentry of the 10th Manchesters – no wonder I couldn't understand him, his dialect was so broad.

A keen lookout was being kept for spies, especially down at the beachheads, and this resulted in a number of false alarms, one of which Norman Burge recounts in his entry for 15 May.

Maj. Burge RMLI, Cyclist Coy RND, Saturday 15 May 1915

Jameson [one of the Cyclist Company subalterns] thought he'd caught a spy in British Officer's uniform at the beach and had him marched down to HQ Office. The unfortunate man was identified as a mechanic of the Flying Corps and had certainly been acting in a way to cause suspicion. He was arrested by one of our Sergeants who covered him with a rifle and said, 'Hands up,' and marched him off. Of course a huge crowd collected at once and off he went to the accompaniment of 'That's right Sarjint', 'Shoot 'im Sarjint', etc. When half way down to the Office he plaintively asked if he might put his hands down! – the Sergeant having forgotten to let him do so!

Failure to recognise one's own side actually caused a number of casualties. One of the most unfortunate was also recorded by Norman Burge, a few weeks after the above occurrence. Lieutenant Colonel

Bendyshe, CO of the Deal Battalion Royal Marines, had been killed on the night of 1 to 2 May.

Maj. Burge RMLI, Cyclist Coy RND, 1 June 1915

Heard the true story of how Bendyshe was killed – it ought to be more widely known as there are such a lot of rumours about. It appears that one Coy of the Deal Battn were holding a bit of very awkward trench. They had lost [Major] Muller that afternoon and most of their NCOs – leaving mostly raw lads who had had a dreadful doing. Also they had been warned that the Turks were largely using Australian uniforms for their spies – which was quite true. Anyway they were jumpy. It appears that they were to be relieved by Australians that night and Bendyshe was showing the Australian Major round the lines. Just at dusk an Australian Private and Major, followed by Bendyshe, suddenly jumped into the trench – the men round about state they challenged but got no answer – so they fired, poor B dropping – they made for the Australian Major with their bayonets – he warding them off with his hands and getting wounded of course in doing so. They were quite convinced they had shot one and taken another one prisoner, both spies, and as the Australian Major was naturally very excited and doubtless a bit incoherent, they handcuffed and blindfolded him and sent him down to the beach under escort. Tupman, who was on the beach, heard, by some mysterious rumour, that B had been killed and came along to this trench to see if it was true. The men in this trench said of course they knew nothing about their Col. and hadn't seen him, but that they had shot a spy. Tupman found the body and the men would hardly believe even then what had happened. The Australian Pte, an orderly, had managed to hide himself away somehow – but was able to explain later. The men were naturally horrified – as B was dearly loved by all of them – but the general impression seems to have been that it would not have happened if B had come into the trench first, instead of the strange Australian. It is very regrettable but quite understandable.

The existence of 'friendly fire' was accepted as one of the unfortunate aspects of war, even if the term had yet to be coined. It was just another way in which one might die, in a war which brought a generation into contact with death on an unimaginable scale.

7

The End of the War: Aftermath

At 11 a.m. on 11 November 1918, the Armistice came into effect that marked the end of the bloodshed. For many of those in the front line there was, if anything, a sense of anticlimax. A feeling of weary relief that it was over at last took precedence over a sense of victory. Charles Jerram, now a Lieutenant Colonel serving as a Staff Officer with the 46th North Midland Division, wrote a very short entry in his journal.

Lt Col. Charles Jerram RMLI, 46th North Midland Div., 11 Nov. 1918

The Armistice of November 11th found us occupying an outpost east of the little town of Sains du Nord, not far from Mons where it all began in 1914.

There was little else to be said. Let the euphoria of relief and victory sweep those at home. Yet even back in Britain, not everyone was making a fuss over the end of more than four years of fighting. The Commandant of the Royal Marines Depot at Deal certainly took it calmly. Arthur Chater, recently promoted major after Zeebrugge, was Adjutant at the depot. He had been invited to the Commandant's for dinner on the evening of the 11th, in order to discuss giving the men more sense of direction in drill, and later recalled his meeting with the Commandant during the morning.

Maj. Arthur Chater DSO, RMLI, Adjutant RM Depot Deal

When on the morning of that great day, I went in to report the Armistice to him [the Commandant] and said we should do something to celebrate the event, he agreed to our holding a mass parade at noon, and to the rest of the day being a holiday, but added, 'Don't forget that you are dining with me tonight to discuss my idea of sense of direction': and that was how I spent Armistice night 1918.

For the serviceman there was the question of 'What now?' Men had left their trades and professions, students their studies and thousands of schoolboys had gone from school uniform straight into khaki without ever experiencing a 'normal' world. Adjusting to peacetime civilian life would not be easy, and for all those who took up the strands of their old life in factory or office, there were the others who could only be at ease out of doors. One who clearly missed service life was Cornelius Moynahan, who told of his own feelings on discharge in *The Globe & Laurel* early in 1920.

Cornelius Moynahan, late Private RMLI, *Globe & Laurel*, **January 1920**

Believe me, the feeling of freedom one experiences on being discharged soon wears off; the collar and tie become distasteful; one sighs, but sighs in vain, for the collar-badges one has just discarded, the comradeship of the mess-deck, and of the barrack-room, a comradeship that has no equal in any other sphere of life.

Far worse was the situation of those who had lost limbs, their eyesight, or were crippled by the effects of gas. Some did manage to find new trades but others would never work again, and would have to rely on the meagre pension and little better than begging. The sight of blind men with the three war medals commonly known as 'Pip, Squeak and Wilfred' on their chests, selling matches on street corners, became part of town life into the 1930s. There were also a large number of men whose mental health was destroyed, and who ended up in mental hospitals, or unable to hold down a normal job and family life. In 1920 the British government was paying disability pensions to about 65,000 men who had suffered neurasthenia and related conditions. In 1922 there were nearly 17,000 men in hospitals, and just before the Second World War there were still over 3,000 men in mental institutions. The last man to have entered an asylum as a result of the Great War did not die until the new millennium.

Even those who came home unscathed faced problems. For all too many the job they had left was not awaiting them on their return. 'A land fit for heroes' was the political rallying cry, but the 'heroes' swiftly became the unemployed and disaffected of the 1920s and 1930s.

Despite the fact that they had to struggle through the inter-war years, and that the younger ones fought in the Second World War, for many the years 1914 to 1918 remained the climax of their lives. Nothing could be as bad as the things they had seen and heard, no fear could be as sharp, nor any camaraderie as close. A silent gulf existed between those who had been part of it and those who had not. While other memories faded, those of the Great War stayed in sharp focus. Sixty years later the television pictures of the Dardanelles and Gallipoli, calm and peaceful as the bays and beaches had become, could reduce men to tears as if it had all happened yesterday.

Finally, there were those who never saw the end of 'the war to end all wars' – men like John (Jack) Barnes, Norman Burge, Arthur Tetley, Gerald Rooney, Fred Logan and Herbert Pare. They had no homecoming, even to a peacetime with problems.

Norman Ormsby Burge was killed, aged 40, leading his battalion, Nelson Battalion RND, in action at Beaucourt on 13 November 1916. He is buried in Hamel Military Cemetery, Beaumont-Hamel, 6½ kilometres north of Albert, in Plot 2, Row D, Grave 20.

Arthur Stanley Tetley died two days later, on 15 November 1916, aged 36, from wounds received leading the Anson Battalion RND in the same action. He lies in Varennes Military Cemetery, 24 kilometres north of Amiens, in Plot 1, Row C, Grave 37.

Gerald Rooney, like the majority of those lost at sea, has no grave, but he is remembered on the Plymouth Naval Memorial on Plymouth Hoe. It is of the same design as those at Portsmouth and Chatham, also in prominent positions.

'Paddy' Logan and Herbert Pare were killed at Passchendaele on 26 October 1917, whilst serving with the 2nd Battalion RMLI. Their graves, like that of Jack Barnes and Christopher Andrews, whose names appear on the Helles Memorial, could not be located after the war and they are commemorated along with 34,887 other men killed in the Ypres Salient after 26 August 1917, and who have no known grave, on the Tyne Cot Memorial to the Missing. Their names will be found on Panel 1. Many of the graves in Tyne Cot Cemetery are of unknown soldiers, sailors and Royal Marines. It is possible that they lie there or within another cemetery. More likely their remains are beneath some Flemish farmer's beet fields. In a sense it does not matter, as long as it is remembered that every name on a panel, every grave, represents a real person and not just a statistic of history.

Material from the Royal Marines Museum Archive

Each entry shows its archive number.

1 The Outbreak of War

Kershaw, Edwin, Sgt RMLI   11/13/208
Rooney, Gerald, Maj. RMLI   11/13/005
Stapleton, Frederick, Clr Sgt RMLI   11/13/156

2 The Dardanelles

Brookes, Frederick, Cpl RMLI   11/13/005
Hedges, Reginald, Clr Sgt RMLI   AQC135/94
Kershaw, Edwin, Sgt RMLI   11/13/208
Oppenheim (later Orde), Godfrey, Capt. RMLI   11/13/034
Pare, Herbert, Pte RMLI   11/13/036
Stapleton, Frederick, Clr Sgt RMA   11/13/156
Wells, W. E., Bugler RMLI   11/13/062
Wilcox, Henry, Pte RMLI   11/13/252
Wyvill, Percy, Pte RMLI   11/13/149

3 Jutland

Blount, Harold, Capt. RMA   7/17/4/(3)
Bourne, Alan, MVO, Capt. RMA   7/17/4
Cauchey, Harold, Cpl RMLI   11/13/071
Grattan, Arthur, Maj. RMLI   11/13/114 (for letter of Francis Harvey, VC)
Hill, Chandos, Capt. RMLI   7/17/4
Hughes, Evan, Capt. RMLI   *The Globe & Laurel*, May 1919
Jago, Norman, Sgt RMA   11/13/199(a)
Jollye, Godfrey, Capt. RMA   7/17/4
Neasham, G., Pte RMLI   7/17/4
Saunders, Albert, Cpl RMA   11/13/002

Smith, Charles, Bugler RMLI   11/12/4 (176)
Swanborough, Thomas, Pte RMLI   7/17/4

4 Gallipoli

'Albert', Pte RMLI   7/17/3(20)
Allen, John, Bandsman RMB   11/13/042
Barnes, John, Lt RMLI   7/17/3
Bramley, G., CSM RMLI   11/13/100
Burge, Norman Ormsby, Maj. (later Lt Col.) RMLI   11/13/163
Chater, Arthur, DSO, Lt (later Maj.) RMLI   9/2/C
Corbett-Williamson, William, Cpl RMLI   11/12/3/(85)
Conybeare, Charles, Lt RMLI   *The Globe & Laurel*, April & May 1919
The Globe & Laurel, January 1917
Inskip, S. Hope, Lt RMLI   7/17/3
Jerram, Charles, Maj. (later Lt Col.)   11/13/24/(A)
Lamplough, Charles, Lt RMLI   11/13/079
Law, Francis, DSC, Lt RMLI   *The Globe & Laurel*, May 1920
Meatyard, William, Sgt RMLI   11/12/8
Moynahan, Cornelius, Pte RMLI   11/13/044
Pottinger, Robert, Pte RMLI   11/13/136
Richards, John, Lt RMLI   *The Globe & Laurel*, February 1920
RND Order No. 26   11/12/4 (87)
Thompson, James, Pte RMLI   11/13/144
Vickers, John, Pte RMLI   11/13/237
Wyvill, Percy, Pte RMLI   11/13/149

5 The Somme

Brown, William, Pte RMLI   11/13/321
Jerram, Charles, Maj.   11/13/24(B)
Meatyard, William, MM, Sgt RMLI   11/12/8
Montagu, Lionel, DSO, Maj. RMLI   7/17/5/(1) & 11/12/13/(33)

6 Zeebrugge

Chater, Arthur, Capt. RMLI   13/1/84
Feeney, James, Pte RMLI   *The Globe & Laurel*, April 1919
4th Battalion RM, Training in 4th Battalion RM, General
  Correspondence 2/10/15; also contains Adjutant General's letter
  concerning deployment of 4th Battalion to France (subterfuge)
Hodgson, Philip, Pte RMLI   7/17/2
Lamplough, Charles, DSC, Lt RMLI   ACQ117/82(4)
Scorey, William, Pte RMLI   7/17/2
Tracey, Ernest, Pte RMLI   7/17/2
Wright, Harry, DSM, Sgt RMLI   ACQ336/78(A) & 11/13/69

7 Day-to-Day Life on Active Service

Black, W., Sgt RMLI   11/12/18
Brookes, Frederick, Sgt RMLI   11/13/005
Burge, Norman Ormsby, Maj. (later Lt Col.) RMLI   11/13/163
The Dardanelles Driveller, Issue No. 1   11/7/16
The Globe & Laurel, August 1917 (sports)
Hallding, Percy, Chaplain   11/12/13
Meatyard, William, MM, Sgt RMLI   11/12/8
Morrison-Scott, R.C.S., Capt. RMA   11/12/18
The Peninsula Press   7/17/3(4)
Rooney, Gerald, Maj. RMLI   11/13/005
Ward, Walter Wyon, Lt RMA   11/13/250
Weekes, B. W., Capt. RMLI   302/77/(11)
Wyvill, Percy, Pte RMLI   11/13/149

8 The End of the War: Aftermath

Chater, Arthur, DSO, Lt (later Maj.) RMLI   9/2/C & 13/1/84
Jerram, Charles, Lt Col.   11/250/9
Moynahan, Cornelius, Pte RMLI   *The Globe & Laurel*, January 1920

Note: The letter from H. A. Holloway to Bugler E. E. Holloway RMLI, and Bugler Holloway's oral reminiscences, are in the possession of the author.

Bibliography

Aspinall-Oglander, Brig. Gen. C. F., *History of the Great War Based on Official Documents: Military Operations – Gallipoli*, 2 vols, William Heinemann, 1929 and 1932

Bennett, Geoffrey, *Naval Battles of the First World War*, Batsford, 1968

Blumberg, General Sir H. E., *Britain's Sea Soldiers: A History of the Royal Marines 1914–1919*, Swiss & Co., 1927

Brown, Malcolm, *Imperial War Museum Book of the Somme*, Sidgwick & Jackson, 1996

Bush, Capt. E. W., RN, *Gallipoli*, George Allen & Unwin, 1975

Corbett, Sir Julian S., *History of the Great War: Naval Operations*, Longmans, Green and Co., 1921

Denham, H. M., *Dardanelles: A Midshipman's Diary, 1915–1916*, John Murray, 1981

Ferguson, Niall, *Empire: How Britain Made the Modern World*, Allen Lane, 2003

Jerrold, Douglas, *The Hawke Battalion: Some Personal Recollections of Four Years*, Ernest Benn, 1925

Jerrold, Douglas, *The Royal Naval Division,* Hutchinson, 1923

Liddle, Peter, *Men of Gallipoli*, Allen Lane, 1976

MacDonald, Lyn, *Somme*, Michael Joseph, 1983

Middlebrook, Martin, *The Bruckshaw Diaries*, Scholar Press, 1979 (Pte Bruckshaw was in No. 4 Company, Plymouth Battalion RMLI, in Gallipoli.)

Murray, Joseph, *Call to Arms*, William Kimber, 1980

Murray, Joseph, *Gallipoli As I Saw It*, William Kimber, 1965

Sparrow, Geoffrey, MC, and McBean Ross, J., *On Four Fronts with the RND*, Hodder & Stoughton, 1918

Steel, Nigel, and Hart, Peter, *Defeat at Gallipoli*, Macmillan, 1994

Warner, Philip, *The Zeebrugge Raid*, William Kimber, 1978

Index

Index

215